T0323411

ADVANCE PRAISE FOR THE CULTURE AND DEVELOPMENT MANIFESTO

"*The Culture and Development Manifesto* seeks to open a path between two disciplines that often seem hermetically sealed, cultural anthropology and development economics. It will be of immense use to any practitioner working at this highly fraught boundary."

—**Francis Fukuyama**, Olivier Nomellini Senior Fellow, the Freeman Spogli Institute for International Studies, Stanford University

"In this highly engaging book, Klitgaard not only brings economics and culture into dialogue with each other, he goes beyond 'culture matters' to demonstrate what 'taking culture into account' may mean in practice. This is a book that only Klitgaard, with his sharp multidisciplinary lens, wealth of on-the-ground experience, and remarkable penmanship, could have pulled off."

—**Dani Rodrik**, Ford Foundation Professor of International Political Economy, Harvard Kennedy School

"In this provocative and thoughtful book, Klitgaard shows that it may take an outsider (an economist, no less) to show how the study of culture holds practical lessons for human development. Rather than seeing 'culture' as an obstacle to development and well-being, he shows how both creativity and collaboration emerge from bringing together on equal footing different, even competing, beliefs and ways of looking at the world. Connecting the dots between theory and policy, he offers a practical and useful 'convening framework' to operationalize this model. Policymakers as well as scholars and practitioners of development should read this book and work to implement its conclusions."

—**Edward F. Fischer**, Cornelius Vanderbilt Professor of Anthropology and Director of the Center for Latin American Studies, Vanderbilt University

"A proposition universally accepted, it seems, is that culture should (must) be taken into account in international development work. However, there is zero consensus as to how best to do so. Worse, the pitfalls on the path to integrating cultural approaches make many duck and avoid the topic altogether. Klitgaard has grappled with this odd dilemma for many years, on the ground and in the academy. In *The Culture and Development Manifesto*, he sets out the challenges and their historic evolution with lucid clarity (and a host of stories), and offers some sensible, if demanding, ways forward."

—**Katherine Marshall**, Senior Fellow, Berkley Center for Religion, Peace, and World Affairs, Georgetown University

"Can cultural anthropology and international development team up in a way that creates mutual respect and contextually sensitive projects, programs, or social movements—ones that fit? How common is an author with kind heart, hard head, and lucid pen; one intimately familiar too with scholars, program designers, and powerful officials? That's right; both disciplines need this book."

—**Parker Shipton**, Professor of Anthropology and Professor of African Studies, Boston University

"This book is a brilliant plea, subtly combining scholarship, examples, and common sense, to mobilize the competencies of anthropologists for a better adaptation of development policies to local conditions. It is based on a robust premise: in the confrontation between the interventions of development agencies and the social contexts in which they are implemented (local cultures), the many failures do not stem from a refusal of development by the populations but from an incapacity of public policy experts to take local cultures into account. The final proposal—convening dialogues between experts, anthropologists, and local actors—is highly stimulating."

—**Jean-Pierre Olivier de Sardan**, École des Hautes Études en Sciences Sociales, Marseilles, and LASDEL, Niamey, Niger; author of *Anthropology and Development*.

The Culture and Development Manifesto

The Culture and Development Manifesto

ROBERT KLITGAARD

OXFORD

UNIVERSITY PRESS

OXFORD
UNIVERSITY PRESS

Oxford University Press is a department of the University of Oxford. It furthers
the University's objective of excellence in research, scholarship, and education
by publishing worldwide. Oxford is a registered trade mark of Oxford University
Press in the UK and certain other countries.

Published in the United States of America by Oxford University Press
198 Madison Avenue, New York, NY 10016, United States of America.

© Oxford University Press 2021

All rights reserved. No part of this publication may be reproduced, stored in
a retrieval system, or transmitted, in any form or by any means, without the
prior permission in writing of Oxford University Press, or as expressly permitted
by law, by license, or under terms agreed with the appropriate reproduction
rights organization. Inquiries concerning reproduction outside the scope of the
above should be sent to the Rights Department, Oxford University Press, at the
address above.

You must not circulate this work in any other form
and you must impose this same condition on any acquirer.

Library of Congress Cataloging-in-Publication Data
Names: Klitgaard, Robert E., author.
Title: The culture and development manifesto / Robert Klitgaard.
Description: New York, NY : Oxford University Press, [2021] |
Includes bibliographical references and index.
Identifiers: LCCN 2020027987 (print) | LCCN 2020027988 (ebook) |
ISBN 9780197517734 (hardback) | ISBN 9780197517741 (paperback) |
ISBN 9780197517765 (epub)
Subjects: LCSH: Cultural property—Economic aspects. |
Economic development projects.
Classification: LCC CC135 .K595 2020 (print) | LCC CC135 (ebook) |
DDC 363.6/9—dc23
LC record available at https://lccn.loc.gov/2020027987
LC ebook record available at https://lccn.loc.gov/2020027988

DOI: 10.1093/oso/9780197517734.001.0001

Hardback printed by Bridgeport National Bindery, Inc., United States of America

For Elaine van Biljon Klitgaard

Always, in all ways

Contents

1

Culture? Development? Manifesto?

"Are you sure you want that title? In some academic circles, both 'culture' and 'development' are dirty words. And *manifesto*?"

Culture may benignly refer to preferences in music, art, and cuisine. People also talk about culture as a set of values and beliefs, customs and norms, patterns of meaning, ways of life.[1] This doesn't seem offensive either. Cultural anthropology grew up more than a century ago to describe and then theorize about the diversity and importance of these "folkways." "I have tried to treat all folkways," wrote William Graham Sumner in 1899, "including those which are most opposite to our own, with truthfulness, but with dignity and due respect to our own conventions." And folkways matter:

> They arise no one knows whence or how. They grow as if by the play of internal life energy. They can be modified, but only to a limited extent, by the purposeful efforts of men. In time they lose power, decline, and die, or are transformed. While they are in vigor they very largely control individual and social undertakings, and they produce and nourish ideas of world philosophy and life policy. Yet they are not organic or material. They belong to a superorganic system of relations, conventions, and institutional arrangements. The study of them is called for by their *social* character, by virtue of which they are leading factors in the science of society.[2]

And so social and cultural anthropology, with the leadership of people like Marcel Mauss, began to document the variations in folkways. Comparison enabled theorists to emphasize the importance of such phenomena as exchange in nonmonetized economies, the evolution of the law, and the influence of seasonality on living arrangements and, indeed, on the "total social fact" of Eskimo life (to name three of Mauss's topics). Across cultures, differences and similarities could be gleaned. Both enabled new vistas into one's own society. Differences suggested that our supposed universal truths

The Culture and Development Manifesto. Robert Klitgaard, Oxford University Press (2021). © Oxford University Press.
DOI: 10.1093/oso/9780197517734.003.0001

might be reexamined as parochial propositions. The fact that others had, for example, such varied property rights, sexual mores, and exotic but often admirable religious beliefs—all could help us question and perhaps recalibrate our own practices. At the same time, similarities across cultures evoked ideas of necessity where one saw before only contingency or happenstance. Both sorts of vistas proved stimulating to social theorists, philosophers, and humanists.

But the comparisons could also lead down unpleasant paths. Differences—even when carefully defined and exhaustively recorded, as opposed to the sketchy and often demeaning descriptions by travelers and so-called men on the scene—could suggest hierarchies, as of civilizations; evolutionary continua and barriers; and, alas, the notion of superior and inferior cultures. On the other side, similarities were used, perhaps abused, to support ideas of human nature and natural law.

Fast forward to today, and surprisingly perhaps, most work in cultural anthropology avoids the word "culture." "Anthropology has an ambivalent relationship with its core disciplinary concept: culture," noted Victor C. de Munck and Giovanni Bennardo in 2019, in a lead article in *Current Anthropology*. "Beyond the rather vague but important notion that culture is shared and learned, there is little agreement about how to define and identify something as culture(al)." We are still, they asserted, "in the 'mush stage' of defining culture."[3]

Mushy, maybe, and potentially offensive. Cultural categories can be sources of stigma. A Zapatista woman spoke to an enormous crowd in the "March for Dignity" in Mexico City in 2001. She said, "Being an indigenous woman is a pride, being indigenous women means that we have thought, that we have dignity, but it is difficult, very difficult, because there is suffering, discrimination, and poverty. This is why we want that constitutional law takes us into consideration." Another Zapatista woman said, "We speak our language, we have our customs, our medicine, our form of praying and our form of dancing. We have our way of respecting our elders . . . and for speaking our language, and for being dark-skinned, we [are] looked down upon."[4] As we shall see, experience with, and fears of, the misuse of "culture" have led to it becoming a dirty word.

Development in the case of a person can refer to growth, improvement, fulfillment. You can develop your mind through education, your body through exercise, your bank account through hard work and good luck. For groups of people, a similar intuition applies. Speaking of a country or state or city, a continent, a class, or an ethnic group, we daily debate how our development (or theirs) compares with the past or compares with others. Education, health, income, equality of many kinds, environmental soundness, civil liberties: political campaigns as well as social scientific descriptions and theories focus on development in these and related senses. And yet, as Jean-Emmanuel Pondi noted, "Few words excite as many hopes in Africa as the word 'development.' Few words irritate Africans as much as this same word 'development.'"[5]

And not only Africans. Writing in 2011, Thandika Mkandawire noted the importance of the Bandung Conference of 1955 of African and Asian nations and its version of development in terms of "catching up," liberation, and "the right to development."

> "Catching up" has been driven by the emancipatory aspirations of developing countries themselves and their understanding of the Western advantage that has sustained its dominance. . . . I share the sentiments and the sense of urgency behind them on unabashedly prosaic arguments that development, if properly defined, will reduce human material suffering, increase people's capabilities and widen their choices.[6]

Development: exciting, but also, annoying. Or worse: the enemy. In many academic circles, *development* was derided as another example of hegemony, a vehicle of inequality, and a destroyer of local cultures. The anthropologist James Ferguson insisted on always putting inverted commas around "development," and he lumped the "development" activities of international aid agencies and of local governments into a stigmatizing stereotype: "The difference here is between the guardians of the global hegemony and those of the local hegemony."[7] In 2017, Jean-Philippe Venot and Gert Jan Veldwisch said that "connections and associations are made to something that is 'Good' in the abstract sense, or to values assumed to be universal (though they reflect a narrow vision of progress, mostly Western and male dominated), such as equity, progress, development, and modernity."[8] A book called *Deconstructing Development Discourse: Buzzwords and Fuzzwords* ascribed to this language *hegemonic* properties.[9] The anthropologist Arturo Escobar praised Wolfgang Sachs's edited book *The Development Dictionary* because it is useful as "a dictionary of toxic words in the development discourse."[10]

And so, *culture* and *development* can become dirty words. Putting them together is double trouble. Since the 1960s, any scholar writing about a "culture of poverty" anywhere would be pilloried for blaming the victim (some newer work is more approving).[11] When "less developed" becomes a slur instead of a description, the concept itself becomes part of the problem, intellectually and practically. The combination of culture and development may be a trigger. "Who are you to classify and pontificate about so-called culture? Who are you to say what is developed and what isn't? How about some respect, some humility?"

If you nonetheless want to join the discussion on culture and development, be ready for another classic problem: both words have many meanings. As with most important concepts in the human and social sciences, definitions and measures are contested—think of sustainability, mental health, democracy, gender equity, intelligence, social justice, creativity. (If you were James Ferguson, you might put each of them in quotation marks.)

In economics, even central concepts like unemployment, wealth, and capital are controversial in concept and murky in measurement. When Angus Deaton won the Nobel Prize in economics, reporters scurried to find out what he'd discovered. They saw he had made influential studies of poverty and the poverty line. They asked him what he'd learned. He replied, "Focusing on the number of people who are below the line is like chasing an [*sic*] unicorn through the woods."[12]

People can spend their academic lives debating concepts and measures of both "culture" and "development," without, I'm afraid, doing much more than clearing their throats. And yet, the miseries and abuses associated with "underdevelopment" (forgive me) are visible to all, and the existence of "cultural differences" (forgive me again) are recognized by all. As we will see in chapter 2, people in the so-called less developed countries are ready to complain about, and witness to suffering from, failures of development. Anthropologists, too, acknowledge the realities of "underdevelopment" even as they flee from that word. For example, Tania Murray Li notes unsparingly:

> For centuries Lauje highlanders had lived in conditions of insecurity as their food production was vulnerable to catastrophic droughts and they struggled to earn enough cash to meet even the most basic needs—salt, kerosene, and clothing. In 1990 they lived in tiny, flimsy bamboo huts; they had little or no access to education; their diets were deficient, and one in

three of the children born did not reach adulthood. Far from being romantic about life in the hills, highlanders considered themselves to be poor and they wanted to change their situation.[13]

About ten years after writing that, Li began a lecture with a reminder of the poverty and suffering that motivates, or should motivate, what we study and do.

> Like many people in this room, I am dismayed by the present state of the world. . . . 10 percent of the world population still lives in extreme poverty (most of them in sub-Saharan Africa and India) . . . conditions of work in many sectors are weak and deteriorating; there is deepening inequality within and between nations; routine insecurity and catastrophic violence affect specific populations and entire regions; there is a scandalous waste of materials and human capacities, and mounting, irreversible, ecological ruin.

"We should all be outraged by these trends," Li continued, "and mobilized to change them, but mostly we are not."[14]

How could we do better? The "missing piece" in all this anthropological research, noted Arjun Appadurai, "has been a systematic effort to understand how cultural systems, as combinations of norms, dispositions, practices, and histories, frame the good life as a landscape of discernible ends and of practical paths to the achievement of those ends."[15]

I agree. Here are two examples of "discernable ends" that need connecting to "practical paths."

Cultural Change and Cultural Preservation in Bhutan

Bhutan's political culture has become markedly democratic, noted the country's former prime minister Tshering Tobgay in 2019, even though multiparty democracy had only begun there in 2007–2008. How did this cultural change occur? "What most distinguishes Bhutan's democracy from the other 160-odd other democracies in the world," Tobgay emphasized, "is that we the people did not want it. We did not fight for democracy or even ask for it. In fact, all the people were decidedly against parliamentary democracy. You see, to put it simply, we were happy with the way things were. So, the King personally educated his people on the democratic process and imposed it in the country."

Tobgay went on to describe some of the unique features of Bhutanese democracy. And then he concluded by reaffirming the planned nature of a huge *change* in political culture—and noted too, that Bhutan's democracy is *attuned* to its culture and has as a goal *preserving* its culture.

> The main point, however, is that His Majesty the king did not just introduce democracy into Bhutan, he had to impose it on the people. But His Majesty went further, he educated and trained all his people in the democratic process. And most importantly, His Majesty the king designed our democracy to suit our unique needs, ensuring that Bhutan democracy is fit for purpose, to serve country and people. So, our democracy is not an end in itself: it is a means to protect our sovereignty, to nurture our unique culture, to preserve our pristine environment, to strengthen our welfare system, and to ensure that political leaders and decision-makers remain faithful to the ideas of Gross National Happiness.[16]

It was King Jigme Singye Wangchuck (sometimes called "King Four" as the fourth regent of the Wangchuck dynasty) who declared that multiparty democratic elections would occur in 2008. Before those elections, he went to his son and said, in effect, "I am going to step down as king, and you will take over." His son Jigme Khesar Namgyel Wangchuck told me this story the first time I met him, and he recounted that he had told his father, in effect, "No, you are so revered and so capable." But his father insisted—"I became king when I was sixteen. If I bring in the democratic order and then you come in afterwards, it will thwart the momentum. It is good that you shepherd in our democracy." And so, his son became King Five in 2006 at the age of twenty-six, and the elections went forward successfully.

King Five has proved to be an agent of cultural change in many ways, from democracy to education to local development. But listen to how he described to me in 2014 the biggest challenge facing Bhutan. "How can we open up our country to outside knowledge and culture, while at the same time preserving and strengthening our unique culture and spirituality?"

Let us reframe this paradigmatic question in the terms of this book. How might knowledge about Bhutan's culture, as well as of experiences around the world with development and cultural change, help the king and his country meet the challenge?

Taking Culture into Account

Other questions about culture and development don't involve cultural change. Rather, they concern adapting policies and programs to cultural realities. Consider Ebola. When this killer disease surges, its victims need to understand how to prevent it and treat it. Knowledge from medicine and public health is key; so is knowledge about the interactions among disease, treatments, and local cultural practices. For example, traditional funeral rites may unwittingly spread Ebola. Indeed, the way those in the health establishment from outside the village arrive, interact with, and treat locals may unwittingly lead to cultural misunderstandings, even violence.

How might both providers and recipients of healthcare do better with detailed understandings of the cultures of both providers and recipients?

The generalization of taking culture into account goes something like this. A problem exists. Treatments exist. But the treatments may interact with cultures to produce outcomes no one intended. How might the design and implementation of treatments—policies, projects, participatory processes, management systems—take account of the interactions in order to do better? In the words of Mkandawire:

> The idea of "catching up" entails learning not only about ideas from abroad but also about one's capacities and weaknesses. "Catching up" requires that countries know themselves and their own history that has set the "initial conditions" for any future progress. They need a deep understanding of their culture, not only for self-reaffirmation, but in order to capture the strong points of their culture and institutions that will see their societies through rapid social change.[17]

The generalization of taking culture into account could aim instead at *not* "catching up." As I will emphasize throughout this book, cultural knowledge might help people oppose, or radically change the paths and meanings of, "development."

About that last word in the title: What kind of *manifesto* are we talking about? The term has a venerable pedigree. Outside of politics, its usages include education, science, and art. Broadly, a manifesto expresses a critique and a call for change, and it often includes examples of how to do better.

All of that here, plus an entreaty. The practical work of applying cultural studies could be, should be, on the side of the disadvantaged, the underpowered, the indigenous. And so, the focus of work on culture and development might be "non-state forces and organizations that challenge the existing dominant order," as James Ferguson put it, "to see if links can be found between our expertise and their practical needs as they determine them."

True, Ferguson admitted, "we must entertain the strong possibility that there will be no need for what we do among such actors." And yet, in a hopeful sentiment I find compelling, Ferguson concluded his book by imagining "a network of researchers committed to forging such links" with the goal of "engaging one's intellectual and scholarly energies with the work of political and social transformations."[18]

He provided no examples of such a network, but it is an attractive goal: one that I hope this manifesto might abet.

2

Is Culture a Key to Development?

It was Don Fernando's first time in Berlin, and his first official act as the newly appointed finance minister of the African nation of Equatorial Guinea. (In that tiny country, even ministers are referred to by their first name, as long as that respectful Spanish "Don" precedes it.) The event was the inaugural cocktail party for the 1988 annual meetings of the World Bank and the International Monetary Fund (IMF). Don Fernando looked lost. Around us thousands of elegant delegates drank champagne and sampled smoked salmon. As we chatted amid the splendor, I wondered whether Don Fernando perceived me, his adviser, as a cog in the mysterious machinery of international capitalism, which could thus assemble from around the globe the heads of central banks and finance ministries, as well as the fine wines and canapés.

Outside the giant convention center, ten thousand police were shielding the eight thousand delegates from thirty thousand protesters. The demonstrators denounced the World Bank and the IMF as neo-imperialists who crammed unsound capitalist policies down the throats of impoverished, debt-ridden nations. Economic austerity programs hurt the poor, they said, ripped up the environment, and promoted only a shell of modernization. They had a point, albeit not one often expressed within the conference hall. Stylistically, too, we were worlds apart. The protesters' shrill newsletters and New Age garb contrasted with the polysyllabic orthodoxies of the Bank and the Fund and with the uniforms, differing but with the constant of colorlessness, of policeman and banker. It was almost like different cultures clashing; I couldn't help reflecting that none of them had much resonance with the cultures of Africa.

In most of sub-Saharan Africa, both socialism and capitalism, in a variety of forms, have disappointed. In those days, our work in Equatorial Guinea was already unearthing some reasons why. Macroeconomic reforms may be required, but they aren't enough. Neither can socialist economies succeed without certain institutional and informational foundations that, in many poor countries, are weak or absent. And when one examines these

The Culture and Development Manifesto. Robert Klitgaard, Oxford University Press (2021). © Oxford University Press.
DOI: 10.1093/oso/9780197517734.003.0002

foundations, one begins to wonder whether culture, in its many meanings and manifestations, is key.

Challenges

The second day in Berlin, Don Fernando took me aside for a long conversation about the economy.[1] What was going wrong? We talked through a few examples.

Take cocoyam, a tuber known locally as *malanga* and a staple of the local diet. It was a good crop for Equatorial Guinea's climate and soils, and our malanga was said to be larger and tastier than those from neighboring countries. It looked like a good prospect for export, yet nothing was happening. Despite Equatorial Guinea's macroeconomic reforms, many obstacles kept freer markets at bay.

One was at the level of village production and marketing. I had interviewed many women who grew and sold malanga. Remarkably, each felt compelled to take her own production to market.

"I don't trust my neighbor to sell the malanga for me," one woman explained. "She would not give me the correct price or would take the money."

"Even a woman in your village, your neighbor?"

"Yes, I do not trust them."

As a result, each woman would spend about three-fifths of her malangas' sale price—twice the amount she spent to grow them—traveling to and from the market and living there for the six days it took to sell her produce in small, retail batches.

The women also complained about "taxes" on their produce. In the Malabo market, municipal officials and policemen tapped them for 15 to 20 percent of the sale price in official payments and protection money. Remarkably, official taxes from small venders accounted for two-thirds of municipal revenues in the country's two largest cities.

The would-be exporter faced further problems. Despite the supposed liberalization of trade, there remained an array of permits and hassles, and the Ministry of Industry and Commerce still slapped on a 25 percent export tax.

"Look here, I have seen things from the point of view of making money," explained one of the traders in the Malabo market. "With exports the government imposes so many obstacles. There are many permits and many payments. I do not believe that I can make money in exports, and there are many uncertainties."

Still other factors helped squelch the market for malanga—a lack of credit, few agricultural extension agents who knew about food crops, and an absence of product grades and quality standards. I explained to Don Fernando that malanga's problems were part of a more general syndrome—not just in Equatorial Guinea but also around Africa. Big economic reforms had taken place; prices and exchange rates were supposedly "got right." But food production and exports had often not taken off. Market institutions, government regulations, and economic infrastructure remained deficient. A culture of trust was absent. And so free-market reforms had made little difference in, of all places, the market.

Better Governments, Better Markets

Over the next days in Berlin, Don Fernando and I talked about other obstacles to economic advance. Property rights, for example, were a mess. It was difficult to buy and sell a piece of property—even, sometimes, to know who owns it. A Spaniard who had lived in Equatorial Guinea for forty years had explained it this way.

"You have to understand the traditional system of property here. The people were hunters more than cultivators, and even the cultivators were nomads. Land was not stable, it would be used and then abandoned. When the tribe moved to a new area the chief would assign the land to the tribal notables, the closest land to the new settlement to the biggest of them, farther out to the rest of the people." Later, in colonial times, as a token protection against exploitation of natives, land was not sold to colonists but was leased for ninety-nine years. "So, the idea remains—land is not yours, it is of the state. The traditional idea also, that land is given by the chief to the notables of the tribe."

After independence, some lands were nationalized. Some were resold by the government but subject to conditions that could lead to renationalization. Property lines were often unclear. Stories abounded of people buying a building or a property only to find that it belonged to someone else. As in other parts of the developing world, unclear property rights were crippling economic initiative.[2]

Don Fernando and I talked about other institutional foundations of successful economies that were weak or absent. The legal system was inefficient and corrupt. Contracts were precarious because the courts, whose judges were often bribed or intimidated, could not be counted on to enforce them. Two state-sponsored banks had recently gone belly-up. For months, it was impossible to withdraw savings, write checks, even exchange foreign currency. The banks had been dispensing loans to government higher-ups and other well-connected people, often with the tacit understanding that they need not be repaid. Fly-by-night "foreign investors" bribed officials to get a deal or a loan and then took off.

Before long, our conversation turned to corruption. Despite macroeconomic reforms, economic regulations and permits were still pervasive. This, plus a lack of accountability and government pay that did not cover a family's basic needs, had spawned widespread corruption. Indeed, as in much of Africa, the lines between the public and private sectors were now vague, even invisible, given all the illicit payoffs, joint ventures, and co-optation.

With so many institutional foundations lacking, the so-called private sector in Equatorial Guinea and elsewhere in Africa did not resemble what we know in the West. A huge informal sector of small traders and producers operated outside the official economic and financial systems. In some cities in Central Africa, it was thought that up to 80 percent of all jobs are in unregistered, unofficial microenterprises with one to five employees. Africa's middle class was meager, perhaps 5 percent of the population in many countries. Many markets were thin and volatile, leading to monopolies and exploitation. Many government officials were themselves in business, in several senses. So, Western concepts of property, private enterprise, and regulation were often out of sync with local cultural and political realities.

Don Fernando's Lecture on Culture

In Berlin, Don Fernando let me be his instructor on the institutional foundations of economic development. When we returned to Equatorial Guinea, it was the new finance minister's turn to lecture me on the cultural and political side.

It was a month after Berlin, and in the interim, while I was in the States, there had been a coup attempt in Equatorial Guinea. Many innocent people, including one of my closest Equatoguinean colleagues, had been tortured, though no charges had ever been lodged against him. Upon returning, I tried to help him, but he was incommunicado. I tried to organize the international community to petition the president for an open investigation of the torture.

I sought Don Fernando's help. I would be leaving the country soon. He stalled me. Finally, late one afternoon, we finally got together at the Ministry of Finance.

Don Fernando had abandoned his necktie and he was smoking a cigar as we walked together up the tattered back stairs of the Ministry and entered his office. He turned on the air conditioner but left the lights off. I sat on the couch, and he plopped down catty-corner on a chair of slick, light green Naugahyde. His face was outlined by the glare from the frosted window behind him: a round black silhouette against a trapezoid of white.

"You know," he began, "in Africa there are certain differences from the West and here even more so. People are suspicious, people are jealous. If you have a car and someone else does not, he starts saying bad things about you. He wants the car, you see, and is envious. Then you find out he has been saying bad things and you try to get him. I will tell you the truth, these recent problems are a lot like that. There is a disturbance, so they round up other people and go after them. The disturbance is within one little group, but they get people from other groups so that people say, 'Oh, they were involved too? Well, that justifies big actions, it's a general problem, a general threat.'"

Don Fernando's speech was animated, his voice certain. He hardly resembled the meek man I'd encountered in Berlin.

"In Africa you have to understand that people do not have a common interest," Fernando continued. "Without a common interest, there are fights. Social conflict. I don't know if you understand me. In Africa first comes the family, then the clan, then the province, then the region, and finally the country. But the country is the last thing. You vote for someone and you say, 'I'll vote for him because he's my uncle.' You have noticed how we all refer to each other—'He's my cousin, she's my aunt.' If no one is a member of your family broadly speaking, then you vote for someone from your clan. Or your district. And if it's a Nigerian involved, you always choose the Guinean, no matter how bad. That's the way it is in Africa, and that's the way it is here."

Fernando told a story about the previous year's preparations for a Central African conference held in Bata, on the mainland part of Equatorial Guinea. People had been conscripted to work on an airport runway extension and the renovation of the soccer stadium.

"Boom, boom, boom—they worked and worked till late at night. And you know when the stadium was done, my God compared to what was there before it was something—and the people were so proud. And when the big jets came into the airport where before the runways were too short, when people saw them land, the people were proud of themselves. Later I saw the president and said, 'Did you notice the same detail as I?' 'What's that?' he said. 'The fact that though the people had to work without pay till late hours, when they finished they were proud.' This work created a common interest, and the people were proud.

"That is what we have to do when everyone is poor. When there is hunger there is no common interest. And everyone thinks of families and clans. So, to create a common interest we need strong leadership—we need to launch works like hospitals, roads, and schools with the people working, where they can see the results and feel proud."

We talked about the coup attempt, about dictatorship and corruption and torture. I said there had to be a strategy for change. Don Fernando said that one had to be realistic.

"There is no equilibrium in our societies," he went on. "The problem of the president is that most of the people in government are incompetent and uncultured, they have no exposure to the outside world. These people are jealous of the few with outside training. But there are too few trained people for the president to have any choice. He needs the Guineans who emigrated to come back, all the lawyers and engineers. They won't come because they talk about democracy and rights. But we won't have that until we have more trained people. The president faces a balancing act—he has to keep the uneducated top people happy, the jealous ones, because they have the ear of the people in the villages. If the president goes only with the educated few, that three or five percent, then he would be out of office in a week. It is a dangerous situation—he has no choice but to humor the backward, the reactionaries."

I told him about other countries that had made progress even in the face of top-to-bottom corruption. But Don Fernando would not let me finish. He repeated his account, with lots of enthusiasm and examples and "I don't know if you understand." Then he continued his lecture on culture.

"Africa is characterized by poverty and tribalism, which render the common interest as conceived in middle-class countries nonexistent. Thus, without a dictator who serves the interests of the masses, the powerful will exploit them. Or else the masses will rise up and exploit the advantaged. Some people see this and commit an error: they figure the more repressive they are, the more stability. In Africa we suffer from this error. We do need a dictator, however. When I say dictator, I mean one that does not permit either the privileged or the oppressed to dominate. There are people who are born to correct these disequilibriums.

"The typical African is poor and hungry. What does he want? He wants three wives and eight, nine, ten children. Then he is happy. If someone has a car, he is bad—it creates jealousy and then instability. This is our reality. There is no common interest to defend. And there is so little education. So, if you allow complete freedom of speech and democracy as in England, you end up with conspiracies and nonsense.

"What has recently occurred must be seen in this light. Something happened within the group, everyone gets excited and casts aspersions on many others, innocent people. Then things happen, a person gets beat up or gets a broken collarbone like your assistant. I am by no means defending torture or anything else. We can and we should do better. But we cannot have a democracy like England's."

I said I appreciated his description but had doubts about his prescription. Could the minister name any dictators who had served the masses and "corrected disequilibriums"?

Don Fernando thought. "Franco," he finally said.

I let that be and asked, "In Africa?"

Don Fernando could think of none. I had a chance to insert a word about the need to begin where we were, yes, but to have a strategy for moving forward. And torture—that had to go, no excuses.

Don Fernando responded dramatically. There was *no way*, he cried, to appreciate this country without having known it under the terrible dictator of the past, Francisco Macías Nguema. Then he said it twice more.

"Without this understanding the parameters of comparison are not objective. You have to compare with the subject itself, not its neighbor. If we were under Macías, there would be sixty people dead now. Including the former finance minister and your friend who was tortured. If you had come to my office like this after hours under Macías then I would be in jail. Now these people are on the streets with their rights."

I reminded him of the torture.

"We started at minus ten. You can't just look at our current situation, say plus five or zero or minus five. Few countries have suffered as we have," Fernando said. "You cannot help but think like an American." I shook my head, but Fernando went on.

"No, listen to me, if you had seen Equatorial Guinea under Macías, you would see that we have come the furthest of any country. That comparatively it's a paradise."

Can We Do Better?

Fernando was implying that there were cultural dimensions to the establishment of just and dynamic economies, good government, and appropriate international cooperation. Other experts on Africa agree. For example, the Nigerian political scientist Claude Ake argued that many past efforts had failed because they did not take indigenous cultures into account. "We build on the indigenous by making it determine the form and the content of development strategy, by ensuring that development change accommodates itself to these things, be they values, interests, aspirations and or social institutions which are important in the life of the people. It is only when developmental change comes to terms with them that it can become sustainable."[3] Summarizing the lessons from decades of rural development work in West Africa by the Centre d'Études Économiques et Sociales d'Afrique de l'Ouest, Piet Buijsrogge said he and his colleagues had learned to begin with local cultures. "We come to the conclusion that the structures and traditional values of different villages have been the point of departure of a dynamic of development, a conclusion that destroys the theory that affirms that the obstacle to development resides precisely in these structures and values of tradition."[4]

In an eloquent presentation to the Sociedad del Quinto Centenario in Madrid, Carlos Fuentes posed questions concerning culture and development in Latin America:

Both capitalism and socialism, in their Latin American versions, have shown themselves incapable of extricating the majority of our people from misery. . . . And the cultural question therefore is this: is there another solution, a solution of our own? Don't we possess the tradition, imagination, intellectual and organizational reserves to elaborate our own models of development, consonant with the truth of what we have been, what we are, and what we want to be, responsible before the civil societies which have been expending themselves in our countries from below and from the periphery?[5]

Fuentes pointed out that there will likely be more than one solution, even within a single country, given the existence in Latin America of so much "cultural plurality."

Beyond the Global South's "own models of development," does the world need new "epistemologies" grown in the Global South? Their aim, writes Boaventura de Sousa Santos,

> is to identify and valorize that which often does not even appear as knowledge in the light of the dominant epistemologies, that which emerges instead as part of the struggles of resistance against oppression and against the knowledge that legitimates such oppression. . . . [Epistemologies of the Global South] aim at a bottom-up subaltern cosmopolitanism. Rather than abstract universality, they promote pluriversality. A kind of thinking that promotes decolonization, creolization, or *mestizaje* through intercultural translation.[6]

The failures of so-called development have for many years been blamed on cultural insensitivity, even cultural irrelevance. "The importance of adapting each development project to the culture for which it is planned seems so obvious that not much more needs to be said about it here," wrote anthropologist T. Scarlett Epstein.[7]

Important and obvious, perhaps, but *how* to adapt? Can what the social sciences know about cultural plurality help in what Fuentes calls the process of redefining development? How can development policies, ways of management and organization, educational techniques, and political processes adapt to cultural diversity? What is known from a practical perspective about how cultures change (purposefully, inadvertently) or can be kept from changing? How might public policy and management take advantage of the creative energies of the "civil societies" at the bottom, at the margins? And how might the disciplines that study culture help in rethinking the ends and means of "development"?

3

La Problématique

And so I began to study culture. Hosted by the Centre d'Études et des Recherches Internationales in Paris, I dove into French anthropology from the founders of the field up to contemporary thinkers.

My approach was chronological. First came the complete works of Marcel Mauss, one of the founders of French anthropology, who wrote from the 1890s to the 1940s. Mauss proved to be a kind of Sherlock Holmes figure, who to his contemporaries seemed to have an encyclopedic command of every fact about every culture in the world. Next came Georges Balandier, whose youthful failure in the 1940s to impress Camus with his first novel led him to change career plans and head for Africa, where he become an anthropologist.[1] Balandier never lost his literary and philosophical aspirations, which he combined with a certain worldliness and an aura of effortless superiority. If Mauss was the Sherlock Holmes of French anthropology (or perhaps the Nero Wolfe, who like Mauss never left home to do field research), then Balandier was the Humphrey Bogart.

In 1954, anthropologists, psychologists, and other specialists held a five-day conference in France on issues related to culture and development. Balandier was the rapporteur. His detailed notes recounted the reminders that become rituals on occasions like these.[2] For example:

- Culture is difficult, perhaps impossible, to define.
- No matter what the definition, culture is not something static and historical as often posited but ever evolving and dynamic.
- Culture is not something unitary and uniform either but, metaphorically, a blend or a colloid or perhaps even something akin to multiple personalities.
- Differing cultures deserve respect.
- Too much has been made of the negative features of traditional societies and not enough of the positive features, from which so-called modern societies can learn.

The Culture and Development Manifesto. Robert Klitgaard, Oxford University Press (2021). © Oxford University Press. DOI: 10.1093/oso/9780197517734.003.0003

- Cultures manifest their own "configurations" of motivations and incentives as a consequence of their "specific cultural capital."
- There are no necessary or sufficient cultural preconditions for economic or political development.
- Policies and economic systems adapt to culture and cultures to them, policies can change cultures, cultures have their own dynamic of change, and valuations of developmental ends and means are themselves shaped by culture.
- Indeed, or especially, "development" itself is a culturally loaded term, ready to succumb to ethnocentrism.

And so forth. Alas, these classic prefaces to hard work—which are, of course, not merely scientific but are themselves freighted with cultural content and political correctness—occupied much of the conference's five days. (And one sees them repeated again and again, up to today.)

Next came Pierre Bourdieu, an influential figure who ceased referring to himself as an anthropologist about the time he accepted a "juicy" professorship in sociology at the College de France.[3] Like Don Fernando, the finance minister of Equatorial Guinea, Bourdieu criticized Westerners for ignoring cultural and social diversity. Of particular relevance to our endeavor are Bourdieu's increasingly virulent critiques of economics.

Bourdieu grew up in a humble family in a rural region of southern France. He escaped to Paris at age seventeen as a brilliant scholarship student, eventually turning to the study of philosophy under Maurice Merleau-Ponty. Military obligations intervened. Bourdieu ended up in Algeria as a twenty-five-year-old soldier, and after his tour of duty he stayed on for a year as a teacher. He returned a few years later to do research among a Berber ethnic group called the Kabyle. He was surprised by what he learned.

He described his "conversion" from his French and market-conditioned ideas as he discovered through interviews that many Kabyle people were baffled by practices that in Bourdieu's culture were simply assumed:

- Working for pay.
- "The very possibility of impersonal transactions between strangers."
- Saving for the long term.
- Lending with interest charges.
- Indeed, thinking of "the future as a site of 'possibles' that are open and susceptible to calculation."

Behavior thought natural in the world he knew could be unnatural to people with different "dispositions" and "habits." The people he was meeting differed in "their tastes, needs, propensities or aptitudes" and in "a refusal to calculate." Yes, he noted, some aspects of gift-giving, even to a deity, are with the express hope of a gift in return, as Mauss had noted. But not all aspects: not at all.[4]

Bourdieu argued that many Algerians had been "pitched into" an economic game for which they were "not equally prepared and equipped, culturally and economically." Policy reforms and seemingly benign development programs would systematically favor the culturally and economically advantaged. What's more, he noted, the less advantaged found themselves "defenseless, particularly in cultural matters." They were forced to "convert" from their "universe of belief" to a different "principle of reason (or, if one prefers, the principle of economy)," a conversion that is often "very costly and painful."[5]

Two conversions, then, both distressing. As a result of his own conversion, Bourdieu abandoned the abstractions of philosophy in favor of the realities of anthropology. His research on the Kabyle was published to acclaim. Among its implications—which Bourdieu elaborated in further works—was how erroneous both theories and policies could be when they ignored those differences in "tastes, needs, propensities or aptitudes." Economists in particular were misguided in their universalism and in their emphasis on rational, individualistic calculations. Moreover, Bourdieu argued, whole areas of life, from religion to family to art, were outside the scope of the maximizing logic he thought economics entailed. And when he discovered that economists, such as Gary Becker, were modeling family decisions as maximization problems with interesting equilibria or talking about *art appreciation* in terms of investment risks and returns, Bourdieu was horrified. Economics was, anthropologically speaking, a monster.

> *Homo oeconomicus*, as conceived (tacitly or explicitly) by economic orthodoxy, is a kind of anthropological monster: this theoretically minded man of practice is the most extreme personification of the scholastic fallacy . . . by which the scholar puts into the heads of the agents he is studying . . . the theoretical considerations and constructions he has had to develop in order to account for their practices.[6]

Back in France, Bourdieu applied his methods to the French elite and education system. He went on to analyze diverse domains such as photography, the media, the housing market, the funding of arts in America, and the behavior of political groups. He also examined some of the poorest members of French society, including immigrants. Everywhere he found patterns of thought and social classifications that distinguished subgroups, reinforced elites, and interacted with policies and institutions. In short, culture matters. Ignoring it, as simple economic models do, leads to lamentable (if not monstrous) errors of design and management.

What, then, to do?

Well, to begin (and alas, perhaps also to end), don't ignore cultural complexity and diversity. But can one do more that *note* them? Can one characterize (classify, measure, model) those "dispositions and habits"? Develop a theory of how cultural capital and social capital are used by their "carriers" as a function of the setting (he calls it "the field") and the challenges individuals and groups face? A theory of how these variables change?

The answers would have important applications. Consider two of the practical challenges noted by Bourdieu. First, some cultural groups lag behind others in academic achievement, even when going to the same schools. He cited differences in their *cultural capital* as a cause.

Second, when confronted with the same market opportunities, locally and internationally, groups respond differently—in particular, some groups respond more profitably than others. Here, Bourdieu used explanations based on *social capital*. (He later lamented the fact that James Coleman had taken his idea to the "highly protected market of American sociology" and got academic credit for it.)[7] To some, cultural capital and social capital are similar in function. To the political scientist Francis Fukuyama, "social capital is shared norms or values that promote social cooperation, instantiated in actual social relationships. Social capital in this view is a utilitarian way of looking at culture."[8] To the anthropologist David B. Kronenfeld, culture enables "collective action that is based on varyingly complex divisions of labor."[9]

Bourdieu said that differences in social and cultural capital are evident. His inference: economists and others who ignore cultural and social causes are fundamentally in error. Don't assume that what works in culture X will work in culture Y.

But couldn't there, shouldn't there, be more? For example, how might a group's cultural capital be taken into account in the design and implementation of education and training to help the members of the lagging group catch up or, if they chose, go in a different direction? If one understood differences in social capital, how might one create better labor and capital markets, more socially relevant and effective policies, and—if so desired by those feeling less culturally integrated—less "costly and painful" ways to "convert" some of their dispositions and habits: to change their behavior if not directly or necessarily their attitudes and values?

Bourdieu's vast and influential work, to my knowledge, never addressed these questions. As we shall see later in the chapter, years later many of Bourdieu's followers resisted applying his concept of social capital to development work.

Intrigued, I plunged into the pool of contemporary French anthropologists and Africanists. Differences within Africa were immense in commonly cited components of culture such as religion, kinship systems, and the like. Visiting the former French colony of Guinea, for example, I learned that the people of one region were highly individualistic, another strongly hierarchical, and a third "communitarian." Some parts of Africa were matrilineal, others patrilineal. And yet, many social scientists as well as many Africans cited some common features such as "the politics of the belly," strong family and clan ties, magical beliefs, even what the Kenyan scientist Thomas Risley Odhiambo called an anti-scientific mentality.[10] As noted, Bourdieu noted among the Berbers not only different "values" concerning work for pay, savings, and trust of outsiders but also an inability or unwillingness to calculate the benefits and costs of different alternatives: a different rationality, he asserted. Another scholar characterized sub-Saharan Africa in terms of "economies of affection" instead of impersonal exchange.

Some of these characteristics and contrasts can be identified beyond Africa. But my interest was not primarily in arraying whatever "cultural differences" there might be around the globe, but in thinking about how we (again, in that broad sense) might take culture into account. Shouldn't an agricultural credit system in Guinea take account of regional cultural differences such as individualist, hierarchical, and communitarian, for example, in the use of group credit and co-guarantees? Shouldn't a family-planning system take account of whether a locale was matrilineal or patrilineal, not to mention Catholic or animist or Islamic? And those varying meanings of work and saving, of gender roles, of wealth, of power—how might they be countenanced in the design and implementation of policy reforms (or, to repeat, in resistance to reforms)?

Just as I was discovering personalities—indeed, characters, heroes, and legends—I also was encountering cultures and subcultures in the very study of culture. In some domains, fervor counted more than science. In my new

French intellectual haunts, to call a work *nuancé* was the supreme compliment, even more than, perhaps, to call it "true" or "useful." "Academic anthropology," wrote the anthropologist Jean-Pierre Olivier de Sardan, "also tends to disregard the problematics of change and to regard the agents of change with contempt."[11]

And yet, many African scholars and activists emphasized the influence of "cultural factors" on various kinds of development. For example, the Kenyan political scientist Ali A. Mazrui sought "to demonstrate that both *ideology* and *technology* are rooted in culture. . . . Certainly differences in skills and technique are, on the whole, more basic than differences in income. And these skill differences are profoundly affected by *culture*."[12] Mazrui characterized traditional African societies as "cultures of nostalgia rather than of anticipation," cultures that move slowly, value prestige instead of achievement, "impressive when judged by standards of charity and solidarity" but where "productivity and effectiveness are less than optimal" (202). The survival of this sort of culture had advantages and disadvantages. "On the negative side, rural culture may be in any case a culture of poverty and indigence. On the positive side, much of the countryside is the repository of what is authentic and distinctive in a particular society" (203). But unfortunately,

> Africa as a whole borrowed the wrong things from the West—even the wrong components of capitalism. We borrowed the profit motive but not the entrepreneurial spirit. We borrowed the acquisitive appetites of capitalism but not the creative risk-taking. We are at home with Western gadgets but are bewildered by Western workshops. We wear the wristwatch but refuse to watch it for the culture of punctuality. We have learnt to parade in display, but not to drill in discipline. The West's consumption patterns have arrived, but not necessarily the West's techniques of production. (5)

Mazrui's recommendation was that rural modernization in Africa should be postponed if possible. "If the 'modernization' of the countryside could be delayed for another generation or two, it could give the society as a whole a better chance to choose a path of 'modernization' which would not be excessively based on 'Westernization' " (203). He left up in the air how this might be accomplished.

"Assuredly," wrote Daniel Etounga-Manguelle about his native Africa, "to revolutionize our culture—and thus our political culture—is the only way to obtain the desired change. To deny that is to accept that we should be marginalized: not only in economic terms—that is clear!—but also in psychological and moral terms."[13] He identified the "principal lacunae that explain our counter-performance in a world based on other values" as the lack of "a critical culture: that is, a system of digestion and assimilation of new cultural events that permit the popular (ethnological) culture to progress" (72). He also cited "the jealousy, the blind submission to the irrational, the lethargy" (125) as African characteristics to be overcome. His recommendation was the opposite of Ali Mazrui's wish to delay modernization, although both agreed that any solution would have to be African. Etounga-Manguelle said Africa needs a "program of cultural adjustment," carried out by Africans, which would transform their "mentality" to one more consistent with values in the rest of the world. "To overcome its underdevelopment," he wrote in 2009, "Africans have to take responsibility, and in every part of society, free themselves and assume individually and collectively the responsibilities implied in the most mundane activities of everyday life. This is, undeniably, a matter of dignity."[14] But he did not describe how such rethinking and transforming might take place.

Similar analyses emerged in a remarkable polemic by the Cameroonian writer Axelle Kabou. African cultures and mentalities are the main obstacles to development, she wrote, yet they never appear on the "long list of official causes of underdevelopment." Indeed, these mentalities, she argued, as well as the very idea of *under*development, have become taboos. The result of "years of disinformation" is that words and realities no longer coincide, that Africans fail to face up to the need to become something new—authentically African *and* different. Africans must understand the depth of their underdevelopment, which is not a matter of capital or resources but "inside the heads of Africans." In order for the Africa to succeed, she said, Africans must become rational—and to do so implies first of all to face up to its deepest problems.[15]

Wariness about Culture

When I would raise these points about culture with economists, their responses were dismissive. I asked one distinguished student of the historical patterns of economic development whether he had ever tried to look at cultural differences among those patterns. I might as well have queried him about the usefulness of phlogiston. "What do you mean, 'cultural differences'?" he replied, rhetorically. It was a question I kept hearing from everyone I asked about culture, no matter what their disciplines; yet it was precisely the question for which I was seeking their guidance. Then he asked, "How would you ever *measure* it?" Vernon Ruttan observed that in development economics, "cultural considerations have been cast into the 'underworld' of development thought and practice."[16] Along with, I began to think, those who wish to study them.

And policymakers—they, too, expressed surprise, if not scorn, at my interest in the cultural dimensions of development. One functionary of an international agency admonished, "We can't come close to understanding the local culture. My wife is an anthropologist. She's been working on Guinea for ten years. I've been an economist for Guinea for three years. She'd be the first to tell you that there are many cultures there, and she isn't close to understanding even one of them. I'm certainly not." Another said, "What are you going to do about 'culture' if you find it? Endorse it, if it's feudal and oppressive? Try to change it? Who has the right to do that?" He meant these as rhetorical questions.

But it was the negative response from cultural anthropologists themselves that puzzled me most. When as a novice in their field I would pose my questions to senior figures in anthropology in France and in America, their eyebrows would also rise. The aesthetics of their reaction was not to phlogiston, as in the economist's start when confronted by a concept thought to be patently unscientific. With the anthropologists, it was more like seeing a Clydesdale loose in their tulip garden. "What do *you* mean, 'cultural differences'?" was still the response, now delivered with a different emphasis and in the fashion of a warning-off. Before providing any answers—and often they never did—the anthropologists would brace me with other questions. "What do you mean, 'taking into account' those differences? *Who* is going to do the taking into account? And to whom?" Was I, if not a Clydesdale, an outsider transgressing sacred turf?

I began to wonder whether one had to inhabit the anthropologists' culture to earn their confidence. The Dogon did not reveal the secrets of their creed to Marcel Griaule until after he had paid a heavy price in terms of learning their language and culture and demonstrating his sincerity and solidarity by living among them. Was I lacking the anthropological equivalent of rites of passages, native language, and customs of the initiated?

Among the anthropologists themselves there were signs of cultural boundaries. Those who belonged to the various sects of so-called applied anthropology seemed cast out by the theorists. And there was resentment in the other direction. When I would ask applied anthropologists what anthropology as the science of man—as the comparative and analytical study of culture, among other things—could contribute to development policy, I would sometimes receive yet another variant of the raised eyebrows reaction. It was the response one might discern in a master mechanic talking about research engineers. "What do *they* know about what's really happening with my machines on the shop floor?"

Perhaps Culture Is Not Important for Development

In search of culture, the first cultures I encountered were intellectual ones. Indeed, within intellectual cultures I began to perceive a kind of split personality with regard to "culture." It is alleged to be an important "factor," yet it seems entirely elusive. It should be taken into account, but not used to make cultural prejudgments. A culture should be preserved—unless, that is, it needed to be radically changed.

Don Fernando's words about culture's importance kept coming back to me. But were there not counterexamples? For instance, consider this list of apparently negative cultural traits and try to guess the country to which they refer:

- Hypocrisy
- Lack of public spirit
- Factionalism
- Immaturity
- Groupism vs. individualism
- Persistently childlike
- Fond of festivals
- Not logical but intuitive

Here is a hint: the list comes from a book entitled *The Anatomy of Dependence*, which was written by a distinguished psychologist from the country in question.

Before learning the answer, consider two other questions. Do you think this country has enjoyed economic success? What sort of governance do you think it has?

To many people, the list sounds like a classic description of an economically and politically backward society, whose "culture" or personality somehow prevents or at least inhibits "development." But the country is Japan.[17] And Japan is an economic powerhouse, a thriving democracy, a country where the average IQ score is thought to have increased by more than 5 points per decade from 1950 to 1975.[18] Its culture has clearly not prevented development.

This example raises a big question about culture and development: So what? Studies often show that supposed "cultural barriers to development" turn out not to be necessary or sufficient conditions.[19] Those who admire scholarly rigor may be suspicious that culture becomes a catch-all, a name for the residual in a regression equation. No carefully specified model of cultural variables is widely accepted—indeed, to my knowledge, none exists. Without agreed-upon concepts and measures, economists (and others) ask, in what sense can social science examine "culture"?

Some of the phenomena of so-called primitive cultures can be understood in economic terms, especially by using game theory and the economics of information.[20] A cultural anthropologist like Tania Murray Li may discover, and be surprised by, the "stealth takeover" of microeconomic principles among impoverished Lauje highlanders of Sulawesi, Indonesia. She found that—given "indigenous concepts emphasizing the value of an individual's hard work," new market opportunities, and "a land regime that enables private enclosure"—rapid change can take the form "outlined in economics textbooks in which competition reigns and market forces dominate, with little 'distortion' from state subsidies, monopolies, or remittances."[21] Nor with much resistance, she noted, by way of local cultural norms and practices. Rapid changes occurred—but not necessarily, of course, with an ending one would call "happy." (Bronislaw Malinowski once put it this way: the native was being "forced to labor on products he did not wish to produce so that he might satisfy needs that he did not wish to satisfy.")[22]

There is another angle to the "so what" question. Suppose one grants that cultural factors are important in determining or shaping a given problem of economic development or governance. This does not imply that the most feasible or desirable solutions are cultural, nor that a problem cannot be dealt with through policies that make no reference to culture. For example, Dele Olowu argued that governments in Africa were "too centralized" for cultural reasons. He cited "the absence of the Parsonian characteristics of a modernized society—universalism, industrialism, etc.—and the non-compliance with Weberian values within the bureaucracy."[23] Some scholars have cited the hierarchical nature of Latin cultures as the cause of overly centralized governments there. Recent estimates suggest that, in terms of promoting economic growth, fiscal decentralization doesn't work as well in poor countries as in rich ones.[24] Yet successful cases of decentralization do exist in developing countries, and they can be analyzed in terms of improvements in information and incentives, rather than as products of cultural change.[25]

Let me clarify the point. Cultural explanations do not mean that what might be called noncultural remedies are out of place. This is not to say that noncultural remedies always work, nor that we cannot do better with them if we take culture into account in how they are designed and implemented. But it is crucial to separate causes from cures, to focus on the size of treatment effects instead of the percentage of variation explained. By analogy: myopia is 100 percent genetically determined, but we have an excellent nongenetic treatment for it—eyeglasses. Proneness to sunburn may be conditioned both by genetic and cultural factors. In either case, sun block works.

Evidence That Culture Matters

Many practitioners and economists are skeptical of culture (as are many contemporary anthropologists). Yet at the same time, experience tells us that something like it does matter. Consider first a remarkable longitudinal and cross-sectional study of Italy's decentralized political development after 1970.[26] Using detailed empirical research ranging from interviews to case studies to survey research to statistical analyses of secondary data, Robert D. Putnam, Robert Leonardi, and Raffaela Nanetti discovered that the best predictor of which states had the most effective governance was not any measure of their economic development but their civic culture—indeed, their civic culture measured a hundred years before. By far the most important predictor of good government was the degree to which social and political life approximated the ideal of the civic community—the extent of their "social capital." The same Italian regions that sustained choral societies and cooperatives also provided the most support for mutual aid societies and mass-based political parties, and citizens in those same regions were the most eager to make use of their newly granted electoral rights. Elsewhere, by contrast, apathy and ancient vertical bonds of clientelism restrained civic involvement and inhibited voluntary, horizontally based manifestations of social solidarity. Economic factors could not explain this historical connection. Time-series analysis clearly demonstrate that economic growth followed cultural conditions, not the other way around: "Like a powerful magnetic field, civic conditions have gradually but inexorably brought economic conditions into alignment, so that by the 1970s economic modernity is closely associated with the civic community" (153).

> Civic traditions have remarkable staying power. . . . Those regions where local choral groups and mutual aid societies were most abundant in 1870 were almost precisely the same regions characterized by civic involvement in 1970. And although these civic regions were not distinctively prosperous a century ago, they have steadily outpaced the less civic regions in economic performance and (at least since the advent of regional government) in self-governance. As between two regions in 1870—one with a civic tradition, but relatively backward, the other relatively more advanced then (healthier, wealthier, and more industrial), but lacking that culture of civic participation, the former has advanced much more rapidly than the latter during this century, and it is benefitting from better industrial performance now. It is hard not to be impressed by the power of the past. (154–155)

The practical implications of these important findings were less clear. The authors first thought of a concluding chapter with policy implications, but then jettisoned the idea; one of them told me, "We are struggling with the implications of our analysis." Instead, they focused their final chapter on such things as game theoretical models of cultural persistence.

But interest grew in applying their ideas to development activities. For example, the World Bank launched a "social capital initiative." Scholars and practitioners considered how to measure social capital, assess its importance for development outcomes, and possibly then adapt policies and projects to the conditions of social capital. Few anthropologists were involved, as it happened. And what ensued? In 2002, a stocktaking volume edited by the World Bank economist Christiaan Grootaert and the political economist Thierry van Bastelaer included contributions by luminaries such as the economist Paul Collier and the political scientist Robert Bates. "On balance," the editors noted in the concluding chapter, "it seems fair to claim that the social capital literature has been more successful at documenting the beneficial impact of social capital than at deriving policy prescriptions or providing guidelines on how to invest in it."[27] And then, the World Bank's "social capital initiative" ended in 2002.

As we saw earlier, Pierre Bourdieu also theorized about "social capital."[28] The application of his concept, too, bore meager fruit, at least to development policies and programs. In part, this is because Bourdieu's brand of cultural theorists has been suspicious of "development." Suspicious, too, of the concept's possible use as yet another way to blame the poor, to make their plight their fault. (Talking about social capital "tends to underplay the crippling impact of inequitable social structures on the very poorest."[29]) Suspicious that social capital would be part of a strategy "for shifting the onus of development from the state to civil society and to third-sector agencies working on its behalf."[30] Or, finally, something typical of critiques of practical applications of anthropology and cultural studies: suspicious that findings about "social capital" would inevitably be "banalized" as "they travel from research to policy, squeezing out all nuance."[31]

Cultural Evolution

A second witness to the importance of culture is Joseph Henrich. He is a rare anthropologist, with deep field experience in three settings (Fiji, Peru, and southern Chile), as well as an affinity for mathematical modeling of the co-evolution of culture and genes. (He is now a professor of evolutionary biology at Harvard.) His laboratories run classic experiments from psychology and from game theory and do so in cultural settings beyond the usual WEIRD subjects of experimental research (people from Western, Educated, Industrialized, Rich, and Democratic countries).

In his 2016 book *The Secret of Our Success*, Henrich summarized a bounty of research on cultural evolution.[32] Cultures to him included everything from customs to habits, values and norms, and as an overarching metaphor, a collective mind. He showed that culture evolves with climates and technologies, with encounters near and far; and culture coevolves with genes. Over time, culture even "hard wires" our minds and bodies.

For our purposes, several points stand out. First, Henrich was unafraid to characterize and measure cultural differences across groups of people, fully aware though he was of fissures within and blurred boundaries across various cultural groupings.

Second, he believed many policies have failed because they assumed what works in one cultural setting will work in another. The science of cultural differences has practical implications, he avers. Indeed, he began studying anthropology with the goal of applying knowledge about cultural differences to the improvement of the lot of the world's disadvantaged peoples.

Third, however, neither this book nor (as far as I can ascertain) any of Henrich's articles describe how to do that applying. The last sentence of his first chapter asserts that culture has "important practical implications for how we build institutions, design policies, address social problems, and understand human diversity" (7). But by the time we reach the last page of his final chapter, these practical implications are just reminders that "the imposition of new formal institutions, imported from elsewhere, on populations often create mismatches. The result is that such imposed formal institutions will work rather differently, or not at all" (331). Henrich provides no examples of policies or programs that took culture into account and did better. No theory of interactions between cultures and "treatments" (policies, programs, etc.) and developmental outcomes. The knowledge is potentially there; the applications, not yet.

Culture as Cause and Effect

An instructive effort to grapple with cultural influences occupied a chapter of David Morawetz's now-forgotten book, *Why the Emperor's New Clothes Are Not Made in Colombia*.[33] Centered at one chapter's start, as if a text for subsequent exegesis, is a quotation from Epicurus: "Hoist sail, my dear boy, and steer clear of culture."

Morawetz took not heed. After reminding the reader (in italics) that "no judgment is being made anywhere in this discussion about which cultural traits are desirable and which are not," he constructed three qualitative models of the determinants of labor productivity, quality control, and punctual delivery. These "are the three most important areas in which East Asian garment exporters have outperformed Colombians."

"Cultural factors" in labor productivity turn out to include physical characteristics (the size of fingers) and seven other variables that seem to be manifestations of policy choices and economic conditions as well as of "culture." What they probably have in common is that the usual economic models ignore them as factors of production.

- The degree to which the labor force is susceptible to organization and discipline.
- The physical characteristics of the workers (in particular, finger size).
- The generalized social training in manual dexterity they have received.
- The degree to which family or government support systems provide a form of insurance.
- The protection that workers have against being fired.
- The degree to which workers identify with the goals of the firm.
- Their innate or culturally conditioned ability to organize.
- The place that money income has in the workers' scale of values in relation to the place of a relaxed and sociable work experience, an easy life, the approval of other people, and so forth.

Morawetz marched through the factors with impressions and anecdotes based on his research in Colombia, Asia, and the United States. He cited some relevant literature, including praise of Confucian cultures. Two authors affirmed that "Chinese and Chinese-influenced civilizations" were, in their own ways, like Western cultures, "more practical and rationalistic, more disposed to physical and mental work as the preeminent—and not perforce simply the predominant—human activity, more inclined to save and invest, and more conducive to social mobility" than the varied cultures of India, Southeast Asia, "the Moslem states of West Asia and North Africa," and Africa. Morawetz adduced statistics indicating that Asian garment workers put in more days per year and hours per day on the job than Latin American workers. In one study in the United States, Asian workers were 30 percent more productive *per hour* than Latin American workers in the same piecework firms in the United States.

Quality control, the second aspect of Asian competitive advantage, is influenced by "the cultural factors mentioned above." But another ingredient is added to the pot: "the place of precision and neatness of finish in the artistic values of the society." Morawetz found it useful to cite as a further cultural factor "the degree of importance the society places on punctuality."

Clearly, Morawetz maintained, cultural factors make a significant difference to success in garment exporting. He was, however, unable to estimate how much difference. His "models," presented in the form of equations in the appendix, are perhaps more systematic than most discussions of culture, certainly by economists. But, as he recognized, they are not defined operationally nor is their functional form specified, and so empirical estimation is ruled out.

This dead-end is instructive; it is one reason why other economists have heeded Epicurus's advice. But equally instructive is Morawetz's text on cultural change. "By nature, culturally influenced variables such as attitudes to quality control and punctuality of delivery might be expected to change only slowly, if at all, over time. Yet outstanding counterexamples exist." He cited Japan's rise from shoddy quality to best quality. Singapore and Hong Kong had also made rapid strides in quality.

Cultural norms can be fragile or robust. Thomas Sowell showed that some cultural values and behaviors persist even when their adherents move to an entirely different culture.[34] But some valued norms and practices prove to be fragile. David L. Szanton studied a fishing community in the Philippines and concluded: "Social organization and political processes, rather than a lack of skills or capital have proven to be the major factors limiting overall economic growth."[35] But when he returned twenty years later, he found that many of the cultural practices he documented had disappeared. He learned why. Before, the village had revolved around the lunar cycle, because with a fuller moon, night-time fishing was lucrative and with a lesser moon it wasn't. All sorts of cultural practices were accommodated to the lunar cycle. During the intervening twenty years, however, technology happened. Powerful, portable lights enabled night-time fishing throughout the month. Cultural practices changed accordingly, and some vanished. Szanton was shocked that even many of his key informants could barely remember the way things were.[36] When will a cultural norm be robust? A recent study suggests these conditions: (1) how much a norm is embedded with other norms, and (2) "the absence of legalization and norm entrepreneurs." Norms that are both procedural and ethical in character will tend to be more robust.[37]

Morawetz noted an old study of Korea, which committed the error that those uncomfortable with "culture" seem to find conclusive. The study said that Confucianism was the reason Koreans did *not* work hard: "the traditional ideal of Korean Confucianism did not have much respect for technical and physical or manual labor. . . . The traditional values of Korea, however, do not always encourage the virtue of diligence or hard work." To us today, this seems obviously false. Therefore, it is hastily concluded by some, the whole idea of cultural explanations should be abandoned.

It is the reflexive reaction to these three facts—some "cultural traits" can sometimes change rapidly, some group is said to be X when some years later it is said to be not-X, and the same belief system used to explain Y is used by others to explain not-Y—that I wish to bring to our attention. A mistaken inference is this: "If these three statements are true, then we need not consider 'culture' or 'cultural variables' of any kind." But upon reflection, this conclusion is evidently invalid. Some practically important cultural conditions "might be expected to change slowly, if at all, over time." But if they or others can under some circumstances change rapidly and with economic and political consequences, the implication would seem to be to study cultural phenomena more carefully, not to dismiss them. That cultural labels can be hastily applied or misapplied is, as we will see, crucially important. But it does not of course imply that all cultural variables are without predictive power or that they must be misused.

The reflexive dismissal is an example of binary thinking about what should be a multiply determined question of degree. This error is common on all sides of the cultural debate. If one can show that X is neither necessary nor sufficient, it is thought to excuse setting X aside intellectually. Thus, anthropologists criticize economic simplifications for not being sufficient, and economic recommendations for not being necessary, for the end being sought. Both criticisms may be true, and yet the economic simplification may enable worthwhile predictions and policy improvements. And in the same way economists may dismiss cultural variables, not only for their inability to be quantified but also by citing counterexamples (a particular "culture" is neither necessary nor sufficient) and, as employed by different practitioners, contradictions (there is no consensus yet). The dismissive reflex is the same, and in each case unfortunate. The reflex may itself be a characteristic of an intellectual culture or predisposition.

Tackling the Practical

Even among writers who take culture seriously as a factor in economic and political development, we discern less success in their analysis of what to do about it. How might cultural factors be taken into account in the design and implementation of economic reforms, be they socialist or capitalist, massive or provisional? Or in transitions toward or away from multiparty democracy? Or in designing and implementing policies, systems, and projects in

culturally loaded areas like health, education, agriculture, and the environment? Or in resisting them? Putnam and his colleagues were not sure. Like
many others, Henrich noted that "new formal institutions and organizations
have to fit with a people's social norms, informal institutions, and cultural
psychology" but doesn't go on to say how to design or implement such "fitting."[38] Etounga-Manguelle and Kabou agreed that change is needed and will
have to be indigenous but are less helpful on the how-to.

Despite its many apparent advantages, the application of cultural knowledge to development—or to resisting development—has not, in the opinion
of most anthropologists, economists, and policy analysts, been auspiciously
successful. Anthropology seems to relish a critic's role, in particular lam-
basting economists and "development" based on alien assumptions. But
when asked for better methods or assumptions, the anthropologist's answer may be a shrug of the shoulders. In her book *Development Economics
on Trial: The Anthropological Case for a Prosecution*, Polly Hill was typically
evasive about how to do better. "Just as an art critic seldom gives artists practical advice on how to improve their work, so it would seem the height of
arrogance for an anthropologist like myself to make practical suggestions on
working methods or subject matter to economists. Nothing like that is to be
found here."[39]

Similarly, after years of fieldwork about cash transfer programs in Niger,
the anthropologist Jean-Pierre Olivier de Sardan avoids any verdict on what
works. All anthropology can do is describe "local contradictions." Peasants
don't behave the way the planners anticipated. "Our focusing on these aspects
enables us to treat them in depth, but in no way permits to give any good or
bad points to the operations of cash transfer programs, nor to propose any
overall assessment of the delivery of this public good in Niger."[40]

After working more than a decade in Indonesia, the anthropologist Tania
Murray Li said she often got asked to provide "a bridge between my research
describing the dynamics of rural life and the world of projects. . . . Such a
bridge eludes me." Why? It's not, she wrote, coyness or any lack of concern.
In fact, *caring* is what originally drew her into fieldwork in Indonesia. But she
drew back from how to improve "development" (or for that matter, practical
resistance to development). Instead, she focuses on the problems that "development" creates via the "technification" of political issues and thereby the
thwarting of true transformation, as well as via the frictions, inequities, and
cultural misunderstandings of the everyday and fraught processes of developmental activities. "My predicament is diagnostic," she wrote. "It enables me

to ask what ways of thinking, what practices and assumptions are required to translate messy conjunctures, with all the processes that run through them, into linear narratives of problems, interventions, and results."[41]

It is not that the study of cultures inherently lacks applicability. Many anthropologists, at least when they talk to or write for non-anthropologists, seem bullish on that score. Tim Ingold hypes anthropology in his textbook: "We face mounting inequality, escalating political violence, warring fundamentalisms and an environmental crisis of planetary proportions. How can we fashion a world that has room for everyone, for generations to come? What are the possibilities, in such a world, of collective human life? These are urgent questions, and no discipline is better placed to address them than anthropology."[42] Or consider these declarations from a volume of supposed successes in applied anthropology:

> The anthropological difference is apparent at every stage of the problem-solving process: Anthropologists design programs that work because they are culturally appropriate; they correct interventions that are under way but that will be economically unfeasible because of community opposition; they conduct evaluations that contain valid indicators of program results. They provide the unique skills necessary for intercultural brokering; they collect primary and "emic" data necessary for planning and formulating policy; and they project and assess cultural and social effects of intervention.[43]

But if this is so, it is a puzzle that anthropologists and the study of culture seem to make little difference in the real world. "Given the expertise of anthropologists in studying and explaining community organization and human dynamics," wrote the editors of another collection of applied anthropology, "it is a paradox that our research findings and recommendations have relatively little impact on public and international policy."[44] Roger Bastide believed in applied anthropology, "but it is necessary to add that sadly, we still know only a little concerning the laws of change. In any case, the failures of anthropologists stem less, it appears, from not having a good understanding of one or another society ... than from the fact that anthropologists are still poorly armed in theoretical terms to give applied anthropology a solid base upon which it could support itself without fear."[45] Maurice Bloch concurred: "Anthropology is of as much use in practical problems as almost any other social science, and no more important than common sense and the ability to listen to people. . . . I am still hoping that there will be some successful applied anthropology."[46]

In his 2019 book *An Anthropology of Anthropology*, Robert Borofsky asked an essential question:

> With its in-depth research techniques and broad comparative insights, it can make a difference—a real difference—in the lives of many people around the world. At its best, cultural anthropology represents an antidote to hate, provincialism, and despair. In stressing the fluid nature of group identities through time and space, it helps soften ethnic violence. In valuing cultural diversity for how it enriches our world, cultural anthropology fosters tolerance of difference. In emphasizing how context shapes behavior, it encourages people to reshape the contexts needed to reshape their lives—medically, economically, socially—so as to find new meaning, opportunity, and hope. But unfortunately, cultural anthropology frequently falls short of this potential. A key question this book deals with is *why*.[47]

This same question drove my own investigations. It became, in the new lingo I was learning, *la problématique*.

4

Cultures Approaching Cultures

If culture matters so, and people have studied culture for a century or more, why don't we have well-developed theories, practical guidelines, close professional links between those who study culture and those who make and manage development policy? Why haven't anthropology and related subjects been more helpful to those resisting "development," or developing cultural revolutions?

The Evolution of Anthropological Culture

Some of the first anthropologists and sociologists hoped for something more useful and foundational. Marcel Mauss's famous manual of ethnography insisted on "total description," both in the sense of painstaking documentation on every dimension of the local culture's life (from economic to religious to social to technological) and in the melding of these dimensions into the "total social fact." These facts are somehow linked in ways that have been compared to a language: they have to be understood as a whole, not as a set of discrete pieces.[1]

And then compared, and (Mauss hoped) the resulting knowledge applied. Yes, there was Modernization, even Civilization, in the minds of some; but there was also the preservation of local cultures, the empowerment of local people through devolution and "indirect rule," and indeed the call for "native anthropologists" to apply ethnographic techniques to the colonial cultures themselves. In the 1920s and 1930s, even as Bronislaw Malinowski called for taking local cultures into account in what we would now call "development," he also criticized both the mechanisms and ends of development. Big capitalism, materialism, deadening science: all drew his scorn. "The Westernization of the world . . . [is] one of the greatest crises in human history." He said he had an "extreme pessimistic view about 'progress' [and of] . . . the endless drive of modern mechanization," and he hoped the application of anthropology could temper the negative effects of "inevitable

The Culture and Development Manifesto. Robert Klitgaard, Oxford University Press (2021). © Oxford University Press.
DOI: 10.1093/oso/9780197517734.003.0004

rationalization." Malinowski was colorful in his critiques of the culture of the development apparatus, "the chaos of maladministration and predatory politics," and "the blunders of administration."[2]

All this sounds quite contemporary. In the 1920s and 1930s, anthropologists expressed many of the same critiques one finds today: linear and mechanical thinking, planning, the implementing agencies of government, and outside experts.

In principle, anthropology could have stayed scientifically astride these various and conflicting propositions, testing their empirical bases and checking their logical projections. But history intervened. After World War II and with the arrival of independence in Asia and Africa, a new generation of anthropologists questioned the roles and therefore the work of their forefathers and -mothers. Hadn't anthropology been "the handmaiden of colonialism"? Hadn't their intellectual ancestors ludicrously oversimplified? Hadn't they done violence to the idea of culture by making it static, as homogeneous as language, and an obstacle to some unanalyzed and suspect "modernization"? Indeed, by what "authority" had anthropologists asserted that they understood a culture or social structure? The anthropologist Michael Horowitz characterized this emerging view as

> an ideological position that an anthropologist involved in development is culpable of accelerating the process of incorporation or, worse, of legitimizing it. Having at first ignored relations of dependency between rural non-Western peoples and the industrial northern countries for 100 years, anthropologists today are prepared to recognize their intellectual centrality, but as an evil to be fought through diatribe. Their hostility draws strength from the clear participation of some anthropologists *on the wrong side* in the internment of Japanese-Americans during WWII, in Project Camelot in Latin America, and in Southeast Asia during the Vietnam war.[3]

Previous studies of culture were criticized for both bad science and bad conscience.

Criticizing the Science of Culture

And so, many anthropologists veered away from the practical application of anthropology as science toward the humanities, posing questions about the Self and the Other and about the creation of meaning itself. The new advocates undercut the science's old objectives: "While it is true that [these critics] were interested in 'honoring' cultural differences, they seemed to have an even greater interest in dishonoring the attempt to achieve a science of society."[4] Ethnographic work continued, leading to an accretion of microstudies with few attempts at synthesis or the development of substantive theories. "The predicament of modern social and cultural anthropology, then," George Marcus and Michael Fischer pointed out, "is that it settled for the primary function of systematically describing cultural diversity across the world, while the encompassing project of achieving a generalized science of Man had effectively withered."[5]

But then, what remained that was specifically anthropological? The method, the locale, and the sympathy remained. Careful ethnographic description; exotic places or at least locales at home different from one's own (or academic) culture in jarring and presumably insight-inducing ways; and standing up for the disadvantaged—these stayed the same. But fewer people bothered to read the ethnographies. Exotic locales became less so, and Third World countries once independent were less welcoming of anthropological research. Standing up for disadvantaged peoples meant a lot in the colonial struggle, but after independence, did it mean siding with socialist experiments in developing countries, preserving local cultures, questioning "development" itself, or . . . what? Cultural relativism began to sound hollow as young anthropologists, especially women, examined traditional practices such as female genital cutting, male domination, and exploitative child labor. Human rights and anthropological relativism cohabited uneasily.

What is left for cultural anthropology to offer? A standard set of "answers?" As Katy Gardner and David Lewis put it, "anthropologists have tended to call for the same solutions: local participation, awareness of social and cultural complexities, and the use of ethnographic knowledge at the planning stage."[6]

Perhaps a set of methods: careful description, born more of long field experience and patience rather than of analytical modeling. Surprisingly, many graduate students in cultural anthropology found (and find today) few courses on these methods.[7] Adam Kuper described his acculturation as a graduate student at Cambridge: "We also all imbibed the faith that field research in the Malinowskian manner—by participant observation—would yield a more accurate view of another way of life than any other method. But how was it done? We put nervous questions to the faculty but were told that there was no fixed procedure, nothing that could be taught."[8]

Whatever: fieldwork provides detail, the grist for theory. "I challenge any high theorists' triumphant put-down that ethnography is 'just descriptive,'" Judith Okely wrote in her 2013 book on fieldwork methods. "They are immune to the detail of human possibility. The minutiae in the anthropologists' testimonies carry profound theoretical implications, if the reader will only surrender to the emergent flow of knowledge."[9]

Thick description, not just description, said the great Clifford Geertz.

> There is a certain value, if you are going to run on about the exploitation of the masses in having seen a Javanese sharecropper turning earth in a tropical downpour or a Moroccan tailor embroidering kaftans by the light of a twenty-watt bulb. But the notion that this gives you the thing entire (and elevates you to some moral vantage ground from which you can look down upon the ethically less privileged) is an idea which only someone too long in the bush could possibly entertain. . . .
>
> Ethnographic findings are not privileged, just particular: another country heard from . . . . [Anthropology's protracted descriptions] present the sociological mind with bodied stuff on which to feed. The important thing about the anthropologist's findings is their complex specificness, their circumstantiality.[10]

Criticizing "Development"

Anthropologists became critical in a second sense: decrying neo-colonialism and neoliberalism. Postcolonial scholars emphasized the effects of colonialism, mostly pernicious, on native peoples. Their research said that classic anthropological descriptions and theorizing categories about the indigenous were mostly negative and wrong. True, sometimes the indigenous way of life was extolled, as when in 1931 Stuart Chase wrote as if addressing Mexican peasants:

> You have in your possession something precious; something which the western world has lost and flounders miserably trying to regain. Hold to it. Exert every ounce of your magnificent inertia to conserve your way of life. . . . Hold to your disregard of money, of pecuniary thrift, of clocks and watches, of hustle and bustle and busy emptiness. Hold to your damned wantlessness.[11]

Fine, said the new generation of students of culture. But don't essentialize people. Don't dichotomize peasants as working in what Pierre Bourdieu called "the round of time" (every year's cycle is more or less the same) and planners working in "the arrow of time."[12]

The policies? They earned the epithet "neoliberal." They undercut social bonds and cultural value systems. Neoliberal policies fueled inequalities of three kinds: among nations (and cultural groups of nations); within nations between center and periphery (and among ethnic groups); and, within ethnic groups and tribes, among individuals. In recent years, what Sherry Ortner called "dark anthropology" has described in ethnographic detail some of the consequences of neoliberal and neocolonial policies, including within the supposedly most developed countries: racism and exclusion, disease and unemployment, brutality in many guises.[13] Dark anthropology draws attention to these issues in revealing detail in order to raise consciousness and challenge development "narratives."

Practical Applications Recede

But returning to our theme: seldom do these studies analyze how to do better in prevention or cure. This evolution of cultural studies has tended to underplay practical ways to help the most devalued people, those most in need. Boaventura de Sousa Santos and César A. Rodríguez-Garavito noted "a hermeneutics of cynicism" in anthropology, in which nothing any actor does can amount to a potent challenge to what exists or even produce a novel thought. Other anthropologists criticized the critiques for staying on the sidelines of action and not being committed to practical steps for reform.[14]

This is so even when cultural anthropologists have "engaged" with these phenomena in ways that blur traditional lines between the ethnographer and the activist. Aimee Meredith Cox, a black woman doing her Ph.D. fieldwork among black girls in Detroit, was told by them, "You can't just sit around here and take notes."[15] Other anthropologists have straddled the lines between scholar and activist in domains such as illegal border crossings from Mexico to the United States or Afghanis resorting to suicide bombing in a time of changing (and weakening) tribal authority and successive waves of internationally funded and often delivered violence. The culprits in such studies are "various mixes and intersections of racism, sexism, capitalism, and militarism," Ortner noted in a 2019 review of "engaged" anthropology. The research "is driven by what are felt to be urgent problems, to be addressed with whatever methodologies provide maximum insight, and even perhaps some solutions."

Perhaps some solutions—but not a one is presented in the studies Ortner reviewed. Typical is the conclusion of a book whose author, Ortner noted, "recognizes not only that it is difficult to come up with solutions to the environmental crisis, but that it is difficult to imagine what activist politics themselves look like in the contemporary moment. Such politics, she says, were once grounded in the idea of 'progress,' but the idea of progress was part of an earlier and more hopeful era, and has 'stopped making sense' today."[16]

The pattern persists: describing terrible outcomes, attributing them to neoliberalism and development, but not engaging with how to do better. Critical, not constructive. In the field of public health, noted the anthropologists Marc-Éric Gruénais and Fatoumata Ouattara, while practitioners seek solutions, "the anthropologist is content to describe all that is going wrong, all that it is convenient to call 'dysfunctional,' all the time abstaining from formulating recommendations."[17]

The anthropologist Arturo Escobar lamented the cultural destruction that has accompanied "development" and the application of Western "design principles." "Almost overnight, a diverse range of rich and vibrant traditions were reduced to being worth, literally, nothing: nondescript manifestations of an allegedly indubitable fact, 'underdevelopment.'" What to do? Lots to reject, he said, including neoliberalism, globalization, and "the constitutive teleology of patriarchal capitalist modernity." What might people with those rich traditions do to resist, to maintain, to be resilient? Escobar refused to go there: "I want to emphasize, more than anything, that this book is not another attempt, no matter how well-intentioned, to teach others how to be or what to do, especially not those communities struggling for their autonomy."[18]

Some anthropologists have called for a more constructive approach. For example, Edward F. Fischer, in his 2014 book *The Good Life: Aspiration, Dignity, and the Anthropology of Wellbeing*, hoped for "ethnographically informed positive alternatives that engage public policy debates."

> If the ends of economies and politics are to have folks live more meaningful and fulfilled lives—and not just increase income and consumption—then we should look to ways to help people realize their longer-term goals and an affluence that is seen in all of its multiple dimensions.[19]

Three years later, Fischer told interviewers, "Anthropology is more comfortable offering critiques than positive alternatives, but the possibility exists to combine our critical proclivities with non-prescriptive, ethnographically informed positive alternatives that engage public policy debates."[20]

Any examples of anthropology providing them? None is mentioned in his book or in the interview—but the possibility exists.

"Diversity is our business," wrote Ulf Hannerz in 2011, trying to "brand" what he called sociocultural anthropology. The discipline "is primarily about" mapping "the variety of human life," and "a study of diversity remains the best antidote to unthinking ethnocentrism." Moreover, "just about any claim that anthropology can have to unusual critical insight is in fact based on its special relationship to diversity." The goal of "cultural critique should be grounded in an ethnographic understanding of alternatives."[21] Hannerz did not draw the conclusion I would: the constructive (as well as critical) use of sociocultural anthropology depends on a science of diversity. Otherwise, one does not have an "understanding of alternatives," which depend on if-this-then-that inferences, always imperfect, from and to that mapping of the diversity of human life. I like a critique of a recent effort to define what a culture might be, and it applies to Hannerz's admirable goal: "Without a clear and empirically supported account of what cultural models are and why they deserve a place in our scientific ontology, it is difficult to evaluate many of the target article's claims regarding what is shared and what is not, what possesses causal force and what does not, and what should count as a basic unit of culture and what should not."[22]

To advance public policy debates in these ways, anthropology should be able to contribute more than a detailed ethnographic description of one place, then another—"another country heard from"—and more than a field report on a dark problem, valuable as these descriptions are. "By generating a matrix of difference and similarity across cases," wrote James Ferguson and Tania Murray Li in 2018, "we aim to give central place to empirical specificities. But in interrogating those specificities via a set of categories and questions that travel across cases and regions, we also hope to advance the project of identifying large-scale patterns and arriving at comparative insights."[23] This is an indispensable start; we also need theory and an understanding of the interactions between problems, policies, and settings.

Such an aim was not alien to many of the founders of anthropology, who emphasized the potential practical importance of their science. Marcel

Mauss, for example, hoped anthropology would contribute to "the art of directing a society, action, administration, command."

> The first stage of a positive political science is this: to know and to say to societies in general and to each one in particular what they are doing and where they are going. And the second stage of morality and political science properly called consists in telling them frankly whether they do well, practically and ideally, by continuing to go in a particular direction. The day when, along with the sociologists, some political theorists or some sociologists themselves, pointing toward the future, arrive at this firmness in their diagnostic and at a certain sureness in their therapeutic, in their propaedeutic, in their pedagogy above all, on that day the cause of sociology will be won.[24]

Us versus Them

"Words like these of Mauss's are exactly what we fear," one senior anthropologist told me. Against any semblance of "directing a society, action, administration," many anthropologists have gone into opposition. Why help those developmentalists (governments, international agencies, even NGOs), who deep down just want to use anthropologists to blame local cultures for the failure of their ostensibly well-defined projects?

I think they really want anthropologists to tell them that the reason their policies are not working is because the local people have bizarre and exotic superstitions. You as anthropologists will be able to tell us that, they think, and therefore you the anthropologists will give us good excuses for the fact that nearly all development projects fail. But anthropologists who know the place are very unlikely to say such a thing.[25]

A companion in the blame game is the almost automatic condemnation of the developmentalists by the anthropologists. The cast of characters here is long, but just to name a few of the leaders of this pack:

- James Ferguson, showing how developmentalists in Lesotho would do almost anything to avoid facing up to politics.[26]
- Arturo Escobar, claiming that what look like efforts to help local people develop are often tools to keep them underdeveloped.[27]

- Jean-Pierre Olivier de Sardan, noting chronic mismatches between the modernizing assumptions of the developmentalists and the way things work "on the ground."[28]
- Tania Murray Li, who posits that "development" policies and projects automatically imply such things as "technification," anti-politics, and ignoring the deeper causes of poverty—and therefore fail.[29]

Conflicts in Intellectual Cultures

And so, within American and European anthropology and cultural studies, there emerged and remains a reluctance to apply cultural knowledge to policymaking and management. It is better to stay theoretical and pristine, with clean hands; or to call for radical change and dismiss practical efforts that fall short of some vague, programmatic agenda. A tension between applied and theoretical branches, and between gradualism and radicalism, can be found in every academic field. But in anthropology the stakes seem higher somehow, as if the field's own cultural values are at stake in application.

In some senses, the application of anthropology to the problems of development remains a marginal activity within the discipline of anthropology. An anthropologist working on education once described the situation to me this way:

> The dichotomy of theoretical versus applied anthropology and the status associated with it has become very closed. "Oh, he's an applied anthropologist" is a put down. But there was a time when people like Sol Tax and Margaret Mead were very much interested in improving the world and weren't looked down upon for doing so. Today I think it's very hard for anthropologists to talk about this. Then you get the James Clifford stuff, which say that even modest claims by anthropologists to truth are themselves false. If we can't even write a valid ethnography, how can we tell people what to do? It's a funny position—the main thing we accomplish is to say that all you other people coming up with solutions are being simplistic. It's useful when you're around people who think they've found the answer—you need a few cynics around—but it's a very easy role to play. Too easy.

The Swiss anthropologist Annick Tonti was blunt: "Social anthropologists, coming from the university generally don't know much, some of them nothing at all about development, but this does not prevent them from regarding the subject of development negatively."[30]

In France I encountered many similar phenomena. As Gérard Lenclud showed, "the productions of applied anthropology, or of empirical applied ethnography, can only be partially anthropological and are rejected from, or consigned to the margins of, the normal sphere of knowledge of the same name."[31] In Mondher Kilani's brusque summary, "Anthropology, in fact, never has succeeded in establishing itself as an applied anthropology."[32] Thierry Berche noted that "rarely does socio-anthropological research have durable connections with a problematic of action: on the side of anthropologists, there is a strong reluctance to enter into application, doubtless because of the possible consequences of the manipulation of social groups."[33] In 2012, Marc-Éric Gruénais wrote an article entitled "L'anthropologie Sociale: Est-elle Inapplicable?" His conclusions were pessimistic:

> Social anthropology's data are not evidently valid or reliable. Its focus is relentlessly critical, on what might not work, on conflict. It does not fit easily with data for decisions, with policy analysis.
>
> The epistemological, theoretical and methodological foundations of social anthropology thus often differ radically from the approaches that prevail in development projects that call for "socio-anthropology." Social anthropology as a discipline may be difficult to apply.[34]

Many anthropologists define themselves in terms of what they oppose: ethnocentrism, developmentalism, economics, maybe even science. When Clifford Geertz gave a pep talk to his peers—later published as a "distinguished lecture" in the *American Anthropologist*—he entitled it "Anti Anti-Relativism." This brilliant polemic reinforces a central tenet of cultural anthropology by arguing against those who are against it. Geertz defines anthropology's contribution in terms of the others it upsets: "We have, with no little success, sought to keep the world off balance; pulling out rugs, upsetting tea tables, setting off firecrackers. It has been the office of others to reassure; ours to unsettle."[35]

We oppose because we have ourselves been the victims of academic hostility and prejudice. Consider this rendition by the anthropologist Michael M. Horowitz:

The economists' dismissal of the field-oriented anthropologist—surely a defense of turf against the new boy on the block—is often couched in a broad-based attack, supported with the same kind of anecdotal "evidence" that they claim constitutes anthropological verification.

Anthropology is dismissed as: a. soft, unquantitative, without adequate statistical basis for its judgments; b. antiquarian, protective of tradition for moral and aesthetic rather than scientific reasons; c. slow, requiring long-term intense field study; d. negative, elaborating a multitude of reasons why not to carry out some program of change, and ignoring all the, to economists, persuasive reasons to adopt it; e. arcane and esoteric, unable to communicate why its findings are germane to some proposed action; and f. non-collaborative or non-team-playing, unresponsive to the requirements of the host country and donor organization to move rapidly from design to implementation (stemming in part from the anthropologist's tradition of working alone, of not welcoming visitors to the field, and in part from the opposition between the consultant, often an academic, and donor-organization career personnel).[36]

As we know from ethnic studies, language like Horowitz's, with enemies unfairly protecting their turf against us, is symptomatic of a minority group's consciousness. There may be another similarity: hidden envy of that same, resented, powerful Other. The anthropologist Polly Hill's polemical attack on development economics contains, about halfway through, a short chapter that she calls "a pause."

I think that many anthropologists have a secret reverence for (perhaps combined with a fear of) economists. Anthropologists cannot avoid being overawed by a powerful academic discipline which commands financial resources vastly superior to their own, and which continues to exert so much authority in the world despite its inability to solve the problems of inflation and unemployment in industrialized countries.[37]

Like most scientists, economists tend to favor rigorous mathematical models; in contrast, cultural anthropologists admire detailed and for the most part non-mathematical description—those "classic ethnographies." Economists favor cross-sectional and longitudinal data analysis where hypotheses are tested. Ethnographic research is defined by the long-term, in-depth microstudy, the generalizability and value of which economists tend to criticize—especially when anthropologists themselves emphasize that each village is different. "Anthropology's claim to rigor," noted Olivier de Sardan, "is in the way it produces its data, not in falsifiable predictions."[38] When the anthropologist Sol Tax published his study of ten years of analysis of the economic activities in a village of 800 Guatemalans, he asked an economist what she would have done differently with the data. "The considered reply was unexpected to me, yet wholly obvious," he reported. "As an economist, she would not have spent years in a community of 800 people."[39]

The anthropologist Renato Rosaldo related this anecdote:

> On a foggy night a short number of years ago I found myself driving with a physicist along the mountainous stretch of Route 17 between Santa Cruz and San Jose. Both of us felt anxious about the weather and somewhat bored, so we began to discuss our respective fields. My companion opened by asking me, as only a physicist could, what anthropologists had discovered.
>
> "Discovered?" I asked, pretending to be puzzled. I was stalling for time. Perhaps something would come to me.
>
> "Yes, you know, something like the properties or the laws of other cultures."
>
> "Do you mean something like $E = mc^2$?"
>
> "Yes," he said.
>
> Inspiration unexpectedly arrived and I heard myself saying, "There's one thing we know for sure. We all know a good description when we see one. We haven't discovered any laws of culture, but we do think there are classic ethnographies, really telling descriptions of other cultures."[40]

Description vs. science, and *we know description*. But even that was questioned, first by scientists, and then by anthropologists themselves.

Different Ends?

Does this exchange exemplify C. P. Snow's two cultures of scientific and humanistic knowledge?[41] Oliver Wendell Holmes's "life is painting a picture, not doing a sum"? Do we have here a question of different ends being sought?

One objective is Mauss's science, built on the careful collection of facts and the construction of something like scientific laws. "It is through the particularities of institutions that we seek the general phenomena of social life," Mauss wrote. "It is only by the study of the variations in institutions, or in similar notions that societies follow, that we define either the constant residues that these variations leave or the equivalent functions that one and the other fulfill." But not just the points in common: "We detain ourselves, on the contrary, through this method, before the differences that characterize special environments; it is through these characteristics that we hope to uncover laws."[42] In 1952 Margaret Mead led a team of authors in a UNESCO (United Nations Educational, Scientific and Cultural Organization) volume trying to apply anthropology to the problems of development; two years later Georges Balandier wrote two volumes on anthropology applied to the problems of Africa.[43] Or take the accomplishments and agenda of evolutionary anthropologists such as Joseph Henrich, who trace the linkages among geography, culture, psychology, and behavior—and do so over time and place.[44]

How different are many contemporary agendas in cultural studies. The objective is not the collection of facts, the construction of scientific laws, or the instrumental use of cultural variables to improve interventions in real life. In a description that could apply to the objectives of many cultural anthropologists, Steven Seidman noted the rejection, or redefinition, of science in postmodern science.

> Postmodern science is oriented to discerning differences and analyzing heterogeneous forms of life; it is more accepting of theoretical incommensurabilities and pursues innovation and experimentation rather than theory-building, integration, and consolidation. Paralleling its epistemological break from the foundationalism and theoretism of modernism, postmodernism stands for a political agenda that highlights diverse local struggles.[45]

When Donald Trump yammered about "alternative facts," it galled many cultural studies aficionados. *He's using our lingo.* "What are the ramifications," asked the anthropologists Karen Ho and Jill R. Cavanaugh, "when progressive academic critiques of (often colonialist) 'objective realities' get thrown back at us, with very different assumptions of power?"

> One clear ramification is to disavow such rhetoric when it comes from the white patriarchy. Anthropology, and cultural studies more generally, stand

on the side of the nonwhite non-patriarchy; they treasure "the minoritized, feminist, postcolonial, and critical race and ethnic studies scholarship that has been so crucial in providing the tools to conduct an anthropological excavation of presentist hierarchies and exclusions."[46]

To be counted as legitimate, applied anthropology must stand against the status quo. So admonished James R. Veteto and Joshua Lockyear in an essay that introduced five case studies of anthropology of correctly radical varieties. Veteto and Lockyear acknowledged that most anthropologists with graduate degrees would not find university jobs and therefore would work in business, government, and civil society organizations. But they should not be gradualists, meliorists, or corporate facilitators.

> If we train future anthropologists with the normative assumptions of neoliberal capitalism and Western cultural values, albeit with a multicultural bent, we can expect no change in the direction global society is headed (see Escobar 1991 for similar insights on development anthropology). If we champion anthropologists who have made careers for themselves in fields that promote the capitalist project, in practical and ethical terms, we do not see how anthropology has any higher moral ground than other disciplines such as business studies or classical economics.[47]

Science is not quite the right word to describe what this sort of ethnography attempts. Some contemporary renditions of anthropology begin with dogmatic answers: clearly, *the system* needs a revolution, "development" needs to be jettisoned, we need a new cultural foundation for politics. If you're not starting there, you're not doing real anthropology.

Marginality

When anthropologists talk with economists and policymakers—or indeed with psychologists, sociologists, and philosophers—one may discern some common traits. For example:

- the identification with the marginal—defending them—while at the same time demystifying and condemning the "dominant culture"— anthropologists are the people who respect every culture but their own;

- the call to recognize cultural differences and diversity and celebrate them;
- the unwillingness, however, to take those differences seriously from the point of view of allocating resources, people, attention;
- in fact, to undercut constructs like "culture" itself;[48]
- and to question radically any current enterprise of allocating resources, "governmentality," and "development"; and
- to pull out the rug, upset the tea cart (in other words, violate civility with the bad boy quality of the *enfant terrible*).

This constellation is familiar: it is that of the marginal man and woman who are seeking their own identities—understanding their otherness—and at the same time justifying and defending *being different*. Like the subjects of their study, many anthropologists feel themselves marginal to the dominant culture.[49] "A loosely connected crowd of coteries and losers, innovators and stragglers, curmudgeons and mavericks," wrote the anthropologist Ulf Hannerz in his *Anthropology's World: Life in a Twenty-First-Century Discipline*.[50] "Marginal natives abroad and marginal academics at home," noted the anthropologist Morris Freilich, who edited a book entitled *Marginal Natives: Anthropologists at Work*.[51] But marginal, often, in a different sense. "Both British and American ethnographic enterprises," observed the anthropologists George E. Marcus and Michael M. J. Fischer, "attracted women, foreigners, Jews, and others who felt themselves marginal," but who were at the same time privileged members of their own societies.

> The twentieth-century tradition of cultural criticism in anthropology had its roots in this qualified marginality of its practitioners. Thus, anthropologists as cultural critics developed a liberal critique . . . ; they expressed sympathy for the oppressed, the different, the marginals, as well as emphasizing the modern dissatisfactions with privileged middle-class life.[52]

John Murray Cuddihy compared anthropology and Marxism. Both are "an uneasy mélange of cognitive relativism and ethical absolutism." Both subjects appeal "to an intellectual clientele at once cynical about the 'situation of social action' and utopian about the 'ends of social action.'"

Thus, the allure of these ideologies for a dissociated theoretical sensibility consists of their appeal to moral passion in the language of social science.

A passionate social conscience is licensed as dispassionate cognitive science. . . . A pitilessly punitive and skeptical objectivity unmasks a given world of fact; a homeless revolutionary longing projects a new world of value.[53]

Can We Overcome Our Cultural Divides?

It is difficult for me to judge the validity, indeed the meaning, of these analyses. Whatever a cultural critique may accomplish when applied to the very fields that study culture, it does make evident that something like cultural differences exist between fields like economics and anthropology, and between the practical application of science and cultural criticism. Different ends are sought. Different means are employed. Misunderstandings and communications that fail to connect are common. Common, too, is suspicion, and perhaps hostility, in ways that can be compared to ethnic or cultural groups in the society at large.[54] Table 4.1 schematizes some of the differences.

What does it entail that there are different cultures concerning the study and the importance of development and indeed of "culture" itself? Let us consider what it does not entail. The hypothesized origins or sociological correlates of a proposition or theory should be irrelevant to its validity, predictive power, or "decentering" impact. Just as in the case of communication across the cultures of this world—say, between an Argentinian rancher and a Hindu Brahmin—cultural differences do not mean that communication or agreement are impossible. They do not mean that a compelling logical and empirical argument, indeed a moving aesthetic presentation, cannot occur across cultures. Some, perhaps many, principles and values are shared across academic cultures and subcultures—just as across cultures themselves, such as Chinese, Arab, Dogon, and Balinese, some, perhaps many, principles and values are shared.[55]

The existence of cultural differences *does* mean that we should be attentive to our premises, predilections, and academic reflexes. Cultural anthropology (and cultural studies more broadly) often pose different questions than does economics (and predictive social science more broadly). The concerns overlap. Yes, Clifford Geertz was correct that a sonata is not a set of rules for writing sonatas; yes, the philosopher Stanley Cavell was right that a language is not a set of rules of grammar plus a frequency table of word usage.[56] But it is also useful for some practical purposes to know the rules for writing sonatas

Table 4.1 Some Differences between Economic and Anthropological "Cultures"

The more modern, the better.	The less modern, the better.
Assume identical utility functions.	Assume (indeed celebrate) diverse utility functions.
One system can be said to be strictly better (more efficient) than another (Pareto preferred).	Cultural relativism precludes cross-cultural judgments of better or worse.
Everything is connected to everything else, as in a thermodynamic system.	Everything is connected to everything else, as in a language, a literary text, or a personality.
Individualist.	Sectarian (egalitarian).
Construct.	Deconstruct.
Marginal improvements.	Radical critiques.
Analytical; mathematical.	Holistic; literary.
Questions of degree: variables are continuous and cardinal. Fact and value can be separated.	Questions of type: "variables" are ordinal or binary. Fact and value cannot be separated.
Surveys (across localities, often cross-sectional, random samples).	Thick description (local, long-term, nonrandom samples).
N is important.	N is not important ("another country heard from").
Policy analysis: top-down use of model to enable individuals to create better outcomes.	Policy analysis: bottom-up process without preconceived model to enable a group to affirm itself (its meaning, confidence, solidarity).
Prescription: instrumental.	Prescription: listen, learn, reflect, leave nature as you find it.
Anthropology is the description of preferences, capabilities, and institutions that affect contracts, information flows, and incentives—and how they change.	Anthropology is a means for reconsidering meaning, person, authority; a commitment to stand up for diversity and autonomy.
Economics is a science of choice built on simple behavioral assumptions, leading to better predictions of social and economic phenomena.	Economics is a view of the world and a language that oversimplifies to the extent that the most important features of life— even economic—are distorted or missed.

Source: The author.

and forming sentences—or, concerning a "culture," to discover patterns of meaning and rules of behavior and to develop predictive models that are not, themselves, behavior or culture.

This discovering and modeling is not the only end of the study of culture, but it is a valid and potentially important one. I think it is consistent with what the French anthropologist Jean Copans advocated: "For the periphery (African, American, Asian) also has a need of an anthropology tuned to today, to the crisis; of a social anthropology in the classic sense of the term, that of social and cultural change."[57] And with what the editors called for in their lead-off to a special issue of *Anthropological Theory* in 2019: "a robust and specific engagement with politics is necessary for anthropology and increasingly urgent given the global conjuncture."[58]

5

Are the Scientific Problems Too Hard?

Let's remind ourselves of a practical goal and, therefore, of a scientific agenda. (Later in the book, we will broaden both goals and agendas.)

- A goal: Design and implement better policies (programs, treatments, etc.) by taking into account the cultural setting. Or—to remind ourselves that resistance is a policy—how to understand the government's culture (or the donor's or the NGO's) and one's own so as better to resist.
- A scientific agenda: Estimate the effects of various policies (programs, treatments, etc.) on desired outcomes, given the cultural setting and other features of the local environment.

In this chapter, we consider the daunting complexities of the scientific agenda. They are, I think, one, at least, subliminal reason why many anthropologists and other students of culture have shied away from applications to policy design and implementation. Fortunately, there is nonetheless hope, and we conclude with humbler but still valuable ways to address this practical goal.

What Is "Culture"?

The first set of complexities surrounds the very term "culture." In previous chapters, we heard people using "culture" to refer to values and norms, patterns of behavior and belief, and meaning-imbued social structures. Don Fernando, the finance minister who lectured me in chapter 2, was talking about values. In Africa, or at least in Equatorial Guinea, he said the hierarchy of values moved from family to clan to country so that "the national interest" had little salience. And he implied that "torture" is a culturally loaded idea, one that a Westerner like me could readily misapply in his context.

As with most important concepts in the social and behavioral sciences, "culture" is a latent variable, meaning it cannot be directly perceived or

The Culture and Development Manifesto. Robert Klitgaard, Oxford University Press (2021). © Oxford University Press.
DOI: 10.1093/oso/9780197517734.003.0005

measured. It is a construct, and as such it is inherently contestable. And in cultural studies, *contestable are us*.

In 1952, Alfred Kroeber and Clyde Kluckhohn published a 223-page, double-columned monograph entitled *Culture: A Critical Review of Concepts and Definitions*.[1] They arrayed 164 definitions under categories such categories as the following:

- descriptive
- historical
- normative
- psychological
  - problem-solving device
  - learning
  - habit
  - "purely psychological"
- structural
- genetic

In their conclusion, the authors reassured perhaps worried readers that they would not offer up definition number 165. Rather, they opened their arms wide: "We believe each of our principal groups of definitions points to something legitimate and important. In other words, we think culture is a product; is historical; includes ideas, patterns, and values; is selective; is learned; is based upon symbols; and is an abstraction from behavior and the products of behavior" (157).

The United Nations Educational, Scientific and Cultural Organization (UNESCO) has also adopted a wide definition. "Culture should be regarded as the set of distinctive spiritual, material, intellectual and emotional features of society or a social group, and that it encompasses, in addition to art and literature, lifestyles, ways of living together, value systems, traditions and beliefs."[2] *Eclecticism are us*.

Did I mention the unit of observation? Are we talking about countries or smaller (or larger) units of cohesive cultures? For example, studies in Africa have looked at the level of subnational cultural/linguistic units. Interestingly, given the way colonial powers demarcated national borders, some of the cultural units spill over into two or more countries. When one estimates the effects of country and cultural unit on measures of development (proxies such as fine-grained geographical portraits of the light visible at night from

Table 5.1 Four Archetypal Cultures or Ways of Life

	Strong Grid	Weak Grid
Strong Group	Hierarchical culture	Egalitarian or sectarian culture
Weak Group	Fatalistic culture	Individualistic culture

satellites), it turns out that culture "matters more" than the country does, other things equal—even though countries differ in development-related policies.[3]

What about cultural diversity within whatever of those units we choose?[4] The anthropologist Mary Douglas arrayed cultures along two dimensions, grid (how important are rules?) and group (how important are group differences?).[5] The four resulting quadrants represent four different cultures (see Table 5.1). She contended that all cultural aggregates, say countries or tribes, possess all four of the grid-group cultures in different proportions.[6] This implies that taking culture into account should be at least that fine-grained, too.[7]

Faced with these definitional complexities, many cultural anthropologists have simply stopped using "culture." At the same time, some economists have begun using cultural "variables" in quantitative studies across countries.[8] In economics, ethnography is not high on the list of methodologies, although case studies are occasionally included (for example, of cultural dissonance between Greeks and Germans and its effects on European integration).[9] *Econometrics are us*; and therefore, in the morass of definitions and measures we have just seen, economists seek comparable data that fit into cross-country models. One economic study defines culture as "customary beliefs and values that ethnic, religious and social groups transmit fairly unchanged from generation to generation."[10] Some empirical studies focus more on values and preferences, while others use a belief-based definition.

How do these quantitative studies measure culture? Consider four (of many) indicators that have been used in recent research.

Individualism

One popular cultural variable is individualism-collectivism continuum or the closely related spectrum from independent to interdependent.[11] The sociologist Geert Hofstede and colleagues created a widely used country-level measure of individualism,

> defined as a preference for a loosely-knit social framework in which individuals are expected to take care of only themselves and their immediate families. Its opposite, collectivism, represents a preference for a tightly-knit framework in society in which individuals can expect their relatives or members of a particular in-group to look after them in exchange for unquestioning loyalty. A society's position on this dimension is reflected in whether people's self-image is defined in terms of "I" or "we."[12]

Within-country differences in individualism have also been studied by comparing different ethnic groups, generations, and social class. People from higher classes are frequently more individualist than people from lower classes.

Hierarchy

Hofstede et al. also created a measure of "power distance." This variable

> expresses the degree to which the less powerful members of a society accept and expect that power is distributed unequally. The fundamental issue here is how a society handles inequalities among people. People in societies exhibiting a large degree of Power Distance accept a hierarchical order in which everybody has a place and which needs no further justification. In societies with low Power Distance, people strive to equalize the distribution of power and demand justification for inequalities of power.[13]

Traditional-Rational

Since the 1980s, the World Values Survey has surveyed individuals in countries around the globe about demographics, economic status, and values and beliefs. In a data-reduction exercise, Ronald Inglehart and Christian Welzel derived two main "cultural dimensions" for each country.[14] One cultural dimension moves from "tradition to reason."

- Traditional values emphasize the importance of religion, parent-child ties, deference to authority, and traditional family values. People who embrace these values also reject divorce, abortion, euthanasia, and suicide. These societies have high levels of national pride and a nationalistic outlook.
- Secular-rational values have the opposite preferences to the traditional values. These societies place less emphasis on religion, traditional family values, and authority. Divorce, abortion, euthanasia, and suicide are seen as relatively acceptable.

Survival-Expressiveness

Inglehart and Welzel's second cultural dimension runs from "survival mode to individual expressiveness."

- Survival values place emphasis on economic and physical security. This variable is linked with a relatively ethnocentric outlook and low levels of trust and tolerance.
- Self-expression values give high priority to environmental protection, growing tolerance of foreigners, gays and lesbians and gender equality, and rising demands for participation in decision-making in economic and political life.

Over the thirty-five years of the World Values Survey, country scores on survival-self-expression have been remarkably stable ($r = 0.89$). Inglehart shows how this dimension is closely related to individualism and another construct, autonomy-embeddedness.[15]

What Is "Development"

Before considering what has been learned about these variables and development, it behooves us to turn to that fraught concept: What do we talk about when we talk about *development* as a set of goals or outcomes? Imagine the possibilities. Here are some of my ideal attributes: human flourishing and social justice; less cruelty, more kindness; a chance to be what one chooses to be. I know: vague concepts, nonexistent measures. But beyond just economic prosperity.[16] And beyond just "democracy" (itself a notably contestable term). Under the rubric political development, people talk about political rights, civil liberties, and "the rule of law."[17] In public health, many studies use disability-adjusted life years (DALY), a measure that takes account of diseases and disabilities as well as longevity (as scaled, lower numbers are better).[18]

Increasingly, people measure national levels of self-reported well-being and happiness. There is now a World Happiness Report,[19] which reports national averages of responses to this question:

> Please imagine a ladder, with steps numbered from 0 at the bottom to 10 at the top. The top of the ladder represents the best possible life for you and the bottom of the ladder represents the worst possible life for you. On which step of the ladder would you say you personally feel you stand at this time?

Country averages show remarkable range, from 2.57 in Afghanistan to 7.81 in Finland.

Is this because different cultures want different things? In 1999, the *Journal of American History* sponsored an international discussion on translations of the Declaration of Independence. Among other things, the authors considered how different cultures interpreted "the pursuit of happiness."

In Japanese, "happiness" seemed to pose no problems, but "the pursuit of happiness" as opposed to "the wish to enjoy happiness," proved baffling.[20] In other languages, "happiness" conjured up different values. For Americans, the pursuit of happiness was thought to be everyone's right and was, in a materialistic world, achievable. But for Chinese or Japanese, especially those who believed in Buddhism, "happiness" seemed chimerical, its pursuit futile, a vanity of human wishes. Joaquim Oltra claimed that "'the pursuit of Happiness'... goes against the Spanish understanding of the Catholic teaching on happiness, since this was always understood as attainable only in the other world."[21]

But the life ladder allows for that. It asks about *your* best life, given your culture. And it turns out that a country's scores on the life-ladder measure of happiness are highly correlated with individualism, aversion to hierarchy, traditional/rational, and survival/expressive. So are more conventional indicators of "development," from income per head to various measures of political development to disability-adjusted life years (see Table 5.2).[22]

Table 5.2 Correlations between Measures of "Culture" and "Development"

	GDP per capita	Liberty	Corruption	Rule of law	Happiness	DALY
Traditional-Rational	0.54	0.43	−0.53	−0.64	0.22	−0.55
Survival-Expressive	0.53	0.57	−0.68	−0.58	0.72	−0.53
Individualism	0.54	0.49	−0.65	0.66	0.36	−0.49
Power Distance	−0.37	0.58	0.62	−0.67	−0.42	0.43

Source: The author.

Following that pursuit-of-happiness notion, let's concoct a composite measure of development that tries to encompass *life, liberty, and the pursuit of happiness*. For *life* we'll use those "disability-adjusted life years." For *liberty*, the sum of two measures developed by the American think tank Freedom House ("political rights" and "civil liberties") and an aggregate measure of the rule of law from the World Justice Project. For *pursuit of happiness*, the country's score in the *World Happiness Report 2020*.

After taking logarithms of DALY, a principal component analysis reduced these variables to one composite indicator, which we'll call LLPH. The top-ten countries on *life, liberty, and the pursuit of happiness* are Denmark, Finland, Norway, Sweden, Netherlands, Austria, New Zealand, Germany, Canada, and Australia. The bottom-ten countries are (beginning with the lowest) Afghanistan, Zimbabwe, Cameroon, Mozambique, Ethiopia, Uganda, Tanzania, Mali, Cambodia, and Guinea. (Thomas Jefferson would not be pleased to learn that the United States ranks only 21 of 103 countries.)

How does LLPH relate to the measures we have seen of a country's "culture"? Again we see significant patterns. Countries with more individualistic cultures tend to have higher LLPH ($r = 0.65$). More hierarchical cultures tend to have lower values ($r = −0.67$).

LLPH correlates 0.62 with the traditional-rational dimension from the World Values Survey and 0.74 with the survival-expression dimension. In a linear regression, these two cultural variables alone explain 72 percent of the variance in our measure of life, liberty, and the pursuit of happiness.

But it is a long way from noting these significant correlations to assessing causation from culture to development. It could be the other way around. Ronald Inglehart points out that, since the World Value Survey began, growing prosperity around the world has led to higher levels of happiness and to cultural change. The survival-expressiveness dimension tilts toward expressiveness as countries grow richer.[23] Ditto for individualism: as countries, regions, and generations have more income, they become more individualistic.[24] In China, for example, young people are more individualistic than older people.[25] Regional differences, in China and elsewhere, can be large, with rural areas and places where indigenous people reside often showing up as less individualistic and more oriented toward the survival end of the survival-expressiveness spectrum.[26] Many studies show how changes in various economic factors lead to changes in measures of culture. Institutional dispensations have also been shown to impact culture; for example, Alberto Alesina and Nicola Fuchs-Schündeln studied the differential evolution of cultural values across East and West Germany.[27] And of course, Marxist theorists (including some anthropologists) have long argued that cultural manifestations are reflections of economic structures and class dynamics.

How Culture May Matter for Development

The causality cuts both ways: culture and development feed each other. And, more to the point of our endeavor, if we are seeking policies that advance development given culture (and other factors that affect development), we would end up with a complicated dynamic equation.

Consider the complexities. "Culture" matters for development in many ways, as noted in the last chapter. Culture affects what people want, loathe, fear, and cherish. Culture may influence whether and how different development-related policies and practices are adopted. The effectiveness of those policies may depend on the cultural setting. And cultural features may themselves respond to policy choices.

These many ways that culture matters can tumble together. Levels and changes in levels may both matter. ("To be sure," Göran Hydén intoned, as if saying so were helpful, "culture is both constant and changing and the analyst must recognize this distinction.")[28] Many debates spin around and around in confusion over culture as a determinant of utility and meaning; as an independent variable that interacts with and perhaps helps determine policy choices (among other things) in the creation of economic, political, and social outcomes; and as a dependent variable whose composition and change may be affected by policy choices. One reason for the confusion is a lack of theoretical development; and apart from the points made in the last chapter, theoretical development is retarded by the sheer difficulty of doing the needed modeling and empirical research.[29] In both high theory and high statistics, understanding the roles of culture (in various senses) faces formidable problems, far beyond those contemplated in most early assays.

Theoretical Challenges

Institutions and cultures interact.[30] General equilibrium models with endogenous preferences and capabilities have many solutions. Multiple equilibria can emerge. This means that history—including chance—affects which path a society follows.

Moreover, cultures may develop features that lead away from the maximization of social value-added, even on a society's own definition of that. An existing solution may well be demonstrably nonoptimal.[31] Anthropologists, too, have noted this fact. "The more hierarchical the society with respect to sex, age, class, caste, and ethnic criteria," Marvin Harris asserted, "the greater the degree of exploitation of one group by another and the less likely it is that the trajectory of cultural evolution can be calculated from the average bio-psychological utility of traits"—in other words, in hierarchical societies, cultures can evolve in pernicious ways.[32] A more recent study concludes: "The in-group favoritism inherent to collectivist societies is likely to engender corruption, nepotism and clientelism in the public sphere. In individualist societies, the relative weakness of in-group pressures and an emphasis on personal achievement and worth will contribute towards a more meritocratic and efficient public sector."[33]

To make things even more complicated, cultures and outcomes coevolve. Indeed, since policy choices affect both cultures and outcomes—and both cultures and outcomes affect future policy choices—we have a complex dynamic system. Even with simplifying assumptions, "very little can be proved in general about the non-linear dynamical system," admitted Alberto Bisin and Thierry Verdier in their mathematical explorations of the joint evolution of culture and institutions.[34] Their quantitative models yielded humbling conclusions: the trajectories of cultural evolution depend on starting points; can face dead ends and irreversibilities; and can simply not be seen as something determined, much less optimal.[35]

The authors concluded hopefully: "Focusing more systematically on the positive or negative interactions between culture and institutions along the development process might result more fruitful in terms of historical understanding as well as in terms of policy implications" (45). But the mathematical models for doing so are fraught with indeterminacies.

Deep Roots of Culture and Development?

Over the length of history, sunny, humid climates have enabled the rapid evolution of pathogens and infectious diseases. Over centuries, these diseases affected human populations through genetic and cultural adaptation. In turn, these adaptations plus migrations led to cross-country differences today in some "cultural variables"—and these differences in turn affect some development outcomes.[36]

The research exploring these connections crosses many disciplines. Enrico Spolaore and Romain Wacziarg reviewed a large body of recent studies of what they call "the deep roots" of development, in particular geography, climate, and genes.

> A first message from this research is that technology and productivity tend to be highly persistent even at very long horizons . . . the second message from this literature: long-term persistence holds at the level of populations rather than locations. The third message from this literature, then, is that long-term genealogical links across populations play an important role in explaining the transmission of technological and institutional knowledge and the diffusion of economic development.[37]

Randy Thornhill and Corey Fincher assembled and extended a large literature linking climate to pathogen burdens and these two to a variety of social and cultural adaptations.[38] Across countries, parasite prevalence is strongly associated with lower measures of intelligence.[39] Individualism as a cultural value decreases in proportion to a group's typical pathogen burden. Pathogen burdens increase in-group favoritism and out-group negativity and promote adherence to rigid behavioral sanctions. In turn, compliance with these sanctions in disease-endemic regions is reinforced by socializing children to obedience rather than autonomy. This constellation of tendencies reduces the potential for innovation and trust.

Another strand of literature connects patterns of culture with patterns of genes. Proponents of dual inheritance theory, such as Joseph Henrich, argue that gene-culture coevolution has affected human social psychology, including social norms and institutions.[40] Jüri Allik and Robert McCrae connected "societal personality differences" with differences in gene pools.[41] Kevin Laland, John Odling-Smee, and Sean Myles reviewed a large literature showing how human evolution has been shaped by gene-culture interactions, and Samuel Bowles and Herbert Gintis estimated models of this coevolution using genetic, archaeological, ethnographic, and experimental data.[42] Nicholas Christakis showed how "our genes have shaped societies for our welfare and that, in a feedback loop stretching back many thousands of years, societies have shaped, and are still shaping, our genes today."[43] Novel econometric work shows long-standing, partly genetic differences across populations in attitudes like risk aversion, trust, and altruism.[44]

Imagine trying to specify all the mechanisms and feedback loops over time, even conceptually. And then ponder the chore of statistically estimating culture × policy interactions in a given setting.

Statistical Challenges

Even at the level of national averages—which of course do not countenance the cultural diversities within countries—the difficulties of quantitative comparative studies have been brought forward many times.[45] Available measures are theoretically incomplete and partial. For instance, we do not have data on the disease environments at historical dates relevant for evolutionary change. Changes in technology make estimates based on historical data difficult to interpret; Alan Barreca and his colleagues showed how the effects of heat on mortality have changed greatly over the last century thanks to innovations such as air conditioning.[46]

And, of course, causation is difficult to validate statistically. For example, because of selective migration, observed variations across countries in culture (and other important factors, including genes) could in theory be a function of development outcomes today, rather than (or as well as) being causes of development outcomes. Cross-country econometric studies are also limited by the small number of observations and the many interconnections among possible causal variables. The machine learning research scientist

Tim Salimans noted ruefully: "The data set we consider contains 88 countries and a list of 67 potential explanatory variables, giving 267 different possible subsets of regressors to include in our model. All of these variables can reasonably be expected to influence economic growth, and we cannot be sure a priori which subset of variables we should use."[47] A quantitative study of social indicators and economic development concluded: "The danger of more and more studies using some or all of the social and political indicators is that 'results' will emerge which are not robust. With other indicators and other specifications, as we have seen, one or another variable may show up as more important than another."[48]

An Analogy: Aptitude-by-Treatment Interactions

Let's return to interaction effects. One goal of taking culture into account is understanding how cultural factors interact with policy choices to produce "development." The history of an analogous problem is instructive: the search for aptitude-by-treatment interactions in psychology. The question that the psychologist Howard Gardner once called the Holy Grail of educational psychology is this: "What pedagogies work how well for what combinations of subject matter, personalities, and aptitudes?" For decades, psychometricians have been attempting to estimate how learning is a joint function of aptitudes, pedagogical "treatments," and other variables. The difficulties they have encountered point to several reasons why the analogous challenge of modeling the interactions between cultures, policies, and outcomes is so hard.[49]

First, estimating interaction effects is plagued by different kinds of effects—on the rate of change, the immediate or starting level, the asymptote or equilibrium toward which the development in question progresses, or hybrids thereof—and these may differ across groups. Within-group effects may also cloud across-group comparisons. And, of course, in work on culture and development, it will usually be impossible to allocate policies or treatments randomly across cultural groups.

Second, errors in measurement make it difficult to discover interaction effects. As a result, statistical simulations show that interaction effects may be discovered where they do not exist, and they may be masked where they do exist.

Third, lags almost certainly exist. The lag structure is likely to be different for different policy and cultural variables and combinations, and the lags themselves would have to be modeled.

Fourth, in the case of cultural questions, long-term longitudinal research would be needed. But since cultures (and much else) are changing, even if we had such a detailed and well-specified longitudinal study about the past—which we do not—the results pertaining to a cohort from many years ago might not be valid today, nor for the future with which we are concerned. The research dilemma, as George Psacharopoulos memorably said of educational research, is fundamental:

> The uncertainty is rooted, not in the inadequacy of social scientific methods to locate the relative areas of research, but in the fact that the effects of education become apparent within a time span exceeding in duration the life of the generation that implemented any specific educational policies. The dynamic evolution of interconnected social phenomena prevents us from isolating variables for the purpose of establishing unambiguous causal relationships.[50]

Finally, as we have seen, many kinds of culture, levels of analysis (local, regional, national, etc.), and types of development exist, and they arguably interact. Data do not exist for all of them. This is the worst of worlds for an aficionado of Marcel Mauss's "total social fact": theory uncertainty, complex dynamic models, incomplete data, and a wide array of plausible estimation techniques. No wonder a recent "exhaustive review" of the economics literature on culture and development concludes:

> Overall, our understanding of the determinants of cultural change remains very limited. Evolutionary models help understand the dynamics, but say little about initial triggers for change (technology, institutions, climate, war, . . .) We know even less about the determinants of cultural change in developing countries.
>
> Understanding the origins of cultural diversity and cultural divergence across the world is probably even more challenging than understanding the determinants of cultural change. This is in part because it requires a comparative perspective, i.e. the same theory or set of mechanisms must explain different outcomes at the same time. Not surprisingly, we know even less about the origins of cultural diversity than about the determinants of cultural change.[51]

The anthropologist Monica Bell and several co-authors declared that culture contributes to "the production and reproduction of poverty." But how? It's "slippery," they said, because the many studies they review neglect interaction effects:

> Further theoretical development may be facilitated by a concern for systematically disentangling social psychological processes (often focused on perceptions) from cultural processes that involve intersubjectivity and shared meaning-making (e.g. symbolic boundaries, classification systems, and repertoires), in their interaction and articulation with social and institutional processes. These various levels should be examined in their interaction with access to a range of social, material, and other resources that act as determinants of poverty and inequality. . . . To consider a part of the equation will by definition result in an inadequate (because incomplete) understanding of crucial causal pathways.[52]

In a different domain of anthropology—the cultural attraction theory of cultural change—a similar quandary is noted: "Especially when characterizing their theoretical framework, they embrace causal excess."[53]

Even with the best of theories and imaginary worlds of data, we would face tremendous difficulties in estimating the evolution of culture or its many interactions with policy choices.[54] But our situation is harsher still. Neither anthropology nor economics provides an agreed-upon model of the interacting dynamics of development outcomes, policy choices, cultures, and other aspects of the local setting. Valid and reliable measures and data are scarce. The number of countries (or cultural units) is small, while the number of potential variables is large: statistical power is therefore meager. The estimation of culture by policy interactions is crippled by complexity, even assuming well-specified models and excellent data; and the empirical study of culture has neither.

Are these reasons why students of culture shy away from this scientific agenda? The anthropologist Alan W. Rew noted how "years of patient scholarship analyzing the social and cultural aspects of a particular society may convince [anthropologists] of the complexity of human cultural forms and processes and lead to their skepticism about the realism of applied research and consultancy rather than to any expectation that social analysts will find solutions with valid cultural content."[55]

His and their skepticism is warranted. But there is hope.

Analogies from Psychology, Soil Science, and Medicine

Consider a less daunting recalibration of the scientific agenda. Imagine you had a limited amount of time and money but nonetheless wished to have information about the "cultural conditions" in several local settings.

1. What would you want to know?
2. How would you go about knowing it?
3. How would the information you collect be helpful to local people and policymakers?

Some anthropologists might divert the questions. For example:

"Your questions don't make sense without knowing more about the problem. What you want to know about the local cultural setting depends on what you're trying to do or predict. Anyway, you can't measure culture. And cultural conditions aren't static or uniform. So, from the start these questions are at best contestable, at worst meaningless."

Fair points. But to capture the spirit of a different and more practical response, let's review answers to these questions from hypothetical practitioners in three other fields—psychology, soil science, and medicine.

1. What Would You Want to Know?

Suppose you had a limited amount of time and money and nonetheless wished to have information about

- the personalities of several individuals (for the psychologist)
- the soil conditions in several local settings (for the soil scientist)
- the health of several individuals (for the physician)

The psychologist might nod at the anthropologist's response and say, "Good points, what you say holds for the psychology of individuals as well. But you know, it turns out that for many purposes having data on a few of a potentially infinite number of variables is quite helpful. For example, quick personality tests capture the 'Big Five' personality traits of openness, conscientiousness, extraversion, agreeableness, and neuroticism."

A soil scientist might continue in a similar vein. "It does depend, of course. But in my field, too, there are a few crucial aspects of soils that are pretty easy to study and turn out to be important for a variety of agricultural decisions. For example, the United States Department of Agriculture has a handy soil quality test kit for measuring things such as soil respiration, the ability to take in water, compaction, electrical conductivity, pH, nitrate, and so forth."

And a physician might say, "What I'd like to know would depend, but my basic data would include blood pressure, pulse, height, weight, and age, and a half dozen more pieces of readily available information—answers to a series of questions about what hurts and how much, what's recently changed, what I hear with my stethoscope in a quick listen to the heart and chest, and so forth."

Our imaginary experts in these three fields would probably add that collecting such basic data would not replace careful interviewing, nor would having basic data preclude the addition of other information, based on the problem at hand. If asked whether these basic data somehow "summarized" or "measured" a personality, a soil sample, or a person's medical condition, all of our experts would laugh and say, "Of course not. These are simply useful data that assist us in making diagnoses in a highly imperfect world, so that the people we are assessing can make better decisions."

2. How Would You Go about Knowing It?

Ideally, we want to know how the desired information is obtained and the resulting data's reliability, validity, and costs.

Our psychologist would have a lot to say. The field of psychometrics studies the statistical properties of various psychological constructs. Practicing psychologists would be acutely aware of the costs of data collection, ranging from low in the case of short tests to high in the case of information obtained through psychotherapy.

Detailed answers would also be forthcoming from the soil scientists and physician. For example, an ideal physician would understand the properties of each test he could give to a patient—its reliability (surprisingly low in the case of blood pressure), its validity (in the sense of how well it measures the theoretical construct it purports to represent), its costs (financial and psychological), and its predictive power (for various health outcomes).

3. How Would the Information Be Helpful to Local People and Policymakers?

The question might be answered in generic ways: "By helping people understand themselves, their soils, and their medical conditions." True. Or: "By reminding people of the importance of personality, soil, medical differences." Also true. But our hypothetical experts would add further points.

The psychologist: "Let me give you a few examples about how this basic information would be useful. If I have even a rough psychological profile, I can help my clients understand the kinds of jobs they are likely to enjoy. We have data on the kinds of personalities that thrive in various professions. My clients can still decide to choose whatever they want, but it can be useful information to them. In pedagogy, it's been shown that university students with high anxiety and relatively low fluid intelligence do better with highly structured curricula, while students with low anxiety and relatively high intelligence learn more through pedagogies that are less structured. Another example: educators and policymakers might allocate more resources to youngsters with certain identified psychological profiles, in hopes of helping them before their problems become ingrained."

The soil scientist: "I advise farmers concerning the kinds of crops that will grow best in soils like theirs. Also, I help them evaluate ways of treating the soils. I help them think about interactions among crops, soils, and agricultural practices. For example, for some crops, they should use nitrogenous fertilizers in some kinds of soils, and phosphatic fertilizers in others. In some soil conditions, contour planting will be worth the effort, whereas in others it won't. To be helpful, I must offer more than just a set of data on the type of soil they have—I have to say how soil types interact with different plants and with different soil treatments.

"Policy makers may want to know about soil types because they may use such information in their allocation of resources, say for irrigation or fertilizer, or in programs to educate farmers to adopt certain crops or certain soil treatments."

The physician: "The basic medical information I collect helps me with diagnoses, when I combine that information with what the patient tells me. Often, I then make further, detailed tests and assessments of the particular patient's condition. The information is useful in prescriptions as well as diagnosis. Obviously, the prescriptive recommendations I make depend not only on the illness I diagnose but also on the patient's general physical condition.

Such data can also help me advise patients about preventive strategies suited for their particular situations—exercise, diet, and so forth. A lot of medicine is about changing those 'underlying variables.' "

A Humbler Agenda

These analogies suggest useful kinds of answers that we might seek in our studies of cultural variables. Unlike psychology, soil science, and medicine, in the fields of cultural studies "garden-variety" answers to our three questions often remain adversarial and unhelpful.

"What *cultural information* would I like to have? It all depends. What problem are you working out? Tell me that and maybe I can help you." After being told the problem, a cultural expert's answers may remain highly schematic. "The main thing is not to assume that all cultures are the same, or even that any one so-called culture is static and homogenous. Look at all the differences! Glory in them! Don't assume that what works in one place will work in another. Be humble!" And so forth: but seldom is a description supplied of which specific data should be collected with regard to a particular practical issue or class of issues.

Moreover, many students of culture feel compelled to belabor the truth that no set of data can ever enable someone to define, comprehend, or somehow capture a culture. Also, they point out that cultures are not static but changeable and that cultures are not uniform or monolithic. Although logically similar points hold for personality, soil, and medical conditions, in those fields they do not tend so to preoccupy researchers or so to forestall conceptual and empirical research.

And when it comes to our third question—the use and usefulness of cultural data—some anthropologists would instinctively recoil. "The only use I hope for is greater understanding, not only of the Other but of the Self. We need to put culture at the center of our intellectual awareness, as something beyond material determination. As far as policymakers go, I don't trust them at all."

The challenges of applying scientific knowledge about groups of people—cultures, let's say—are not qualitatively different from applying scientific knowledge about individuals. Psychologists, too, worry about vague terms, incomplete data, the reliability and possible biases in what measures are available, and the weaknesses in theory linking treatments, individual characteristics, and outcomes. They, too, worry about the misuse of data, including stigma and self-stigma. They, too, have to ponder their power relationships and imbalances, their own weaknesses and strengths: *they* are part of the problematic. They have to think about the tensions between trait-taking and trait-making.

In practice, they have to take into account the various institutions through which "treatments" are delivered. And there is more to take into account: the political and economic conditions, group and neighborhood characteristics, and the dynamics of change involving, perhaps, all those "factors."

The problems are general. Doctors face them. Teachers face them. Soil scientists face them. The tensions are chronic, not particular, and the ways we can deal with them without giving up are also subject to study.

6

The Misuse of Culture

In conversations with anthropologists and in reading their work, I have come to believe that they know much that could be of practical importance. Things beyond the ethnographer's abilities to describe carefully, mix and empathize with the natives, serve as interlocutors, and the rest. And beyond their roles as critics of big-D development as a set of desired outcomes and little-d development as the panoply of neoliberal, so-called free-market reforms and limited-scope, through-the-government projects. I believe that many students of culture have knowledge of rules of thumb, typical potholes and dangers, and generalizations and tendencies (if not laws) that connect types of cultures, types of policies, and types of outcomes. Anthropologists know many useful things, yet their knowledge is underutilized. Why?

In part, I think, because of the differences in intellectual "cultures" described in chapter 4 and the scientific difficulties detailed in chapter 5. But the more I became acquainted with anthropologists, the more I became persuaded that behind their reluctance to apply, or even to write down, what they know about cultural pluralism was their fear that it would be misunderstood and misused.

This danger of misuse is apparent in some of the great collective crimes of modern times. Nazi Germany is foremost, but consider also the cultural engineering in the Soviet Republics, the Chinese Communists during the Cultural Revolution and more recently with the Uighurs, the cultural tailoring of education under apartheid in South Africa, and the justification of colonial occupation on grounds of cultural superiority. Each of these examples coexisted with anthropological, psychological, and sociological studies, often quackery and glorified prejudice but sometimes, too, social science of publishable quality.

In his 2019 book *Why Culture Matters Most*, David C. Rose connected cultural beliefs—specifically moral beliefs—to trust, which in turn is crucial for development.[1] Without the cultural norm of generalized trust, free riding and corruption emerge, with disastrous implications for efficiency, equity, and the environment. Imbuing trust involves education (especially

The Culture and Development Manifesto. Robert Klitgaard, Oxford University Press (2021). © Oxford University Press.
DOI: 10.1093/oso/9780197517734.003.0006

stories: repeated and valued stories). Once present, he showed, our continued trustful responses actually change the connections in our brains. Culture becomes wired. And yet, it is not pre-wired: Rose rejected biological causes of trust and other cultural traits. Even talking about biology and culture can raise well-known red flags of racism and discrimination. "Many scholars began to treat cultural explanations as one step removed from genetic explanations. Saying that a society's culture might explain a bad outcome was taken as a code for the problem being that a given society's people were genetically inferior" (15).

Trust was also a theme in Nicholas A. Christakis's 2019 book *Blueprint: The Evolutionary Origins of a Good Society*.[2] He emphasized something more than that: altruism. Both trust and altruism are learned and imbued with cultural norms. And yet, he argues, they are also biologically conditioned. Evolutionary forces, driven in part by the challenges of collaboration in large groups, favor trust and altruism. If not hard-wired, they are pre-wired.

Both authors are nervous about their findings being misunderstood, even misused. (Christakis spends most of his concluding chapter fighting off binary thinking and negativity. His message, he keeps saying, is optimistic: human beings are increasingly wired to be good.) They are right to worry. Cultural stereotypes lurk, indeed barely lurk. Human history, and American history, are replete with bigotry and oppression against cultural groups. Even when discrimination and oppression have diminished or become illegal, many people from these groups recognize vestiges in their own lived experiences. They acutely perceive current disparities between themselves and the groups guilty of oppression. They feel angry and humiliated.

Enter here the study of cultural differences. Painfully and controversially, increasing amounts of research contend that some of the group differences, historically and today, stem in part from deep roots of culture.[3] These findings may be taken, often incorrectly, to imply that some cherished public policies will have weaker effects than believed (formal education, for example). Seeing that one's group is still at a disadvantage—even if not the current subject of bigotry enfranchised in custom and law—and learning that researchers (mostly not from one's group) are discovering deep cultural causes of those disadvantages, will spur understandable if sometimes nonproductive responses:

- The methods of these studies are wrong. Their concepts, measures, and models are incomplete, biased, and therefore invalid.

- The people doing these studies are serving other ends besides science, even if unwittingly. Their work is undergirding the white patriarchy.
- And this extension: any study of cultural differences, especially with applications to policy, can only lead to discrimination and failure.

Taking Culture into Account: Trait-Taking and Trait-Making

Long ago, Albert O. Hirschman identified a different dilemma in taking culture into account in making or resisting policy—the choice and the balancing of *trait-taking* and *trait-making*.[4]

> The dilemma of project design is then the following: if the project is planned, built, and operated on the basis of certain negative attributes of the status quo, taking them for granted, as inevitable and unchangeable, it may miss important opportunities for effecting positive changes in these attributes—on the contrary, it may even confirm and strengthen them. The achievements of the project would then be far below what they might have been and the net result could even be negative from the point of view of some "social progress function." The project planners will stand convicted as men without imagination who do not really believe in change and perhaps do not desire it. If, on the other hand, success in the construction and operation of the project is made to hinge on a prior or concurrent or subsequent change in some of the attributes of backwardness, then the project's fate becomes a wager; if the wager is lost, so that the needed change does not occur and the project's success is thereby jeopardized, the project planners will be accused of ignoring local circumstances, traditions, and sociopolitical structure and of incorrigible naivete and lack of realism in general.[5]

"Trait-taking" takes local attributes such as "culture" as given and builds projects around them. The advantage is realism; the disadvantage, fatalism (isn't taking the existing situation as given in effect giving up on change?).

"Trait-making," in contrast, declares that changing the underlying attributes, including culture, is one of the goals of the project. The danger here is sheer failure, that the traits will not change; and to this will be added, predictably, the charge that one is insensitive to local realities.

Hirschman pointed out that the dilemma is fundamental and inescapable. I believe it is one reason why anthropologists (among others) are uncomfortable applying their cultural knowledge to practical choices of policy or resistance. Roger Bastide noted:

Curious thing. White anthropology is often more concerned with this relativity of civilizations, stressing the discovery of indigenous solutions, than are local politics or the anthropology of people of color. It appears perhaps to these latter parties, who have studied at Western universities, that the ethnologist, in underlining the importance of cultural diversities and the necessity of respecting them, remains a "colonialist" or a "neo-colonialist," desirous of slowing down progress more than of accelerating it, in this way maintaining the superiority of the White world and the dependence of the emancipated ex-colonies.[6]

To their credit, anthropologists have characteristically been sensitive to the weaknesses as well as the needs of traditional societies. (Some anthropologists in calm moments also acknowledge the accomplishments of "development" as well as the disappointments and pathologies.) Few anthropologists trumpet local cultures as democratic or egalitarian. Consider this example from Thailand from the anthropologist Jonathan Rigg:

The problem is that village life and the aspirations of villagers in Thailand, and in all developing countries, are fundamentally different from those that existed as recently as 20 years ago. The bases upon which traditional village life and livelihood were founded are arguably incompatible with the modern, commercial world. With this in mind, drawing upon populist conceptions of rural life (even faithfully), and incorporating them into rural development strategies, may well be a blind alley with little to offer rural people who rarely (rightly or wrongly) wish to return to "the good old days."[7]

Moreover, he argued, existing village institutions often do not allow "the people" to make effective choices about their futures. Even in supposedly participatory programs "projects are very rarely assessed in a democratic fashion, and the opinions and desires of individuals and cliques are extremely influential."[8]

Suppose in a particular case Rigg is right. What to do? Does one rely on its given "culturally appropriate" mechanisms for decision? Does one try to introduce change? Does one support or aid only the local cultures that are deemed appropriate, leaving the rest to fend for themselves? On what facts do the answers depend?

Hirschman was correct—one cannot escape criticism no matter what one's choice. If one opts for changing cultural traits, one may be accused of neocolonialism, even if one is a member of the culture in question. And, as Bastide noted, the very same accusation may arise when one calls for preserving the cultural manifestations that now exist.

Other Dilemmas of Taking Culture into Account

Suppose anthropological research shows that a treatment (or policy, program, etc.) benefits some cultural groups more than others. "In Indonesia, private sector support programs must take account of the issue of indigenous Indonesians vis-à-vis ethnic Chinese [who are also Indonesian citizens]. This is a highly charged and important social issue that, like many, is context-specific."[9] More broadly, Amy Chua argued that market-oriented economic reforms around the world systematically favor certain ethnic and religious minorities.[10] What does it entail to take these facts into account? Should one adopt ethnically discriminatory policies to contravene the distributional implications of privatization? Change policy because it affects groups differently?

In 2004, Robert Horne and colleagues documented in Great Britain large cultural differences in attitudes toward medication. People of Indian background were more suspicious of "modern medication" than people who reported a European cultural background. The Asians "were significantly more likely to perceive medicines as being intrinsically harmful, addictive substances that should be avoided."[11] So what? The best the authors could do was to recommend that somehow these cultural differences be taken into account in "the conduct of prescribing-related consultations" and in the provision of information about medication.

If cultural differences exist, are studied, and are publicized, may this not hurt people's feelings, lead to stigmatization, and foster prejudice? The problem is perfectly general. It concerns the value but also the misuse of group information in predicting and making decisions. What do we consider valid use and invalid misuse? If we had perfect knowledge, what would we do to use such information and prevent its misuse?

Similar problems arise in teaching about cultural differences. Many professions call for the training of practitioners in cultural knowledge—this, for example, was Bronislaw Malinowski's recommendation for how anthropology should be applied. Cottage industries in the United States and around the world strive to imbue "cultural competence."[12] But when such training has taken place—as in teacher training—it has not been free of criticism. If cultural differences "explain" differences in academic performance, it may lead prospective teachers to brand minorities, even to blame them for not learning. "Anthropology," wrote one scholar, "has given education students a new and somewhat more sophisticated set of rationalizations for giving up."[13] Since anthropology teaches that each culture is different, "teachers will not know in advance which patterns of interaction will be prevalent in their students' communities, and which of those lead to learning difficulties"—at least, not without a detailed ethnographic study of each locality, which is clearly infeasible, as it "requires intense observation, by a trained observer, over an extended period of time."[14] With the needed knowledge unavailable, teachers may fall back on cultural stereotypes, which may only make matters worse. They may start thinking in terms of "cultural deficits."

And students themselves may imbibe the stereotypes. An evaluation of culturally relevant education for Māori students in New Zealand suggested that "even a professional development initiative for teachers with the ultimate goal of raising student achievement can be misinterpreted as something remedial that is directed at student deficits"—and *deficit* is a dirty word. "If students are led to believe that the focus is on remediating underachievement among Māori (rather than remediating teaching practices), deficit theorizing can undermine students' identities."[15]

Let's extend these ideas to research methods. Suppose we devised measures for a few "cultural" variables (ascriptive-achievement, group-individual, tight vs. loose locus of control, religion, and matrilineal-patrilineal). Suppose we combined these in a predictive model of certain behavior of interest. And suppose that we showed that such variables had significant predictive power, after allowing for other pertinent causes and conditions. Our model would be imperfect, but suppose we could make better predictions by using it than by forgoing it.

Even so, might such a model lead to unfortunate results? With regard to culture, does it not badly miss the point to say that one has developed a predictive model with a few ad hoc variables that "explain" some percentage of the variance in an outcome?[16] Does this not do violence to the kind of inquiry that cultural studies should represent?

Relief and Misunderstanding in South Sudan

Let us now consider an example that illustrates several points. First, how taking anthropological insights into account might have helped a relief program do better. Next, why, nonetheless, the application of anthropological insights can make anthropologists so uncomfortable:

- For reasons that Hirschman's dilemma captures—when it comes to taking cultures into account, you'll be criticized no matter what.
- And a second thing: the cultural knowledge you capture, summarize, and apply can itself be misused.

"You'll Be Criticized for Whatever You Recommend"

Consider food relief in southern Sudan in the late 1990s. With limited funds, international organizations wanted to target food to the most vulnerable—children and geographical areas facing the greatest risk of famine. But the local people, the anthropologist Simon Harrigan reported, rejected the alien practice of "targeting the neediest."[17] Among the Dinka people, food aid was "not seen as belonging to anyone, even to the extent that someone accused of stealing aid can reply, 'what did I take from your mother?'" What's more, targeted aid would create a stigma because some people and regions were defined as "needy"—and therefore, some of the neediest people wouldn't take the food. As a result, local authorities did not comply with targeting and redistributed the food along kinship lines rather than territorially.

Harrigan's cultural justification may grate some Western audiences:

Having a large family is the ideal to which Dinka aspire (cieng). In practical terms, having more than one wife allows a man to have many sons to bring fame to the family name, many daughters to bring bride wealth cows into the family, and plentiful labor in an unmechanized subsistence economy where the main constraint to increasing production is labor shortage. Penalizing those who have attained the kind of success to which people aspire and rewarding the unsuccessful has a questionable logic in a war where aspiration and hope of better times sometimes seems to be all that remains. (311)

But there are other explanations. When I visited South Sudan in 2004 to help the Sudanese People's Liberation Movement think through regional autonomy, my interlocutors shared a remarkable document, "The Draft of the SPLM Policy on Dialogue." It contained a lot of generalities.[18] But for our purposes here, notice how its author, James Wani Igga, recognizes the realities of power and the struggle for freedom (the jungle) and the abiding need for equity (the elephant is peace and freedom):

Politics is a *jungle* torn between doing the right thing and staying in office. Whether before or after the formation of the Government of South Sudan (GoSS) the SPLM must take the lead to include and involve others outside its circumference in the upcoming government and related posts.

The SPLM ought to view itself like a good hunter who goes to the forest. If he kills an elephant the animal doesn't belong to him alone. The entire village has the right of taking knives and cutting the meat, though traditionally the hunter retains the prerogative to distribute the leg, neck, ribs, etc. to whosoever he pleases.

Yet it would be totally uncustomary for him to deny inclusiveness, sharing and participation of others in this big meal. The elephant in the SPLM context is the peace and freedoms it shall certainly bring about.[19]

Because of this norm of inclusiveness, Harrigan argued that targeted aid would fail in its goal of getting to the neediest. Kinship groups would take the aid and allocate it their way, and the military would, too. "On the ground reality meant it would be hard, perhaps dangerous, to keep food aid from soldiers" (319).

At times, Harrigan seem to imply, "Don't target aid, just give it equally to everyone." In other words, in Hirschman's terms, aid givers should be trait-takers in this case.

But to his credit, Harrigan pulled up short from that conclusion.

There is a danger that listening to the local value system and adopting a distribution system that targets the majority of the population will result in an inadequate amount of assistance going to the most needy. A finite amount of aid spread thinly across the whole population reduces its value to almost nothing. There is also the mandate of certain aid agencies to address the needs of particular groups such as children or the elderly. If a local value system reproduces gender inequalities, should it be supported? The arguments are valid ones, and the counterarguments sometimes sound like one is taking sides or idealizing the egalitarian nature of non-western societies. (322)

Harrigan also felt uncomfortable doing what he was doing—trying as an outsider to describe and present "local Sudanese culture."

There is strong feeling among relief workers that they should speak out on behalf of the oppressed in the places where they work—for example, for Médecins Sans Frontières, temoinage (literally "witnessing") is written into the mission statement of the organization. However, there is a danger that overzealous "representing" of their opinions leaves the poor without a voice and leaves relief agencies believing that the poor cannot think or act for themselves. (324)

And so, in the end, Harrigan, like many anthropologists, refused to make recommendations. His cultural knowledge was in tension with his acknowledgement of the humanitarian reasons for targeting aid to the neediest—and he experienced discomfort as seeming to endorse local cultures or, for that matter, as seeming to represent those cultures to outsiders.

Trait-taker or trait-maker: he'll be criticized, no matter what.

"Someone Will Misuse Your Anthropological Findings"

And now to the second risk of applying knowledge of local cultures: oversimplification and misuse. Years after Harrigan's study was published, the psychologists Hazel Rose Markus and Alana Conner retold it and drew big lessons. Here is an excerpt from their book *Clash!*:

In early 1998 a famine descended upon southern Sudan, despite a United Nations-led effort to monitor and alleviate food shortages in the region. Aid workers suspected that military and tribal chiefs had been hoarding the food, so they began delivering rations directly to the most vulnerable people: nursing mothers, children, the ill, and the elderly. To the workers' dismay, however, these beneficiaries rerouted the rations right back to their leaders....

We agree that culture is partly responsible for charity gone wrong. Unlike many of these experts, though, we lay the blame not on any one culture, but on the collision between the cultures of donors in the Global North and recipients in the Global South.

. . . Despite their amazing diversity, the people of the Global North have in common a sense of their selves as independent. For them, including the aid workers in Sudan, people are unique individuals, separate from their groups, in control of their fates, equal in rank, and free to act in their own self-interest....

In contrast, the amazingly diverse people of the Global South have in common a sense of their selves as interdependent. For them, including the Sudanese famine victims, people live their lives through relationships, and see themselves as strands in a web, nodes in a network, or fingers on a hand. As a result, ties to kith and kin drive individual actions.

When the Global North attempts to help the Global South, the clash of independence and interdependence undermines many of its efforts.... On the poorer, southern side of the equation, what donors call "irrationality," "corruption," and "inefficiency" are what many aid recipients call "sound operating principles." The mistrust that pervades West Africa, the cronyism that besets India, the conflicts that pepper the Middle East, and the slow pace that hobbles Mexico are the flip sides of interdependent qualities, including a profound sense of history in West Africa, of duty in India, of honor in the MENA region, and of *simpatía* (Spanish for "pleasant and harmonious social relations") in Mexico. The culture cycles supporting these different aspects of interdependence have brought meaning and order to the Global South for the past few millennia.[20]

One can imagine Simon Harrigan and most anthropologists cringing at these generalizations. To apply a point of Olivier de Sardan's, made regarding aid projects in Mali:

The multiplicity, complexity and interweaving of the variables involved in any social intervention, no matter how small, make any attempt to reduce it to a single explanatory variable illusory. Nevertheless, this illusion persists in certain sectors of the social sciences governed by a positivist vision of the world.[21]

And cringing at simplistic inferences: "You can't change those local cultural features. Just accept them. In Hirschman's terms, be a trait-taker."

For these reasons, anthropologists may feel unwilling to apply cultural knowledge to practical questions. Stereotyping lurks, with bigotry in the background. In practice, Hirschman's dilemma of trait-taking vs. trait-making is one many anthropologists wish not to confront. And the oversimplification and misuse of their careful, nuanced fieldwork—whether by aid officials, government officials, or other scholars—makes them ill.

7

Cultural Texts

Early in their marriage, the French anthropologist and literature professor Raymonde Carroll and her American anthropologist husband took their baby girl to Nukuoro, a remote atoll in the Federated States of Micronesia. Even today, Nukuoro's population is under 400 people. Its land area is about 1.7 square kilometers. It has no airstrip, and a passenger boat calls irregularly every few months.

They were welcomed by the English-speaking chief, who placed them in a small house that though humble was the best on the atoll. The next morning, Raymonde found that the chief had slept on the porch.

"Wanted to take care of our things," he said.

He and the villagers doted on the baby girl. It was, Raymonde surmised, the first white baby they had ever seen. They cooed over her, laughed at her every movement, seemed to be totally in love with her.

The chief, especially. He even washed the baby's diapers daily, despite Raymonde's protestations. She thought, he seems to be doing this ostentatiously, displaying for the villagers.

On day four, the chief spoke seriously to Raymonde. "Don't you think it's time to cut the baby's nails?"

Though taken aback, Raymonde agreed. The chief watched attentively as Raymonde did the trimming.

On the morning of the fifth day, the chief made an announcement. Cordially but directly he told Raymonde and her husband, "It is now time for me to take your baby, in adoption."

"That day," she wrote later, "I understood the urgency and distress of certain intercultural exchanges."

But soon matters were clarified. The misunderstanding was at least visible and apparent. A satisfactory resolution was "only a matter of finding an adequate response, which I did, of course, once the first moment of panic had passed."

The Culture and Development Manifesto. Robert Klitgaard, Oxford University Press (2021). © Oxford University Press.
DOI: 10.1093/oso/9780197517734.003.0007

Another point is crucial here. As she and her husband encountered their exotic new neighbors, they were professionally prepared to be aware, tolerant, and forgiving.

But Raymonde and her husband soon encountered other, less visible forms of cultural misunderstanding—in their own relationship. They were occasionally less tolerant and forgiving of each other. It was easy to blame the other person for insensitivity, irrationality, and clumsiness. In Raymonde's words later about intercultural friendships, "I was struck repeatedly by the frequency of intercultural misunderstandings, principally in our close interpersonal relationships, by the number of wounds, deep and superficial, that were essentially due to the profound differences in our cultural premises."

Luckily, she and her husband had an insight. What if it wasn't the other person but the other person's culture? They began unpacking those awkward moments in terms of American culture and French culture. They began to have fun with the analysis. "You weren't trying to hurt me, you were just being American!"

What proved liberating about this discovery was transferring a personal issue to a cultural issue. It transformed what could have been a chronic source of personal conflict into a shared task of cultural discovery and appreciation.

When she returned from the South Pacific, Raymonde Carroll began studying French-American cultural misunderstandings more generally. She found that in conversation, French people often seemed rude to Americans. "The French ask you a question, and then they don't listen for an answer." And vice versa: "You raise a simple topic with an American, and they want to take it back to Adam and Eve." For the French, she generalized, conversation establishes and fortifies a relationship. For Americans, conversation is about the transfer of information. Perhaps American women understand this distinction better than American men. Psychologist Deborah Tannen found that conversation for an American man is about "report," while for an American woman it is about "rapport."[1]

And so it was that Raymonde Carroll began documenting French-American differences in homes, romance, money, telephone calls, friendships, accidents, and more. Her book *Cultural Misunderstandings: The French-American Experience* is fascinating for what it says about French and American implicit rules and systems of communication, and also for the hints it provides about how to do *cultural analysis*.[2]

Carroll wrote, "I see cultural analysis as a means of perceiving as 'normal' things which initially seem 'bizarre' or 'strange' among people of a culture different from one's own" (2).

> But in order to understand this, I must first become aware of my reading, of the interpretation I bring to the cultural text, of the filter through which I learned to perceive the world. In other words, before learning to understand the culture of the other, I must become aware of my own culture, of my cultural presuppositions, of the implicit premises that inform my interpretation, of my verities. (4)
>
> The first step [in cultural analysis] consists of clearing the deck, so to speak. I must, above all, avoid all attempts at discovering the deep-seated reasons for the cultural specificity of such-and-such a group. That is to say that I must avoid the temptation of psychological or psychoanalytic explanations ("because American mothers . . . ," "because French people can't stand authority . . ."). (5)

She also wants us to set aside explanations that are ecological, geographical, demographic, economic, religious, historical, or sociological. "Indeed, I am not using cultural analysis to find out why things are as they are or to uncover their deep-rooted nature ('what they are'). Rather, I seek to understand the system of communication by which meaning is produced and received within a group" (6).

Carroll wants us to begin with our own views. What are our so-to-speak cultural presuppositions and implicit premises? Then, we can ask the same questions about people in the other culture(s).

Such questions may force us to ask almost etymological questions. Consider evidence about cultural differences. Evidence, defined in one dictionary as "a thing or things helpful in forming a conclusion or judgment," comes from the Latin *evidens* clear, obvious, from *e-* out of, from + *videns*, present participle of *videre* to see. Evidence, in other words, shares a root with evident, defined as "easily seen or understood; obvious." The reason many cultural misunderstandings are so frustrating is because to one of us an answer seems "evident," just as to the person from the other culture a different answer is equally "apparent or obvious to the mind or senses."

Raymonde Carroll's book was originally published in French. Its title was *Evidences Invisibles*, in the plural. What a strange title. How can "evidence" be "invisible," when we have just seen that the word comes from something apparent?

Her answer is precisely those unexamined assumptions, those implicit rules of communication, which shape our views in ways we do not see until we make an effort to do so. That which is most "evident" to us may have roots in something we do not see at all, which within our culture is to us invisible. Thus, the search for that which is evident but invisible *in ourselves* can be the beginning of understanding of the other's invisibles, and then to a deeper understanding of our encounters.

From there it may be possible to move to a constructive new engagement. We can avoid being unintentionally rude. And we can discover and employ, as she did, tentative but scientific classifications of behavior and belief—of culture—in different countries. *Scientific*, in the sense that there are categories, patterns, and empirical differences whose importance, for particular contexts, a scientist could evaluate, and which delighted readers could evaluate more qualitatively with their own experiences. My wife Elaine, who is originally from South Africa, found that many of Carroll's characterizations of French culture fit fairly well with her own experiences. So, we hosted a dinner with three other couples who were legitimately one from France, one from America, giving everyone Carroll's book well in advance and asking them to bring along a favorite passage and be prepared to discuss it. We served French and American wines (as nonjudgmentally as possible), and so we cannot attribute all the liveliness and fun of our dinner-table conversation to the testing of Carroll's anthropological science.

Why don't we try to be more like Raymonde Carroll? For example, use her inspiration to address cultural misunderstandings in development. Consider an example from Senegal.

An Antidote for Poisonous Texts

Some years ago, a remarkable meeting took place. Almost the entire leadership of the government of Senegal—including the prime minister and almost all cabinet ministers—took two days off and had a retreat with senior officials from the World Bank. These *journées de réflexion* included a few outsiders invited by both sides as "resource people," and I was lucky enough to be one of them. The idea behind the event was for both sides to work through their appreciation of current problems and strategies for overcoming them. The hope was that a new partnership might be forged in the process.

I arrived before the event and then stayed after it for a few days in Dakar, meeting with government leaders. Then I spent a week in Washington with the World Bank people. What struck me was hearing various renditions of what might be called cultural "texts" concerning the roles of the World Bank and sovereign governments in Africa: texts that are potentially poisonous.

Here is a paraphrase of the text I often heard from World Bank officials:

I don't think it's any mystery why this country is at a standstill. The government really doesn't care about development. That's all a pretext. They are good at speeches and choosing the right words, but when they choose policies it is to get the most they can personally. Look at the new industrial policy—it's all about ripping off the productive sector. Bureaucracies perpetuate themselves, like a colony of insects. Politicians, even or perhaps especially in a democracy, avoid economic strategy. Instead, politicians search for ways to please in the short run, in order to hold on to their own privileges.

The problem with the Bank's behavior here is that we're not tough enough. We don't see this big picture; we pretend that the government is serious when it isn't. We should force the government to face the truth about their economic situation. We should make them take hard, strategic decisions. For example, make them allocate money to primary instead of tertiary education. Cut the public payroll. Reform those tariffs at last. And many others. If they don't, we should just, at some point, stop pretending and clear out.

The second text was what I heard from the Senegalese ministers. To paraphrase:

We listen and listen to what the World Bank's so-called experts tell us, but their advice is far removed from our realities. They are narrow technocrats. They do not understand our institutions, and they have no appreciation for politics or implementation. They propose some things to us that have never been tried elsewhere, or some other things that no government however conservative in the North would ever accept. They are doctrinaire, guided by a theory that is not culturally relevant in countries like ours.

And they themselves do not bear the risks of failure. We are the ones who must suffer the political consequences of their advice. The money they lend us immediately goes to repay our debts to them. As individuals, their rewards don't depend on how well their advice turns out. Ours certainly do.

And this conditionality—it rubs us raw. It reminds us of the lack of respect that we have always felt in this part of the world—ever since the time our ancestors were shipped off as slaves. The World Bank people do not just give us advice, they coerce us. They treat us like children.

In the context of negotiations, not to mention the creation of collegiality, texts like these can be poisonous. They can furnish an excuse for evasion and dissimulation; they can stand in the way of hard work. These two texts can escalate issues unhelpfully, each side recoiling to levels like "they must face reality," "we must play hard ball," "there is a lack of respect," and "should we (they) be here at all?" But not saying so to each other.

Who knows the extent to which negotiations about development are undercut, and partnerships precluded, by "poisonous texts" like these two?

Would something like Raymonde Carroll's analysis of cultural misunderstandings help? As with her "invisible evidence," texts like these remain in the background, kept from the other side, kept from close analysis. Both texts emphasize the inadequacies of the Other's motivations; they tend to be less aware of inadequacies closer to the Self. In general, texts are poisonous when their interpretation places the Other's character or morality on center stage—and leaves our own in the dressing room.

How might we detoxify poisonous texts? Once we have them on the table—perhaps through the help of anthropologists—we might consider three stages: externalizing, criticizing, and using problem-solving exercises.

Externalizing the Texts. Once a poisonous text is discerned and described, the next step is to externalize it. This means objectifying it, putting it in some third person's mouth. In this process we try to extract the text from the particular country and the particular international institution. We try to remove the texts from *these particular* Selves and Others, just as Raymond Carroll and her husband externalized those French and American texts about money, love, and so forth.

The World Bank's text about Senegal, for example, might be externalized through readings from public choice theory, concerning the universal and unfortunate tendencies of governments to watch out for themselves. "It's not about Senegal per se, it's about governments." For the second text—the

Senegalese criticizing the World Bank—one might read pieces that criticize foreign aid, from the perspectives of the new political economy, organization theory, or game theory. "It's not just about you, it's the nature of donors." The texts are not unique secrets: we are not alone in what we are experiencing and in our interpretations of it.

Criticism. The next step is criticism: put the texts on the table, to show that they can be analyzed. Again, it is useful that the analysis be removed from the immediate context. For example, those articles on public choice may provide both the basic intuitions of that "text" and a number of critiques concerning its logic, its applicability, and its explanatory power.

What work should criticism hope to do? It should point to lacunae, inconsistencies, places where the text says or seems to say more than is justified— and to misunderstandings that a text may engender. But criticism should also help one to appreciate a text's utility, suggestiveness, and merit. A good textual critique should stimulate creative rethinking.

Problem-solving exercises. Finally, invite those with different texts to step beyond them and work together solving specific problems. One detoxifies a poisonous prejudice by demonstrating, via cooperation on concrete tasks, the Other's helpfulness and intelligibility in one's own terms. One tries to create new texts together, texts that complexify the old reductionisms while at the same time contributing something useful.

For example, in the case of Senegal and the World Bank, joint exercises can tackle problems where both sides bring immediately and tangibly useful contributions—for example, where the World Bank shares its international experience, the government its knowledge of local cultures. Ideally, begin with tasks where short-run success is likely.

Standard negotiations between donors and recipients, between lenders and borrowers, might be recast in this way. For example, as happened in Senegal, a World Bank public expenditure review of a borrowing nation may contain bad news: the country's pattern of spending is unsustainable. When the World Bank brings such news to a country in the form of a study and simply admonishes the country to do more (or live up to its agreements), it may unwittingly reinforce the government's poisonous text. An alternative might be to create an environment in which the unpleasant facts become the basis for the joint analysis of alternatives. One might create such an environment by beginning with a case study of another country that once had similar problems and succeeded in overcoming them. One would analyze the other country's problems together, consider the pros and cons of alternatives, and then make recommendations. Only afterward would one learn what the other country actually did. With this as a warm-up that externalizes the problem and demystifies it, then attention can be turned to the local challenges. (We will elaborate on this technique in the final chapter.)

These three steps of criticism applied to cultural conflicts may have an unexpected effect. Potentially poisonous texts may be corrected or enriched and appreciated at last as texts and not ultimate truths. And, as with Raymonde Carroll and her husband, in the process of mutual criticism, the Self and the Other may themselves change. The texts as a consequence may no longer have their grip.

"How" Matters

In Burkina Faso, the quality of maternal care was undercut by mistrust and misunderstanding between mothers and healthcare providers.[3] Each group tended to possess "poisonous texts" about the other. A team of outside anthropologists and "social mobilization experts" helped the patients and health professionals get together and vet these texts, hoping that the open communication would be salutary. In the event, it wasn't—and the lesson is that how cultural texts are surfaced and analyzed makes all the difference.

Here is a rendition of what the mothers thought about the healthcare providers.[4]

> They don't respect us. They refuse any dialogue with us. There is a lack of explanation about the nature and the purpose of the fees incurred during childbirth. We want to be consulted, especially about the improvement of the conditions in the hospitals. We demand to be engaged directly in this process.

Based on experience in other maternal clinics in Africa, these texts could have gone much further, to mistreatment and abuse by medical staff. A 2019 study of facility-based childbirth in Ghana, Guinea, Myanmar, and Nigeria documented that more than two in five of the women in the 2016 births observed by the researchers "experienced physical or verbal abuse, or stigma or discrimination. . . . Many women did not consent for episiotomy or cesarean section, despite receiving these procedures."[5]

And in Burkina Faso, the healthcare providers had these texts:

> These patients do not respect our directives about prevention and treatment. They don't regularly make their prenatal consultations. They don't listen: they arrive too early or too late for giving birth. And the people who accompany them: awful. They comport themselves badly. There are too many of them, and they are undisciplined. They have a terrible opinion about health personnel. They blab outside, in town, about anything bad that happens in the maternity ward. These people can be helpful to encourage women during birth, but most of them refuse to take the most elementary protective measures, like washing blood-stained clothes or emptying liquid wastes. They give bad advice to the patients and try to speed up the delivery. They don't respect visiting hours—we tell them, "This isn't the marketplace!"

The team of anthropologists and others in the French-funded Aquasou Programme tried to overcome these negative texts by getting them out in the open. They created "a space for dialogue," actually many spaces. The team selected about twenty patients (some urban, some rural) and about twenty healthcare providers. The team prepared each group in advance. For example, a week before each encounter, the team met with the leaders of health services and explained the principles and objectives of the meeting. Participants were reminded of a local adage: "A dog can't smell the odor of its own head," meaning (the team explained) it is always difficult to perceive one's own imperfections and "to conduct an autocritique."

An easily accessible, "neutral site" was chosen in hopes of minimizing the chances of an "unequal dialogue" (for example, if the meeting took place at a hospital or a city hall). The facilitator was a well-respected, senior midwife.

The first session spawned harsh complaints and angry reactions. In order "to attenuate the tensions," the second and third meetings began with bright spots. "Please provide some examples of aspects of care that struck you as positive. Where have you experienced good interactions?"

Over the period of a year, a total of nine meetings were held. Complaints dominated, in "concrete areas" such as giving birth, accompaniment, cesarean sections, contraception, and medical evacuation. They meetings did lead to "clear communication [*la parole à froid*] about the relations between users and caregivers, a form of 'freedom of speech' among the various actors in face-to-face situations." A number of harmful rumors were vetted and dispelled, such as genital cutting by health staff.

But the encounters proved difficult to sustain. The discourse became stale. And, the team noted ruefully, "the essential element for the continuation of these meetings remains the difficulty for the care providers to envisage discussions with lay people about quality of care. Both users and anthropologists are judged illegitimate sources about questions of the work of health personnel."[6] It was expensive to involve the anthropologists and "social mobilization experts," and when French funding dried up, the meetings were discontinued.[7]

The objective was laudable, the method less so. As Elisabeth Lasch-Quinn has shown with regard to "sensitivity training" in the United States, simply bringing groups together to air grievances and expose their stereotypes is often counterproductive.[8]

Note how different this is from the method I proposed to deal with poisonous texts. The first step was to externalize the texts—extract them from these people in this place and locate them in another country, indeed in an academic literature. Then, critique these now-disembodied texts together, including their reasons, uses, and misuses. After that, seek together a few new ways to collaborate.

Raymonde Carroll and her husband did this. They extracted their quarrels from themselves and their tiny island to a general consideration of cultural texts in France and in the United States. Then they analyzed the stereotypes together as "invisible evidences" in their respective cultures. "We're not alone" is often the first step of effective therapy.

Taking Account of the Indigenous

Consider one more application of Raymonde Carroll–like analyses: discourses about "taking indigenous institutions into account." What could be more culturally grounded and distinctive than indigenous institutions and networks? And more important to "take into account" in development activities? I think that something like "cultural misunderstandings" are present in answers to these questions—and that by laying out different cultural texts about indigenous institutions, we might move practical discussions to more productive places.

James Wunsch and Dele Olowu concluded that

> studies highlighting successful African development, interestingly enough, have usually pointed away from the centralized state and the organizations it has spawned. Instead, key roles have been played by organizations it has generally attempted to weaken or destroy: by community and mutual improvement unions; age-grade associations; cooperatives; labor unions; rural, market, social welfare, and trading voluntary associations; local governments; traditional political institutions; religious associations; and others.[9]

In 2018, Claudia Baez-Camargo noted how important such organizations and networks are to the implementation of public policies.[10] "Our focus on social networks carves out the many ways in which they are locked into configurations from which they cannot easily or readily break away. All members of a network, *including* powerful actors, are tied into relations of reciprocal exchange through co-optation and control. These practices are all the stronger as they are frequently underpinned by social norms and values that are used to legitimize extraction and redistribution." Michael Cernea's examination of twenty-five agricultural projects "found local grass root organizations to be a prime factor contributing to long-term sustainability of project benefits, while their absence was identified as a key cause of nonsustainability."[11]

Successful local organizations tend to be *indigenous*—that is, organizations that were not initiated by outsiders, although once they are established, outsiders may help them thrive. Note that these are not "just" "civil society organizations," at least not in the eyes of critical anthropologists who have slated "civil society" as a Eurocentric, bourgeois, and individualist concept.[12] These organizations and networks are indigenous, or spontaneous—meaning self-organized and locally contingent. Milton Esman and Norman Uphoff studied a sample of 150 local organizations around the developing world. They uncovered certain "characteristics of local organizations most likely to function beneficially." Two stood out:

> Informal modes of operation were generally more successful than more formal ones. . . . One of the strongest statistical explanations for local organizations' contribution to rural development goals was their impetus—who took the initiative to start them? *Those established by community members or leaders had much higher performance scores than those created by outside agencies.*[13]

In contrast, many studies document the failure of outside efforts to initiate cooperatives and other rural institutions.[14] The reasons for the failures include co-optation by government agencies or well-meaning outsiders, an unfavorable policy environment for cooperation, and, importantly, the organizations started from outside lack culturally appropriate forms and meanings of cooperation and enforcement. Indigenous institutions, which by definition are initiated by rural people themselves, originate and operate within the local milieu. To be sustainable, they must be culturally adapted.

And so, argue many activists and scholars, it is important for those wishing to understand and improve rural development to "take indigenous institutions into account."

Four Ways to "Take into Account"

But what exactly do the words in quotes mean? How might a cultural analysis à la Raymonde Carroll help us improve our conversations about taking indigenous institutions and networks into account?

Consider four possible meanings of "take into account," which are usually not separated in discussions of what to do and how.

1. Give them resources

"Empowerment," says one text, "means giving indigenous institutions resources and agreeing to go along with whatever they come up with." If one asks why such institutions should not simply be left alone, the answer is that they have legitimacy but lack resources. This text fits nicely into an economic perspective, too: if you want to help someone according to his or her own lights, the optimal gift is a lump-sum transfer, no strings attached.

But this text rings alarm bells, even to those most familiar with local situations. Indigenous networks contain their own dynamics of meaning and power. Some theorists believe that "one is least likely to find internal democracy in grassroots organizations where members are the least well educated, the poorest and of the lowest social status."[15] As we have seen, indigenous institutions are not always paragons of democratic, egalitarian, inclusive organizations. They can be hierarchical, ageist and sexist, and inefficient. "Taking indigenous institutions into account" must countenance their negative as well as the positive aspects.

2. Give them (us) respect; listen to them (us)

  (a) When you listen to locals complain about development projects and
       programs, you may hear above all a version of this text: "Governments
       and donors systematically bypass what is local and unique, seeming
       thereby to devalue it." But when locals are pushed to recommend
       alternatives, they have trouble coming up with more than "consult us,
       talk with us, listen to us."

  (b) "Give them (us) respect; listen to them (us)" may have the purpose of
       emphasizing the "symbolic motor," or the autonomy of meaning from
       material causality, that culture provides and indigenous institutions
       embody. *Respect* means acknowledging this autonomy—perhaps in
       the vein of what the philosopher Charles Taylor calls "the politics of
       recognition."[16]

3. Create an enabling environment for them

An insight of this text is that institutions and networks, even traditional
ones freighted with meaning as well as function, are not exogenous or
static. Indigenous institutions respond to, among other things, conditions
of risk and opportunity, and to both market and non-market failures. They
will be optimally enabled—in some cases strengthened, in others perhaps
replaced—by public policies. A government doesn't have to figure out which
particular indigenous organizations to support directly; it has to create a
policy environment that provides laws, information, and incentives so that
local actors can thrive.

There's a flip side to this text. "Our" trying to help "them" directly can
breed resistance and negative dynamics. Milton Esman and Norman Uphoff
concluded:

> According to our reading of dozens of case experiences, "pump-priming" of
> local organizations based primarily on outside resources seldom results in
> effective, sustainable organizations. The leadership that emerges is likely to
> be less well-motivated and may indeed be bent mostly on self-enrichment;
> members will take what is free without developing a sense of responsibility
> for the local organization.[17]

Offers of direct help from the outside, Bernard Lecomte argued, may excite local mistrust. "Any fresh project will fit into their history as one more

unfortunate episode of outside influence on a rural community. It will be accepted not as something radically new but as one more trial to be undergone, with the need yet again to safeguard the group's own existence as far as possible. Participation in what outsiders have prepared is seen first and foremost as a threat to the existence of the group."[18]

Even local participation that is initiated by outsiders may be dysfunctional in some cultural contexts, argued Jean-Pierre Olivier de Sardan. "The paradox, in this case, is that this participatory approach has on the contrary amplified the suspicions of the local populations instead of dissipating them! The very fact of associating village auxiliaries with investigators for HEA [Household Economy Appraisal] investigations or going through general assemblies convened by chiefs has made the process suspect!"[19]

4. Merge with them

Mamadou Dia argued that a "disconnect" between modern and traditional institutions is at the core of Africa's development problems. A "reconciliation" of these institutions is the answer:

> The central themes . . . are (a) that the widely lamented crisis of capacity building in Africa is more a crisis of institutional capacity (capacity utilization) than a crisis of technical capacity (availability of skills, methods, systems, and technology); (b) that this institutional crisis is essentially due to a structural and functional disconnect between informal, indigenous institutions rooted in the region's history and culture and formal institutions mostly transplanted from outside; and (c) that institutional reconciliation is the key to resolving the crisis.[20]

Two features of this text seem important. Both indigenous and modern institutions have something to offer; they must be reconciled, merged, to create something new. As a consequence, to those relying on this text it is uncomfortable to ask whether for some tasks and in some settings the problem is too much merging of traditional practices into modern institutions, or that in some circumstances merging may lead to cooptation and even demise.

Another feature is the satisfying metaphor of merger: "Don't just give them resources, don't just talk, and don't just enable—somehow we've got to *get together* and both become something new." Exactly what this means, the adherent admits, is unclear; but it is deeply felt; and there is a tendency toward a combination of exhortation and frustrating vagueness. Marie-Dominique

Perrot worried about this text of cultural merger and reconciliation: "Of course, it aims to go beyond the binary nature of the classification between tradition and modernity, but it remains loaded either positively, and at the same time idealistically and simplistically (long live the mixture!), or negatively, when it refers to phenomena such as the liquefaction of identity, cultural disarray, unresolved double-belonging by cultural 'marriage', self-denial etc."[21]

Beyond Texts?

How could indigenous institutions help with some of the chronic challenges of local economic development?

Market Failures

Take credit markets as an example. In rural areas especially, private firms will not provide the optimal levels and types of credit. Credit markets underperform when there is (1) imperfect information about the riskiness of potential clients, (2) imperfect mechanisms for the enforcement of repayment, and (3) unclear or nonexistent property rights. These three conditions are especially prevalent in rural areas of developing countries.

Indigenous institutions and networks may help overcome these problems. For instance, they may have better information on the riskiness of specific potential clients and more efficient screening techniques. They may provide a low-cost and credible way of pooling transactions costs and risks, taking advantage of economies of scale. They may possess both techniques of enforcement and (if carefully designed) appropriate incentives for applying them. The design of credit programs might "take indigenous institutions into account" in all these ways—and some successful programs have done so.

This is only one example of a general idea. Imagine analyzing each project with a set of questions in mind. What are the market failures we see? How might indigenous institutions and networks provide the information, economies of scale, enforcement, incentives, and so forth that could help mollify those failures? What new problems might using them entail (e.g., their managerial inefficiency and their own implicit market power) and how might these problems be mitigated (e.g., management training, accounting systems, oversight, etc.)?

Bureaucratic Failures

Typically, it is difficult to measure outputs in public agencies and therefore difficult to create appropriate incentives within the bureaucracy. Controls, discipline, professionalism, and exhortation attempt to substitute for links between pay and performance. But they are imperfect substitutes, and monopoly plus discretion minus accountability is also a recipe for corruption. In many countries, bureaucracies underperform and even become predatory, perhaps especially in countries with low levels of human resources, weak countervailing institutions, and legacies of colonialism or state-run economies.

How might indigenous institutions and networks help overcome these failures? Once again, the analytical task is to examine the sources of the failure one by one. Might indigenous institutions be utilized to provide better information on the outputs of government agencies? How? Might they provide incentives to government agents? Might they be efficient mechanisms for the delivery of public services, perhaps because they "internalize" some of the costs of predation and therefore have better incentives to deliver the goods? Might they be used to provide "competition" in service delivery? Working through such questions might generate a host of ideas that otherwise would not have occurred to us.

Once again, we must also anticipate the problems that using such institutions might entail—cooptation, inefficiency, the creation of market power, and others—and consider ways to ameliorate or prevent these problems in advance.

The Rule of Law

The administration of justice is often an obstacle to economic as well as political development. How might traditional institutions help remedy some of the failures of the current system? As in the previous headings, we would analyze various dimensions of information and incentives. We would add further headings. Can traditional means of dispute resolution be exploited to replace or supplement more formal mechanisms?

Again, the costs and risks of using indigenous institutions would be analyzed as well. What sorts of training and accountability might render these "informal" mechanisms more efficient and less subject to monopoly creation and arbitrariness? Would these "improvements" themselves threaten the indigenous institution in any way?

Doing this "taking into account" would likely have many forms, depending on the problem, the institutions, and the cultural setting. Sometimes indigenous institutions and networks would be important and sometimes unimportant. Sometimes the result might be to avoid them altogether. The point is that by working systematically in project and policy design through frameworks like these, we might be able to go beyond "texts" and generate practical ideas for taking indigenous institutions into account.

Conclusions

The examples in this chapter have implications for the worries that surfaced in the previous chapters. We sympathized with the fear of the misuse and misunderstanding of cultural analyses, in "development" activities and more generally. Indeed, it was the idea of "misunderstandings" that led the anthropologist Raymonde Carroll to classify, with plenty of ethnographic sensitivity and detail, aspects of French and American "cultures." Her hope, successfully achieved in the case of her own bicultural marriage, was that reframing local, particularized, and highly sensitive misunderstandings as manifestations of "cultural" ones would lead people to relax, understand (maybe even be amused together), and move ahead constructively.

The same techniques might be applied to many areas where cultural texts and misunderstanding deter collaboration. I believe the example of the Senegalese government and the World Bank typifies many "cultural misunderstandings" in development work, including in the work of local governments with local peoples. Indeed, thinking about "indigenous institutions" is plagued by hidden cultural texts, which, I hope, bringing into the open and analyzing generously might result in better ways "taking indigeneity into account."

8

Adjusting to Cultures

Earlier we described a version of taking culture into account. A problem exists. Treatments exist. But the treatments may interact with cultures to produce outcomes no one intended. How might the design and implementation of treatments—policies, projects, participatory processes, management systems—take account of the interactions in order to do better?

In this chapter, we consider several examples of devising and adapting treatments to different cultural contexts.

Cultural Ergonomics

Many examples exist of culturally appropriate ergonomics, or "human factors engineering." Their prosaic nature may help demystify the issue of tailoring treatments (in this case, designs) to cultural differences.

In India, for example, many workers prefer a squatting position. Machines for sawmills have been designed to take account of this preference. The Indian "woman usually prefers to squat on the ground in the preparation of family meals," so a gas oven has been successfully distributed "that can be easily manipulated on the ground or, at most, on a platform 12 or 13 cm above the ground."[1]

Studies in Bengal revealed, contrary to hypothesis, that road signs in Bengali and Devenagari scripts were much less legible than signs in the Roman alphabet. Consequently, road signs used the Roman alphabet.[2] "Japanese language keyboards may contain 100 times as many characters as European typewriters," and the problem of optimal grouping of keys given use becomes crucial for keyboard design. Both language and physique can be taken into account.[3]

One finds many examples in the design of housing. The architect Christopher Alexander once explained to me his technique for adapting low-cost housing to local cultures. He would spend a good amount of time with low-income people in their homes, asking about and observing their

The Culture and Development Manifesto. Robert Klitgaard, Oxford University Press (2021). © Oxford University Press.
DOI: 10.1093/oso/9780197517734.003.0008

preferences and practices. For example, in Lima, Peru, Alexander discovered a cultural preference for having an *antesala* where guests could be received. He was able to incorporate this feature even into very low-cost housing.

The Israeli architect Baruch Givoni pointed out other "dimensions of culture" that matter for town planning and housing design. They include attitudes about privacy, family structure, the role of women, childrearing patterns, recreational patterns, entertainment patterns, shopping habits, cooking and eating habits, patterns of social interaction, and socioeconomic and residential mobility.[4]

Checklists

How can those "dimensions of culture" be ascertained? Short of full-blown ethnographies, one might aspire to something like the appraisals described at the end of chapter 5 in psychology, soil science, and medicine. Like those professionals, we do not possess a dynamic general equilibrium model of all the relevant factors and their interactions. But like them, we may pull together knowledge of what variables may be most crucial in what contexts— and then gather information about them. Sometimes the variables that matter may be relatively obvious, as in some of the examples we have just seen from "cultural ergonomics." Sometimes things are not obvious, as in the case of rural development.

Consider a cultural checklist developed in Africa and ponder how it, and other kinds of checklists, might be developed and used.

A fascinating book from the Centre International des Civilisations Bantu (CICIBA) in Libreville, Gabon, focused on the cultural factors that impinge most on rural development.[5] The Centre developed a long diagnostic checklist, a translation of which appears in the appendix to this chapter. The book discussed examples of how cultural configurations interact with policy choices.

For example, during training, the book recommended separating age classes—particularly young people and adults—and, during agricultural training, recommended "the recognition of traditional chiefs of the land through the offering of a tribute." Respecting the elderly was repeatedly stressed. The book emphasized that "individual innovators are difficult to incorporate" in the group-oriented way of life. "Rural animateurs" who try to organize the people have failed, as have cooperatives. Women are the "surest choice" as administrators of money. But the book also warned against trying to change sexual traditions. One chapter "summarized" Bantu culture by briefly noting the existence of certain features of belief and religion, social structure (e.g., chiefs, social solidarity, the importance of clans, the influence of the elderly), and customs (e.g., taboos and a grand tradition of hospitality).

Working through the checklist in a particular cultural area will, its creators hoped, help "develop a capacity of attentiveness and questioning, and to acquire a method for detecting the points of contact between development and culture" (171).

How might checklists like CICIBA's be developed and productively utilized by practitioners? Atul Gawande's remarkable book, *The Checklist Manifesto*, provides valuable examples and advice.[6] He showed how using simple checklists yields large benefits, even in some of the most complicated tasks and sophisticated organizations in the world—building skyscrapers and flying jets, for example.

One of Gawande's first successes involved hospital operating rooms. The checklist he and his colleagues designed included seemingly obvious things like washing hands, discussing the operation in advance, and having all instruments sterilized and ready. Doctors and nurses may say, "Of course." And yet, at one of the most elite hospitals in the United States, developing and using a checklist led to remarkable reductions in infections and operating-room errors.

A version of this checklist has been adopted around the world, with such success that the World Health Organization called it one of the world's most important health interventions. In each locale, doctors, nurses, and administrators learned about the checklist, saw examples from elsewhere of its surprisingly positive effects, and worked through its steps for their specific situation. Sometimes steps were added ("Make sure the surgical theater has been cleaned and sanitized after the last operation"). But a hospital in Mexico or Mauritania or Massachusetts ended up with a similar checklist and instructions for its use. Despite huge differences in cultural settings, this innovation transferred well.

Similar points might be made in other areas of government, business, and nonprofit organizations. Take breweries. It is notable that good local beer is usually available even in underdeveloped settings. What works here, with regard to brewing, is very much like what works there. Ditto for central banks. And for airports (well, maybe not quite "ditto").

Projects and programs can be arrayed along a continuum that represents *the ease of transferring* what works *somewhere else* to what will work *here*. Two considerations are paramount. First, how much do local settings vary in the objectives being sought, the populations being valued, the particular policies or programs being considered, and the cultural setting? Second, how much do such variations matter? Local variations in things like culture may be apparently large and yet not matter, as in brewing lager, monitoring exchange rates, or processing baggage claims. Or the differences may be small and yet crucial for success.

How would we know? Somehow, we have to assemble knowledge, wisdom, and expertise about our problem and our setting into the design and implementation of policies and programs. How to do this awaits explication in the final chapter, but to give the headline now: ask experts *and* ask locals. Experts on the problem area and on cultural contexts may know enough about the specific problem and context to tell us where variations in the parameters of our equation are large and important. Locals can help us, too, especially to specify crucial features of the setting that may be hard to discern or invisible to outsiders—features of politics, process, precedents, symbolism, timing, and personality.

Culturally Attuned Agroforestry

A celebrated success is Haïti's *Pwojè Pyebwa* (Creole for "tree project"), which began in 1981. Designed, and in the early years led by the anthropologist Gerald F. Murray, the project set up professionally managed nurseries that provided free tree seedlings to Haitian farmers, who planted them on their private plots. The results were dramatic: within four years 110,000 farmers planted 35 million seedlings.

Murray recounted how both "anthropological reconstructions of cultural evolutionary processes and my own ethnographic research on Haitian peasant communities" shaped the project's design and management. Following a number of pre-project feasibility studies by economists, foresters, and anthropologists (including himself), Murray wrote:

> maverick project strategy that began with a fundamental paradigm shift—a radical anthropological redefinition of the Haitian "tree problem."
> . . . . The programmatic result of this shift was a project that downplayed

conservationist and protectionist themes and brought to the fore the theme of introducing the planting of wood as an income-generating crop on the holdings of the Haitian peasant.[7]

Murray's fieldwork revealed that many of the most evidently deforested lands in Haiti belonged to kin groups and were used for grazing. "Farmers are aware, much more than planners, that trees in Haiti are vulnerable to three dangerous predators that can wreak havoc on distant plots or agriculturally marginal plots: (1) free ranging livestock, (2) nocturnal thieves, and (3) one's own kin."[8] Add to them a fourth potential predator: the Haitian state. Peasants perceived *rebwazman* (the Creole term for reforestation) as coercive interventions that forced them to cover grazing land with unwanted trees. Peasants worried that once the trees had matured, kin-held land would be expropriated.

Haïti's prevailing model was to create state-led, ecologically motivated forests that had to be protected from the natives. The anthropological research said this was unworkable in Haïti. When collective economic undertakings have happened in Haïti, they "have been mandated by the state or triggered off by externally funded development programs."

> Ethnographic fieldwork quickly reveals Haïti to be neither a tribal society with communal control of land nor a peasant society with ancient communal traditions. It is instead a Westernized, postcolonial society inhabited by the descendants of involuntary migrants uprooted and transplanted from Africa. Both the Westernized economy and the Westernized land tenure system have been market oriented from the outset; not only crops, but also land itself has been and continues to be freely bought and sold.[9]

Trying to change Haitian cultures and institutions was seen as impractical and unnecessary. Instead, "macroecological needs of the environment would be served not directly but instead indirectly, by meeting the microeconomic needs of smallholding cultivators; and . . . fast-growing wood would be planted, not for protection's sake, but explicitly for harvesting and selling wood, thereby encouraging widespread planting."[10]

In 1989, outside evaluators suggested three reasons for the project's success: (1) Emphasizing wood as a marketable crop, with individual farmers as owners and producers. (2) Avoiding the government, which in Haïti would have led to "certain paralysis and possible death" of the project. (3) Good technical choices about the types of trees, the seedlings, intercropping schemes, and so forth.[11] Ironically, after ten years of unprecedented results, in the early 1990s a new leader for the U.S. Agency for International Development (USAID) abandoned the policy of free seedlings, believing that pure market forces should be allowed to take over. Although rural Haitians were willing to invest cash in cocoa and coffee seedlings, they proved unwilling to do so for wood trees. Many seedling nurseries crashed, and the project came to a standstill. In addition, political unrest and economic uncertainty led to more and more small farmers cutting down their trees prematurely.

But in 1994, after changes in Haïti's government and in the USAID leadership (and a new study by anthropologist Murray), the seedling subsidy was reintroduced. Although trust by the peasants in the project had been weakened, the planting of new trees resumed. By the early 2000s, more than 300,000 peasant households had planted 65 million trees. "Nearly 50% of the households of rural Haiti may have received seedlings or otherwise participated in the project at one point or another during the two decades. Even if these national participation figures are dropped by 10 or even 20 percentage points for 'safety's sake,' the level of nationwide involvement in and enthusiasm for a tree planting project must still be seen as unprecedented in the annals of agroforestry."[12]

Murray is rightly wary of blueprints, but he says some principles may travel. "We suspect that in many other agroforestry settings as well, issues of seedling supply, tree tenure, and harvest rights are more critical than the mission of remedying presumed peasant knowledge deficits by itinerant environmental educators."[13]

Implementation should be culturally attuned. For example, "a remunerated structure of village animateurs turned out to be one of the key organizational breakthroughs that led to the success of the project."[14] These locals were culturally legitimate and knowledgeable, as well as monitored and compensated.

Another lesson: combine both outside expertise and local knowledge.

Educational flows should be bi-directional, moving as frequently from farmer to project staff as vice-versa. While technical information regarding nursery and agronomic practices was valuable and necessary, the knowledge that staff in Haiti carried in their brains was, after 20 years of field immersion, more heavily influenced by farmer inputs than by lessons learned long ago in school. Stated differently, we abandoned the podium and the pulpit. We were neither pedagogues nor ecological preachers, but partners in a long-term joint venture, encapsulated by the Creole slogan used by the field staff "*Plantè se kolèg*" (planters are colleagues).[15]

Though we did not romantically assume perfect wisdom and knowledge among farmers—we have information about tree species and planting techniques they might not have—we nonetheless assumed that farmers also had information about local ecological and economic constraints that they could share with us.[16]

In Haïti the reforms involved improved trees and horticulture, better markets, and appropriate property rights. "I have argued," Murray later wrote, "that the viability of this approach in Haïti is only partially related to the idiosyncrasies of Haitian ethnography. If the approach has enjoyed some success, it is due rather to its willingness to apply to wood the same tenure and usufruct principles which cultivators around the world and throughout history have applied to their other crops."[17] But cultural knowledge shaped the design of the project, and the details of implementation took account of local beliefs, practices, and priorities.

Culturally Aligned Pedagogy

Ethnographic research led to a successful educational reform in Hawai'i. The context was underperformance of native Hawaiian students—more dropouts, more unhappiness with school, lower test scores. Reformers had tried techniques based on more tests, more feedback, more rewards and punishments. These hadn't worked.

And so, the Kamehameha Elementary Education Program (KEEP) tried a different approach. Anthropologists studied children in their homes and then worked with teachers and parents to adapt classroom practices to what they had discovered.[18] Together, they designed educational interventions to get around "mismatches or incompatibilities between the natal culture of the children and the culture of the school *at points that are critical for school success*."[19]

For example, the anthropologists documented that Hawaiian children played together and made a lot of noise. So, the new pedagogy featured more group work and more tolerance of chaos. The new system allowed more helping and sharing in the classroom. "While the teacher meets with each small homogeneous reading group, the rest of the class works in small groups at 'learning centers' located throughout the classroom. . . . Children are allowed to assist each other within the center, and even at times to go to other centers to seek help."

In a Hawaiian home, if a child was singled out by the mother, it was a sign of "scolding behavior." So, instead of teachers' calling on individual students to read or recite, the new classroom style was

> characterized by overlapping speech, voluntary turn-taking, conarration and joint construction of a story. It was as if the change in instructional focus and the openness of teachers to greater variety in student contributions to the lessons opened the door for the students to contribute in a speech style that was linguistically *familiar* to them.

Teachers had typically found it difficult to get Hawaiian students to do their own work, ranging from homework to tests. Praise was directed less at individuals than at groups of students. "Ethnographic work indicated that indirect praise, and praise to a group ("Good. Table 3 is ready.") are more effective than direct praise that spotlights one child."

The results were remarkable, including more industriousness, less disruption, and more learning. "Industriousness, as it turned out, did not require external motivation systems and extreme praise rates or teacher attention. It required school adaptation to the students' culturally based skills and inclinations." Student satisfaction with school increased. And scores rose on standardized reading tests.[20]

Similarly, on an Indian reservation in Oregon, researchers showed that the customary method for praising and punishing children was through groups. This was not a good cultural fit for individual-based praise and punishment in the classroom. The native way of gaining attention was visual, whereas in the classroom it was auditory. Odawa Indian students in Ontario found it culturally uncomfortable to be "spotlighted" for answering "content questions." In both Alberta and Alaska, researchers argued that Athabaskan Indians "think of speech as a privilege of intimacy, and, hence, prefer to speak little, if at all, in contexts such as schools where some of the listeners are not intimate."[21]

These findings suggest that cultural knowledge can be used to improve educational methods and, thereby, student outcomes. And yet as we saw earlier in the book, whenever "cultural differences" are documented, questions arise about whether and how to countenance them. Recall Albert O. Hirschman's inevitable tension between "trait-taking" and "trait-making." Some people argue that "culturally appropriate education" helps keep cultural diversity alive. But others say that doing so may handicap people from these cultures when they enter mainstream society.[22]

> If the people's main concern is to enable Indian children to compete successfully with non-Indians, and so have the *choice* of access to the modes of interaction and life-styles of non-Indians, then there should be a conscious effort made by schools to teach the mode of appropriate verbal participation that prevails in non-Indian classrooms.[23]

Some educators emphasize the goal of cultural dissonance rather than cultural affinity. "Rather than trying to make schooling equally familiar to all students, schooling should be made *equally strange*."[24] (Note that doing so would also require a knowledge of cultural backgrounds, this time to ensure the right kinds and degrees of cultural incongruity.)

What are the long-term effects of culturally congruent instruction (of various kinds and degrees) on student learning, cultural assimilation, cultural preservation, and so forth? A newer study of the Kamehameha Schools and culturally relevant pedagogy did not focus on learning in the classic senses, but on "students' college aspirations, sense of belonging to school, self-efficacy, cultural affiliation, and connection to community"—all of which were well served.[25]

In New Zealand, a culturally tuned curriculum helped Māori students feel proud of their Māori culture and identity. They enjoyed "how their school demonstrated valuing Māori culture and language, primarily through examples of using Māori protocols and customs." They felt more engaged with school. But no increases were reported in "traditional student achievement."[26]

This is typical in other examples of culturally relevant education. Students are happier, their cultural awareness is higher, sometimes social justice issues are raised. But conventional measures of long-term student achievement in mathematics, science, social studies, and the humanities are not always improved.[27] And seldom are the costs of such programs included in the evaluations.

Rural Development in West Africa

Let us now examine an example of culturally appropriate development that illustrates several of the points so far, the West African program called

Association 6-S. Akin to the analysis of cultural texts we saw in the last chapter, the designers and implementers of 6-S were intimately aware of different ways local people and government officials perceived the same activities. They used something like a cultural checklist to describe the strengths and weaknesses of local settings and institutions. They designed the program to build on local cultural practices and strengths, as in the fashion of culturally sensitive pedagogy. And it worked.

In the aftermath of a severe six-year famine in the Sahel, the Burkinabe development expert Bernard Lédéa Ouédraogo sought a new, culturally appropriate model of community development.[28] In his old government job in a village, he had "to supervise the 'official' village groups organized by the government (and not by the farmers themselves). I did my best to help these groups, but I failed."

> The rural extension workers would arrive in a village, and the only concern of the officially organized farmers was to take advantage of the donkeys, bullocks, carts, hoes, and other materials we would make available to them. There was nothing else behind this demeaning form of assistance, no vision, no global conception of development or of the rural world, no doctrine or philosophy. There had been no prior efforts at consciousness raising. It was normal that in such a situation the farmers had but one concern: prime the State "pump" for all it was worth and cheat the extension workers.[29]

Frustrated, Ouédraogo turned to a traditional group in his Mossi culture, the *Kombi-naam*. These youth groups (*Naams*) included young women fifteen to twenty-one years old and young men twenty to thirty-five. Such associations, widespread in West Africa, were organized in an egalitarian fashion, without regard to many of the society's divisions such as wealth and caste. The Naams served as vehicles for both socializing and cooperative labor. Members also saved through these groups, using their combined resources once a year for festivities. Working with the Naams, Ouédraogo helped "the farmers to understand that the traditional functions of the Naam could be transformed into functions adopted to modern development." Over the years, the traditional "KombiNaam" structure was transformed into modernized, grassroots self-help groups open to all. It has been called "Africa's largest and most successful grassroots movements for self-reliance."[30]

Ouédraogo went further, founding a nongovernmental organization called 6-S (or Six-S). (The six S's are *Se Servir de la Saison Sèche en Savane et au Sahel*—"Using the dry season in the Savannah and the Sahel.") 6-S became Africa's largest farmer aid and training network, consisting of federated organizations of hundreds of thousands of members in nine West African countries—Burkina Faso, Chad, the Gambia, Guinea Bissau, Mali, Mauritania, Niger, Senegal, and Togo.

Ouédraogo emphasized the utilization of traditional modes of farmer participation, as opposed to government-created cooperatives or village councils. The latter were, he said, artificial creations, manipulated with political aims in mind. Along with Bernard Lecomte, the cofounder of 6-S, the new organization identified key obstacles that "prevented the mobilization of the farmers."

> The first obstacle was the lack of know-how. The farmers simply did not have the necessary knowledge to face the unprecedented challenges of the drought situation. The second one was the lack of "negotiators." By that I mean farmers capable of negotiating projects with both the local administration and the village elders, without whose consent nothing could be achieved. More and more villages were becoming active, starting peasant groups, but once they started to organize on a regional basis, they were lacking in the funds both to support investments in organization and to initiate larger projects.[31]

6-S took advantage of the unemployment of men in the Sahel during the dry season by utilizing their time for training. 6-S addressed weaknesses in peasant associations, such as planning and accounting, and developed culturally relevant training programs. It allocated funding in a novel fashion. Instead of telling the peasants what to do, as in the usual government program or the usual aid project, 6-S's system of *fonds souples* (flexible funds) made money available without prior knowledge of the projects for which the money would be used. 6-S did insist on certain conditions: no grants to individuals, accounts would be kept, and funds used for profit-making activities would be reimbursed with interest. 6-S distributed millions of dollars annually to "peasant groups that have banded together to form federations."

Over time, membership was opened to those outside the age group, and village elders were included as counselors. "I must mention here," Lecomte emphasized, "that in the work of awareness education that we undertook, we were very careful never to attack any traditional customs. Instead, we built on the positive aspects of these, on the values of solidarity, understanding, brotherliness and friendship, which were already at the heart of the traditional Naam groups."

By the late 1980s, there were over 4,000 Naam and affiliated groups in the Yatenga area of Burkina Faso, with over 200,000 members—one of the largest, most powerful peasant associations in Africa. The founders attributed the success to "letting oneself be mastered by the grassroots."

Pierre Pradervand described the cultural relevance of this success story:

> The Naam is a form of development adapted to local needs, created by the people themselves, which instead of destroying traditional structures from the outside, slowly, like leaven, transforms them from the inside.
>
> This experiment may be the first authentically African experiment aimed at creating a model of social organization that is neither a carbon copy of the West, nor a return to the past out of timorous rejection of modernization or rebelliousness against Western values. It starts with what people *are* (based on a true appreciation of their African identity), what they *know* (respect for traditional knowledge and values, which implies the considerable effort necessary to become acquainted with them), their *know-how* (rediscovery of traditional techniques, some of which, for example in the field of water and soil conservation, have proven invaluable), and what they *wish to achieve* (which implies meaningful grassroots participation in defining the very objectives of the development process).[32]

The organization eventually had many more village associations wishing to join (and be funded) than it could accept. So, it insisted that the village had demonstrated a successful collaborative project before receiving any 6-S support. Delegates from the village groups, meeting as a committee, "apply a number of criteria: volume of own resources pledged, number of people involved, past borrowing record, level of risk in the scheme, feasibility of launching it quickly, and so on."[33] Then, if the village organization was selected and its project funded, it had to pay back the amount (at least for projects that generated a profit). "Gifts, as the farmers I met repeated time and time again, make people passive," Pradervand noted. Six-S allowed around 12 percent of external assistance to go to nonrefundable operating costs of the local organization. Loans, he said, have several advantages: "they guide operations towards the productive sector," they promote social solidarity, and they provide the right incentives ("inasmuch as members realize that by repaying what they owe they will be able to get another loan later").

It usually took several years for a village association to "qualify" for funds—to show that it was serious and had done something on its own. Its members then were trained in "the basic elements of rigorous management (planning, evaluation, and accounting), which are key to their survival in a modern economy." 6-S staffers trained, passed on information and technical advice, and conducted literacy courses. "Above all," one of them said, "the coordinators continually stress the importance of self-reliance and the '6-S spirit,' which forms the basis for all our action. One of the basic principles of 6-S is to help only those who help themselves."[34]

Finally, the expectation is that local organizations will graduate from 6-S support. Once they have managerial training, the spirit of can-do, and a track record of achieving (and repaying loans), "they can now become autonomous: they are able to negotiate loans with local banks. The financial role of the partner is over."

6-S's strategy also addressed incomplete and imperfect credit markets. Local banks apparently would not finance village organizations because of transactions costs and poor information about credit worthiness and would not finance federations for similar reasons. By helping the locals develop a track record and making their accounts transparent, 6-S prepared the way for the normal credit market to take over, efficiently.

This success story combines cultural sensitivity with culture-free policy analysis. 6-S built on traditional organizations. It also strove to change certain cultural practices—for example, part of the savings formerly reserved for festivities were to be dedicated to productive group activities. The emphasis on self-reliance may also have marked a kind of cultural change, at least compared to the dependency and apathy that local governments and other forms of aid apparently induced.

6-S also applied good principles of management: emphasizing transparency, rewarding efficiency and penalizing inefficiency, and addressing problems of incomplete and imperfect credit markets. 6-S accounting featured what the farmers described as "accounts in the sunlight." "Nothing must be hidden," explained one African coordinator. "Everyone must know what we decide and above all must be able to check the accounts. Only in that way can we create trust. And trust is fundamental to understanding and harmony." Lecomte emphasized that accounts include not only expenditures but also who received the money. "What is needed is for each village (or district) covered by the organization to draw up an inventory of its own efforts, the resources involved and where they come from (including local actors), and where they are applied. Accounts that are as transparent as this will be genuinely instructive."[35]

As 6-S grew, new problems emerged, which were understandable in cultural terms, perhaps, but also through the lens of economics. With expansion, some farmers began to take advantage of 6-S funding. Delays and defaults on loans eventually rose; and as one farmer was quoted as saying, "Why should we make an effort to save if we can easily get money from 6-S?" Pierre Pradervand noted, "Without the 6-S spirit, farmers end up seeing 6-S simply as a goose that lays golden eggs." And with expansion, worries grew that loans were misused at the grassroots level. "In Senegal," noted Lecomte, "over-rapid growth makes an association unwieldy and impossible to manage: fiefdoms, feuding and malpractice emerge, mistrust reappears, and the incentive to reach out is lost." *Les fonds souples* may need tightening. A supporter of 6-S, Bakary Makalou, put the point this way. "6-S is in danger of falling into a grassroots mystique. The grassroots can also make mistakes. It's not because the grassroots has proposed something that it's good." Perhaps for this reason, no other donors in the region adopted the 6-S principle of "flexible funds."

What is it, then, that was "culturally relevant" about 6-S? One feature was the use of traditional village institutions like the Naams. Another was the recognition of cultural conflict and resistance. The usual aid project involves a dialectic: local needs and objectives but also the needs and objectives of the donor. If the latter takes too much control of the project, Lecomte observed, "participatory management vanishes, and assistance takes over," which "can kill off the [local] group's initiative, which alone gives permanence and meaning to any activity."[36] So, the 6-S approach placed great importance on local participation. Only in this way could a cultural syndrome of distrust and lack of confidence be overcome—and could local knowledge and resources be tapped. When the donor participates in such processes, it is said to build trust and allay fears. Differences do not disappear, but the hope is that they will be confronted with honesty, good information, and mutual trust.

Another dimension of taking culture into account in this case is its conservatism. Over and over, the refrain was sounded: don't move too fast, don't finance too much, let them make mistakes. In a similar vein, Joseph Brunet-Jailly wrote of Mali:

> Should one contemplate that the many forms of collective action proposed to villagers will lead to social development? One must listen first to villagers

recount thirty years of promises, thirty years of the collection of fiscal contributions gone astray, thirty years of bad management, thirty years of the theft of their payments by their political or administrative authorities, indeed by their old traditional chiefs, thirty years of fugitive interventions and perhaps of swindles on the part of foreign and national NGOs.

Simply calling for collective action, Brunet-Jailly argued, implies a naive belief that the collectivity can repair "all the conflicts that in the past have been born of the deception that has been systematically associated with administrative initiatives in this domain."[37]

Only by proceeding cautiously, said Lecomte, can one overcome local habits of mistrust. "Any fresh project will fit into their history as one more unfortunate episode of outside influence on a rural community. It will be accepted not as something radically new but as one more trial to be undergone, with the need yet again to safeguard the group's own existence as far as possible. Participation in what outsiders have prepared is seen first and foremost as a threat to the existence of the group."[38] Therefore, several years of capacity building (particularly savings and management) must be followed by several years of *fonds souples*; only after perhaps a decade is the organization equipped to handle development projects and to take bankable projects for commercial funding.

I want to note one more point, to which we will return in the final chapter: the comparative advantages of outsiders and locals. In the case of 6-S, the outside agency provided funds, but perhaps its greatest comparative advantage was informational and educational. In the case of credit and savings, for example, the key outside intervention was "to supply the grassroots groups with information about the various methods of establishing and expanding community savings and loan banks." Outsiders shared their knowledge of management techniques, especially accounting. Outsiders contributed technical and agricultural skills and provided conduits among locals to share *their* knowledge. Regarding the almost inevitable rivalries and conflicts that can develop and threaten local groups, the outsiders' most effective contribution may be information.

One remedy is a steady flow of information to the villages and groups. To be effective, this information should be continuous and diversified. As far as possible it should reach the rank and file unfiltered. Groups will receive cassettes, newspapers, audiovisual displays, self-appraisal reports and the like directly, and members will discuss them outside the formal setting of a general assembly of the whole association. By this means members will gradually learn how to lessen the manipulation by their delegates and even how to defuse disputes before they blow up.[39]

The methodology was participatory and educational at once. "The underlying idea is to analyze a situation by comparing the views of all the members of the community as well as the external actors to identify (jointly) the reasons why existing organizations have seized up, and to support (without any preconceived design) the measures and reforms that the group deems both feasible and desirable."[40]

Moreover, Lecomte observed, the very process of self-analysis that can be encouraged from outside can help local people become aware of local realities that remain undiscussed—exploitation and inefficiencies, on the negative side, and potentialities for action, on the positive.

Culture by Policy Interactions in Native American Nations

In 1986, the young Harvard resource economist Joseph Kalt was studying Indigenous nations in the United States. He was puzzled. Two nations in a similar ecosystem, with similar timber and wildlife endowments, were progressing very differently. On a suggestion, he telephoned the "political and cultural sociologist" Stephen Cornell, also at Harvard. Cornell's Ph.D. dissertation on the emergence of Native Americans was en route to becoming a book, and Cornell said, "I had been pondering what to do next." He and Kalt had lunch. They saw the potential for collaboration on the patterns of economic development on Indian lands, commonly known as Indian Country.[41] By the end of their meal, they had outlined a research program. "Little did I know then," Cornell wrote decades later, "that we would still be working on topics traceable to that lunch."[42]

Both scholars cared deeply about the challenges facing the most disadvantaged group in the United States, namely Native Americans on reservations.[43] According to the 2010 Census, their per capita income was less than half that of Americans as a whole, and their poverty rate was three times higher.

Since the Indian Self-Determination and Education Assistance Act of 1975, the hundreds of Indigenous nations in the United States have exercised powers of self-government akin to those of the fifty states. Some have advanced rapidly; others have languished. Even before the onset of gaming in the 1990s, some tribal economies had been growing 8 percent a year, while others had been declining. Unemployment rates, education, and alcoholism rates also varied markedly. Cornell and Kalt wondered what accounted for these differences.

They began by doing the kind of quantitative studies that characterize development economics. For a variety of outcome measures, such as unemployment, they statistically assessed the effects of natural resources, economic conditions in areas adjacent to the tribes, and so forth. Surprisingly, such factors could not account for much of the variation across tribes. For example, the Crows in Montana had coal, timber, wildlife, water rights, and a relatively well-educated workforce, but they were one of the poorest tribes.

Meanwhile, Cornell and Kalt assembled ethnographic descriptions of Indigenous nations. They categorized the situations found before the 1934 Indian Reorganization Act, which had imposed a common governance structure on widely varying tribal systems. Historic tribal political systems ranged from the theocratic structures of the Keres, to the effectively parliamentary, multibranch democracies of the Lakota, to the "presidential" democracies of the Western Apache.[44]

Cornell and Kalt did fieldwork among twelve Indigenous nations. "We asked people to tell us stories," Cornell recounted. Which people? Present and former heads of tribal governments, development officers, investors, and so forth. What stories? About turning points in tribal life, successful and unsuccessful entrepreneurs, resource use and investment. How were native college students welcomed home on the reservation, with enthusiasm or with surliness? What were the attitudes toward native attire? Members of some tribes thought wearing traditional garb was crucial to their identities. Others, not so much. A member of the then-highly successful White Mountain Apache tribe invited Kalt to visit the reservation's booming ski resort. The host sported a pink parka. Later, Kalt ventured to ask him about the importance of Apache clothing for his Apache identity. "I love being a White Mountain Apache," he responded in effect. "What does clothing have to do with that?" Giving the anecdote political force, the chairman of the Apache tribe proudly told Kalt: "The typical Apache teenage girl may not have grown up thinking she would be a ski instructor wearing a chartreuse ski outfit . . . but that's *real* Apache."

Cornell and Kalt made several discoveries about culture and development.

Culture Matters

First, cultural diversity helped explain development outcomes. Higher incomes, lower rates of unemployment, and less alcohol abuse were associated to some extent with specific features of tribal cultures:

- Receptivity to interaction with nonmembers of the tribe.
- Tolerance of hierarchy.
- Attitudes toward resource use.
- The legitimate locus of authority, including the separation of powers.
- "The degree to which tribal members' primary source of identity and loyalty is to the tribe as a whole, as opposed to sub-tribal organizations."
- Viable mechanisms for dispute resolution (current and traditional).

Governance Matters

Across tribes, certain features of governance were also associated with positive outcomes. In a sample of sixty-seven tribes with at least 600 residents, those with constitutionally based, strong chief executives (i.e., directly elected, typically to four-year terms of office), strong legislatures, and independent judiciaries tended to have better development outcomes. On the negative side, tribes with weak formal rules and procedures could not "prevent every new enterprise proposal from turning into a political fight." Haphazard financial systems led to financial troubles. "Insisting on employment for the chair's supporters, dipping into the cash reserves of the tribal enterprise to fund a popular project, or changing lease or royalty terms in midstream—these kinds of actions can discourage investment and effort to the point that they shrink the reservation economic pie."[45]

Culture by Policy Interactions

But the abiding lesson was not to "get the culture right" or "get the institutions right." "The point was to get the *fit* right between formal institutions and contemporary Indigenous political culture."[46]

"Unless there is a fit between the culture of the community and the structure and powers of its governing institutions, those institutions may be seen as illegitimate, their ability to regulate and organize the development process will be undermined and development will be blocked."[47] For example, unlike the impoverished Sioux, the relatively successful Apaches were found to have pre-existing cultural and political norms that matched the structure of their formal constitution imposed in 1934.[48] "What's interesting," Cornell related, "is that the Oglala Sioux turn out to be badly out of synch with their traditions: the Apaches more or less in synch. And guess who was doing very much better?" In fact, tellingly, of the seven contemporary Sioux tribes, only the tribe that had changed its federally imposed constitution had unemployment or poverty rates below 50 percent.[49]

So, Cornell and Kalt emphasized, practical choices should take culture into account. "While all tribes must solve similar problems of separations of powers and controlling rent-seeking as they wrestle with development dilemmas, the answers will be tribally specific, responding to particular sets of opportunities, constraints and cultural contexts. The reason for this note of 'cultural appropriateness' lies in the concept of cultural 'match.' "[50]

To reiterate, the choices tribes make not only have to be appropriate to tribal cultures, they also have to be efficacious. "Solutions that fit with indigenous culture but fail to constrain the power of those who govern will only further undermine the possibilities of politically, socially, and economically successful development."[51]

Bold and Humble

The authors were bold in their analyses. Hard though it may be to hear (or to say), some cultural characteristics seemed to stand in the way of what tribes say they want. Another unpopular thing to note: because cultures are notoriously hard to change, don't start there.[52] The authors faced up to the negatives of nepotism and corruption:

> A staple of storytelling in Indian Country has to do with political interference in business activity. Over and over one hears of voided leases, hired or fired cousins, politicized management, and enterprises drained of funds by tribal council interference. Such problems are not unique to Indian Country—witness Chicago or Boston, or the Philippines or Mexico, where the politics of patronage and personal aggrandizement have memorable histories. While the details vary across reservations and other societies,

their consequences are depressingly similar: costs are raised and competitiveness reduced; earnings are dissipated and capital is not replenished; investors fear being held hostage to politics and turn away.[53]

Cornell and Kalt were also humble. They rejected a universal definition of economic development, recognizing that many goals will be culturally contingent and evolving.[54] Nor did they sanctify a particular form of government. In a 2019 book on the development among Native Peoples in Australia, Canada, New Zealand, and the United States, Cornell rejected the idealization or imposition of "Eurocentric good governance."[55] For example, in earlier work Cornell and Kalt described a New Mexico tribe with traditional theocratic structure in which a single individual appointed all the senior governmental functionaries. Possible abuses of power were checked successfully by a system of religious "kivas."[56] Not James Madison, but effective.

Admirably, Cornell and Kalt have gone beyond analysis to action. "At that original lunch," Cornell explained, "we had realized that if we could explain differential economic outcomes in Indian Country, and if the explanation involved factors over which Indian nations exercised some control, we would have something of practical value to those nations. This became a central purpose of the project: a search for insights that Indian nations could use."[57]

Their activism, too, combined humility and boldness. Don't dictate, indeed don't make recommendations. Provide data to help tribes locate their challenges and opportunities in the contexts of their local economies and by comparison with other tribes. Share success stories through documentation, video interviews, convenings, prizes, and websites.

> Success stories are so important, even when they are stories of some other nation's success. They expand the available knowledge of what's required for change to occur. For example, case after case reinforces what the research conclusively shows: If you don't get politics out of the tribal court, even your own people won't want to invest in the nation's future.
>
> But success stories also do something else of importance. They enlarge the imagination, encouraging people to imagine doing successful things themselves.[58]

And share principles. They and their colleagues launched institutes, first at Harvard and later at the University of Arizona, to help tribal leaders make sense of the interactions among cultural settings, tribal choices, and development outcomes. The institutes provide practical, hands-on training for tribal leaders. What tribal leaders want are data, examples, and principles[59]—and researchers at the institutes aim to supply all three. And notice how they work:

> Since tribal sovereignty and self-determination are paramount, the faculty are charged with making it clear to the tribal clients that projects will not provide specific recommendations or one-size-fits-all solutions. Rather, projects *identify* resources, knowledge, information, and options for the clients to consider in their own decision-making processes. . . . Respect for indigenous sovereignty means that the university provides information, analysis, and education at the request of Native clients with the conscious intent of arming Native decision-makers and communities with, hopefully, high quality raw materials from which those decision-makers and communities can fashion their own solutions to their own problems and concerns.[60]

And there are bold innovations as well. Remarkably, the institutes offer on-line, customizable "toolboxes," where Native Americans can find everything from case studies of tribes that have dealt with their challenges to samples of actual laws, codes, regulations, resolutions, and policies.[61] Since 1998, Harvard has awarded annual prizes for exemplary tribal programs, practices, and initiatives. In addition, the universities convene tribal leaders, enabling them to share their challenges, successes, and setbacks.[62]

The results? Cornell and Kalt, and their institutes, became "conduits for information, not only about our analyses but about what was happening where. The national scope of our project was turning us into a storehouse of information on tribal development efforts and their results—models, tools, and innovations."[63]

Greater Indian control and economic self-sufficiency on reservations has been accompanied by rising social investment. Some tribes improved their formal institutions of government, such as the Osage Nation in Oklahoma and the Ho-Chunk Nation in Wisconsin. Others reformed their corporate boards (Winnebago), appellate courts (Navajo), gaming commissions (Oneida of New York), and tribal administrations (Confederated Salish and Kootenai). "Until recent decades, these superstructures of tribal government reflected outsiders' views of how best to organize and use authority. But these reforms have brought alignment with local cultures, conditions, and preferences, thereby increasing the effectiveness of self-government."[64] From 1990 to 2010, real Indian per capita income and median household income grew by 46.5 percent, compared with 7.8 percent for the United States as a whole.[65]

Let's close this case study with a passage that resonates beyond Indian Country to major themes of the culture and development manifesto.

> But tradition is not the issue here. In some cases, indigenous political traditions are long gone. But in many nations, distinctive ideas about the appropriate organization and exercise of authority still survive and often are starkly at odds with IRA [Indian Reorganization Act] structures or other structures imposed on Indian nations. The crucial issue is the degree of match or mismatch between formal governing institutions and contemporary indigenous ideas—whatever their source—about the appropriate form and organization of political power. Where cultural match is high, economic development tends to be more successful. Where cultural match is low, the legitimacy of tribal government also is low, the governing institutions consequently are less effective, and economic development falters.
>
> Governing institutions have to pass two tests. As we have just suggested, they have to be culturally appropriate. But they also have to be able to get the job done. The tribal governments of long ago were invented to solve the problems of the times. The times have changed. In some cases, traditional forms and practices may be inadequate to the demands of the modern world. If so, the challenge for Indian nations is to innovate: to develop governing institutions that still resonate with deeply-held community beliefs about authority but that are flexible enough to adjust to the demands of contemporary times.[66]

Conclusions

The examples in this chapter have implications for the worries that surfaced in the previous chapters. We have seen how anthropologists rightly fear the misuse and misunderstanding of cultural analyses in "development" activities (and beyond). We appreciated why anthropologists (and other social scientists) might shy away from creating and applying anything like culturally sensitive models of "development" because of scientific complexities, nay impossibilities. Even trying to define and measure "culture" and "development" makes some cultural anthropologists (and I have to say, many economists and practitioners) head for the exits.

At the end of chapter 5, we began to explore pragmatic ways to move ahead nonetheless. The analogies from psychology, soil science, and medicine suggested, but did not prove, how people can be helped by even limited scientific knowledge, shared in ways that respect their sovereignty and utilizes local knowledge.

In the last two chapters, we continued the theme of using cultural knowledge despite theoretical incompleteness and with careful attention to possible misuses and misunderstandings. In this chapter, we encountered other cases where "taking culture into account" didn't require anything like a full-blown, dynamic model, as with the humble examples of cultural ergonomics or in the inspiring case of culturally attuned Hawaiian education. For policy purposes, cultural checklists can be useful even though theoretically incomplete, if they are developed and used in the fashion described by Atul Gawande. The example of 6-S in West Africa shows how indigenous, culturally grounded institutions can be the basis for rural development, even for remaking dysfunctional cultural patterns of citizen-government relationships. The work of Stephen Cornell and Joseph Kalt shows how to appraise and apply culture by policy interactions, in ways that empower Native Americans.

Let's not be put on the sidelines of practice, then, by the fear of misuse of cultural knowledge or by the impossibility of the complete theory of interactions between culture, policy choices, and development. Let's do cultural analysis à la Raymonde Carroll, design together checklists à la CICIBA and Atul Gawande, tailor policies to culture as in Haïti's *Pwojè Pyebwa*, try to find a few culture-by-policy interactions we can test, and look for new ways to collaborate, in the spirit of 6-S.

Appendix

The following is my translation of a checklist, or *aide-memoire*, for "knowing the cultural elements of a local collectivity," as created by the Gabonese research organization CICIBA.[67] After presenting this long array of considerations, the authors ask rhetorically: "Is it necessary to insist? This '*aide-memoire*' is not itself either exhaustive nor limiting. . . . The most important thing . . . is to develop a capacity for attentiveness and questioning, and to acquire a method for detecting the points of contact between development and culture" (170, 171).

1. History

1. Ethnic groups present in the collectivity.
2. Inventory of kinship lineages in the territory (cartography if possible).
3. Age of the groups. Inter-group relations (antagonisms and solidarities).
4. History of relations with the administration.

2. Social organization

1. Patrilineal or matrilineal?
2. Precedence among relatives; the rights and precedence of elders of different lines.
3. Obligations and *"reconnaissances"* that result from parental ties. What and toward whom?
4. Rights of occupation of the land (cartography if possible).
5. Rights over goods and their transmission.
6. The status of women: her *prestations*, role, influence on decisions, rights over people and goods, and particular positions (midwives, healer, etc.).
7. The status of youths in the collectivity.
8. The specific status in the group of healers, blacksmiths, carpenters, artisans, etc.
9. Is traditional education (ritual initiations, wakes, stories, proverbs, etc.) still carried out?
10. Traditional festivals and dances.

3. Beliefs, rights, and customs

1. Beliefs in occult forces, divine or human; presence or influence of a religion of foreign origin; rapport between traditional and modern beliefs.
2. Ancestor cult: how and on what occasions does it manifest itself?

3. Rites and ceremonies (they are important to know because they reveal certain beliefs and form an integral part of socioeconomic activities).

4. Customs (habits and their origins: agricultural, artisanal, medical, regarding food, etc.).

4. Administrative, political, and associative structures

1. Traditional power (when, for whom, and in what domains is it exercised?).

2. Modern power (how is it constituted, by whom? [persons of the same ethnic group as the collectivity?]; who makes decisions and how? with regard to what subjects?).

3. External dependencies: alliances through exogamous marriage, socioeconomic dependencies. Relations between the traditional and modern powers (submission, coexistence, collaboration?).

4. Associative life. Existence of spontaneous associations (rotating credit groups, work sharing, etc.). Participation of women? of youth? Forms of modern association (cooperatives and their functioning: successes? problems? participation of women? of youth, peasants?). Their "leaders": reason? role? origin?

5. Economic and technical environment

1. Traditional knowledge: plants, soils, medicine, minerals, cultural techniques, know-how, etc. Occult forces and knowledge of biochemical elements (limits of knowledge with respect to science).

2. Initiation and the traditional transfer of knowledge. Organized by sex and the consequences thereof? Secrets and taboos.

3. The division of labor (by sex and age). Agricultural. Domestic. What individuals and groups do (construction of houses, schools, wells, managing erosion, etc.).

4. Modern schools. Existence, frequency of attendance, results? Relations with traditional education, with peasant reality?

5. Innovations. Which have taken place? In what domains? Resistance and opening up? Reasons why?

6. Technical and "political" group formation [encadrement]

1. Technical *encadrement*. Specialized *encadrement* through links with the polyvalent peasant (soliciting peasants—coordination). *Encadrement* through links with the role of peasant women? System of traditional communication and pedagogical intervention in group formation? Peasant group formation ("pilot peasant," "progressive peasant," "*animateur*").

2. Political *encadrement*. The political authorities (role? relations with traditional and modern powers?). Pedagogy and content of interventions? Popular participation? (motivations? results on development?).

9

Culture and Corruption

It's painful to be told your country is corrupt—worse still, that your culture enables or even approves corruption. No wonder there are aggrieved responses from many people in supposedly corrupt countries when Transparency International's Corruption Perceptions Index is published each year. To paraphrase: "The concepts are Western and therefore culturally biased, the measures are Western perceptions and therefore culturally invalid, and the effects of supposedly awful corruption can in our culture be positive as well as negative."

But quickly, the narratives get more complicated. As we shall see, outrage about corruption turns out to be widespread *inside* those supposedly corrupt countries, as manifested in opinion polls, electoral campaigns, and popular uprisings. Ishrat Husain asked rhetorically how one knows that corruption exists in his native Pakistan. He cited some effects:

> Inflated contracts, understated or unpaid customs duty, evaded income tax, exaggerated prices paid for land acquisition by public agencies, lower rents for leasing mining, oil and gas rights, illegal connections of electricity and natural gas, apprehension of wrong persons in criminal cases and their release after accepting bribes, weak prosecution of cases, granting of licenses and permits in returns for favors, acquittal of criminals by the lower judiciary, grant of loans by nationalized commercial banks to un-creditworthy persons are some blatant manifestations of the widespread institutionalized corruption in the society.[1]

Popular outrage over corruption sometimes slides into cultural condemnation—of one's own culture. And this condemnation in turn may translate into hopelessness or calls for wholesale cultural change. The result is a potent cocktail of culture, policy, and development.

This chapter tries to recast discourse about culture and corruption, and thereby to represent an instance of thinking more constructively about

The Culture and Development Manifesto. Robert Klitgaard, Oxford University Press (2021). © Oxford University Press.
DOI: 10.1093/oso/9780197517734.003.0009

culture and development. We examine the cross-cultural applicability of definitions of corruption and assess the coherence and correlates of widely used cross-cultural measures of perceptions of corruption. We find that these national-level measures are indeed correlated with certain cultural characteristics. But instead of leaping to condemn or exonerate culture, we focus instead on tensions in norms and values within a given culture. And we arrive at practical ways to make progress despite cultural dissonances—by considering structural changes instead of cultural ones, implemented in culturally cognizant ways.

Who's Corrupt?

From early days, anthropologists have studied activities called "corrupt" by Them or by Us. They have documented how widespread and damaging some corrupt practices are, whereas other practices are often benign. Corruption is especially harmful, anthropologists are prone to note, when carried out by outsiders: those government officials doing development; those supposedly enforcing laws for the public good; and those international agencies that quasi-corruptly extend "aid" in return for UN votes, agreements about migration, help in wars against drugs or terrorists, or investigations of political rivals. Anthropologists have also noted the functions, sometimes contradictory, of corruption and of discussions about corruption. Anthropologists and historians have examined anti-corruption discourse, and "the cultural work it does," even possibly enabling corruption to flourish "materially."

And from the beginning, anthropologists have made two abiding points: behavior that is corrupt to us may not be corrupt to them, and corruption has its positive functions. These points exemplify two anthropological values: cultural relativism and don't blame the victims.

To these findings on the ground, cross-cultural research (usually not by anthropologists) has documented noteworthy facts. First, corruption is a big deal. Around the world, people talk about corruption as one of the most serious problems facing their countries. Political campaigns and popular uprisings feature outrage against corruption. A large literature suggests that reductions in corruption lead to good things, such as more investment; but as I have emphasized, both theoretical and statistical limitations should make us suspicious of these sorts of cross-country findings. What is clear, however, is that around the world citizens, politicians, aid donors, and humanitarians call for less corruption—and they do so in the name of development.

Second, as we shall see, research shows that some cultures (and subcultures) are more corrupt, indeed more dishonest in various measurable ways, than others. Some "cultural traits," such as individualism-collectivism, tolerance of hierarchy, "traditional-rational," and "survival-expressive" are correlated with corruption. Members of some religions tend to be more corrupt than others.

Third, although cultures undoubtedly are fluid, and some measures of cultural traits change over time, it is not clear how much or how policymakers, citizens groups, international organizations, or scholars can make cultural change occur.

So, we have an explosive combination:

1. a big perceived problem,
2. cultural correlates, and
3. hard-to-change cultures.

These three facts have spawned some defensive reactions and, when the facts are accepted, some fallacious inferences.

The defensive reactions. Wait, don't forget cultural relativism, and don't blame the victim. The concepts and measures are culturally biased. Look at the agendas being advanced—locally, nationally, internationally—by all this talk about corruption. When the mouthpieces of monopoly capitalism complain about corruption, that should make us prick up our ears.

The fallacious inferences. If some cultures are more corrupt than others, nothing can be done—just be a trait-taker. Or at the other extreme, we have to be trait-makers: positive correlation means the only way to fight corruption is through a radical change of cultures (the often-heard-in-developing-countries phrase, "we need a change of mentality").

This chapter suggests a different tack. Every culture has norms that oppose corruption and norms that favor it. Some "practical norms" are corrupt in some situations and not in others. If so, the practical challenge is to reform systems so that the norms opposing harmful corruption have more room, the norms favoring it less.

Second, it is a slight play on words to think of a "culture of corruption" this way: as an expectational equilibrium in an *n*-person game where each of us is stuck in a dominant strategy of "bribe" even though (a) in our personal ethics we abhor bribing, and (b) we all appreciate that the preferred collective equilibrium is "don't bribe." People around the world recognize this phenomenon, even if, thankfully, they don't use such unwieldy words.[2]

The conundrum is real, the equilibrium is powerful, and yet both theory and examples show that collective action can reduce systemic corruption. The "what-to-do" turns out to be largely independent of "culture," independent of cross-cultural variations in hospitality, religious belief, individualism, and the rest. And yet, the "how-to-do-it" should be sensitive to culture in those senses and others.

Concepts of Corruption

The *lava jato* movement in Brazil resulted in the unprecedented documentation of systemic corruption—and put some of the most powerful people in the country behind bars.[3] It also led to national soul searching. "Many Brazilians believe that corruption is part of our culture," the Brazilian journalist Juliana Bublitz told me in a telephone interview in 2016, "and that without a big cultural change, we will not be able to fight corruption. Do you agree?" I didn't (for reasons that will become clear), but I apparently didn't convince her. Indeed, the subtitle of her published article included this even stronger question: "A trapaça está enraizada no nosso DNA?" ("Is cheating rooted in our DNA?").[4]

Brazilians are not alone in linking widespread corruption with cultural degradation. In Uganda, Emmanuel Mwaka Lutukomoi, the resident deputy commissioner of Lira, declared: "We live in a rotten country, rotten districts, rotten offices, with rotten people. Corruption has invaded all public institutions. . . . We have lost the moral sense of shame."[5]

Pope Francis lamented that corruption has become "a personal and social statement tied to customs" and "a greater ill than sin."

> The scandalous concentration of global wealth is made possible by the connivance of public leaders with the powers that be. . . . Corruption is a greater ill than sin. More than forgiveness, this ill must be treated. Corruption has become natural, to the point of becoming a personal and social statement tied to customs, common practice in commercial and financial transactions, in public contracting, in every negotiation that involves agents of the State.[6]

Despondency about corrupted cultures is often based on the perceived exaltation of greed and a consequent erosion of traditional ideals. And therefore—sometimes explicit in the argument but usually just assumed—it is believed that without a change in culture (a revaluation of values, a change of mentality), corruption will flourish. In Mexico:

> A President who believes and affirms in public that corruption is fundamentally a cultural problem sends an alarming signal: not much can be done to change it. Worse still: he seems to be saying that he is not even going to try to do anything about corruption, since modifying the culture is not something that can be done in a term of office.[7]

The Latin root of "to corrupt" (*corrumpo*) means to pervert or deprave, to rot or contaminate, and to spoil. Ancient metaphors included the turning of the head of the judge, as with her blindfold removed she looks sideways at the bribe-paying party and tips her scales. The UN Convention Against Corruption (Art. 19) defines "the abuse of functions" as "the performance of or failure to perform an act, in violation of laws, by a public official in the discharge of his or her functions, for the purpose of obtaining an undue advantage for himself or herself or for another person or entity . . . when committed intentionally." Corrupt acts involve the misuse of office for illicit ends—understanding that across contexts "misuse," "office," and "illicit" vary. Corruption is where a market enters where a society says it shouldn't. For example, a society may decide that a good or service should be allocated by popular vote, not by market forces. Or by "merit," seniority, need, or random allotment. Corruption introduces instead an illicit market.[8]

At this level of abstraction,

> corruption is a phenomenon universally understood in a similar manner across cultures. . . . Differences in what is understood as corruption lie in the variation of what counts as (and is the extension of) public goods in cultures, and not variation in whether it is morally wrong to turn a public good into a private good.[9]

All governments have laws against bribery, extortion, and related practices. No culture or religion endorses corruption. Condemning corruption is virtually universal. In late 2011, a BBC survey of citizens of twenty-three countries around the world identified corruption as "the topic most frequently discussed by the public."[10] Anthropological fieldwork agrees. "Stories about corruption dominate political and symbolic discourse in Nigeria. Everyday practices of corruption and the narratives they generate are primary vehicles through which Nigerians imagine and create the relationships between state and society."[11] The historian Steven Pierce concurs, noting that anti-corruption discourse is also widespread in Nigeria.[12] An anthropologist working in northern India "was struck by how frequently the theme of corruption cropped up in the everyday conversations of villagers. Most of the stories the men told each other in the evening, when the day's work was done and small groups had gathered at habitual places to shoot the breeze, had to do with corruption."[13] And it is not just gossipy chatter: in a 2013 poll of 70,000 people in sixty-nine countries, corruption was deemed the world's number one problem.[14]

Measures of Corruption

If people everywhere complain about corruption, is corruption equally distributed? How would one know? Even when corruption is systemic, most corrupt acts are secretive and stigmatizing. Most people will not admit to them. Even supposedly hard data, such as media stories or cases prosecuted, will be biased in societies where the press and the prosecutors are stifled.

As a result, many scholars and policymakers use data about *perceptions* of corruption. These may matter for their own sake, as signals of discontent and harbingers of unrest. Data on perceptions usefully track a concept "being put to work":

> Anthropology, it has been said, did not advance until it turned from the study of witchcraft to the study of accusations of witchcraft. . . . Where accusations abound—where sermons on the sin are copious, where prosecutions proliferate, where laws multiply—the idea of bribery is being put to work. . . . The reality of a concept in the society is indicated by its invocation, even though the extent to which the idea affects official conduct cannot be closely calculated.[15]

One widely used measure is Transparency International's Corruption Perceptions Index (CPI).[16] It is a composite measure derived from twelve different sources from eleven different institutions that capture perceptions of corruption within the previous two years. The CPI is scaled to measure "freedom from corruption," so higher scores are better.

Statisticians have explicated the qualities of a good composite measure,[17] and some of these same scholars have examined the CPI.

> The JRC analysis suggests that the new methodology for the Corruption Perceptions Index (CPI), besides being appealing for reasons of transparency and replicability, it is also conceptually and statistically coherent and with a balanced structure (i.e., the CPI is not dominated by any of the individual sources). Despite the high associations between the sources, the information offered by the CPI is shown to be non-redundant.[18]

Many other measures exist. Besides asking individuals about their experiences or perceptions of corruption, researchers have used numbers of news stories, tweets, and prosecutions.[19] Other research looks at the flip side of corruption, for example government efficiency,[20] perceptions of impartiality,[21] and expert and popular perceptions of the rule of law.[22] Still other researchers have created scales based on the existence and/or implementation of various laws, rules, rights, and institutions in a country.[23] The PRS Group, a for-profit organization, has created a composite measure of political risk, one element of which is the risk of corruption.[24]

Most of these measures of corruption are highly correlated (the following are my calculations). The bivariate correlations among the CPI, the World Bank's Rule of Law Index, and the World Bank's Absence of Corruption measure all exceed 0.90. The CPI is correlated 0.91 with a composite of three quality-of-government indicators of the PRS Group. The CPI is also highly correlated with answers to two questions in the World Economic Forum's Global Competitiveness Index: irregular payments and bribes ($r = 0.90$) and Diversion of public funds ($r = 0.86$). The 2020 Rule of Law Index mentioned in chapter 5 is correlated 0.97 with the 2019 CPI, though they were derived completely independently.

Finally, the CPI is highly correlated with variables ranging from inequality to democracy, from income to the status of women, to happiness and satisfaction with life.[25]

What about with measures of culture?

Links between Culture and Corruption

Family Ties

As we saw in chapter 2, Don Fernando the Equatoguinean finance minister explained family ties this way:

> In Africa you have to understand that people do not have a common interest. Without a common interest, there are fights. Social conflict. I don't know if you understand me. In Africa, first comes the family, then the clan, then the province, then the region, and finally the country. But the country is the last thing.

Göran Hydén emphasized Africa's "economies of affection" in which kinship and tribal obligations inhibit good governance.[26]

Africa is not alone. If it is true that an African proverb says, "Whoever does not rob the state robs his kith and kin," a saying in the former Czechoslovakia was "He who does not steal from the state, steals from his family." From Latin America come accounts of clans and also of *compadrazgo*, or fictive kinship, that provide networks of support and often of corruption.[27] Campaigning in India, Narendra Modi argued that he would not be corrupt because he is single, as opposed to other Indians with strong, corrupting family ties. From Egypt and Afghanistan come detailed analyses of the power of family and clan to distort the good governance that many in these countries say they seek.[28] Edward Banfield emphasized the cultural trait of "amoral familism" as a source of corruption in southern Italy.[29] All these accounts suggest that culture matters in understanding corruption.

As we saw earlier in the book, the World Values Survey (WVS) has since the 1980s surveyed individuals in countries around the world about demographics, economic status, and values and beliefs. Using three questions from the WVS, Alberto Alesina and Paola Giuliano created a composite measure that combines people's beliefs regarding the importance of the family in an individual's life, the duties and responsibilities of parents and children, and the love and respect for one's own parents.[30] They found that stronger family ties were associated with more corruption. "These results remain valid if one exploits the correlation between inherited family values and current institutions and level of development, indicating a strong persistence in family values."[31] Seymour Martin Lipset and Gabriel Salman Lenz also reported strong correlations between their own "familism scale" and corruption.[32]

Other Measures of Culture

Earlier in the book, we examined some other country-level measures of culture, including individualism-collectivism, power distance (or hierarchy), a scale from "traditional to rational," and a scale from "survival to self-expression." It turns out that each of these cultural measures is correlated with the CPI (the following calculations are mine, based on the 2019 CPI). The more individualistic is a country, the less corrupt ($r = -0.69$). The more hierarchical, the more corrupt ($r = 0.65$). And if you take the two dimensions "traditional to rational" and "survival to self-expression," together they explain 65 percent of the variance in the CPI.

Suggestive, but a full model would of course consider other mechanisms. Corruption itself may cause cultural changes. For example, if a country becomes more corrupt, its citizens may move toward the traditional end and more toward the survival end of those two WVS scales. People may revert to family ties:

> Human beings are born with a suite of emotions that fortify the development of social relationships based on cooperation with friends and family. To behave differently—to choose, for example, a highly qualified employee over a friend or relative, or to work in an impersonal bureaucracy—is socially constructed behavior that runs counter to our natural inclinations. It is only with the development of political institutions like the modern state that humans begin to organize themselves and learn to cooperate in a manner that transcends friends and family. When such institutions break down, we revert to patronage and nepotism as a default form of sociability.[33]

Policies may simultaneously affect cultural change and corruption: for example, freer trade, more exchanges of information, greater travel and intercultural contact, and more gender equity. Arguably, some of these policies may lead to less traditionalism, less emphasis on survival, less hierarchy, and more individualism—and therefore to less corruption (let's place the emphasis on "may," because backlashes lurk). Second, policies may address corruption without changing "cultures" (more on this later).

Therefore, just as we saw in chapter 5, full causal models of these multiple and reciprocal effects between culture and corruption (and policies of various kinds) are impossible. Insufficient theory, weak data, endogeneity, competing estimation techniques, and deep heterogeneity: these many challenges reduce our confidence that we will be able to estimate mathematically the interactions among corruption, culture, and policy choices.

Moreover, the measures and correlations can themselves become part of a political discourse: they do their own "cultural work." Around the world, as in Brazil and Uganda and the United States, the putative links between corruption and culture have led to popular vilifications: "This culture has been corrupted—nothing can be done without wholesale cultural change."

Conflicting Cultural Norms

Let us now consider an alternative line of reasoning. It is not "a culture" that is somehow corrupt or corrupted, rather that cultural norms conflict. The head of prisons in South Sudan taught me this lesson.

It was 2004, before South Sudan was to become an autonomous entity within Sudan—in preparation for hoped-for complete independence, which eventually happened in 2012. About sixty South Sudanese leaders from civil society and the liberation army convened for two days in a tented encampment to discuss government after autonomy. It was my privilege to share with them data, examples from other countries, and an analytical framework, with plenty of opportunities to do creative work.

Among other things, we discussed the challenges of corruption. Some of the ideas we'll see later. The one that is pertinent here is the principle of the big fish: early on, successful anti-corruption campaigns fry some big fish or offenders, including from your own party.

When the workshop closed, I invited everyone for a drink. As we mingled outdoors in the dusk, we were tired and stimulated, drained and inspired, confused and celebratory. We ate dinner. I wandered from table to table. The participants were talking about autonomy and the tasks ahead.

One of the groups was discussing corruption. And as I sat down, the head of prisons looked at me and asks, "What do you do if you have to be the big fish?"

Puzzled, I asked what he meant.

He inquired softly, "How did you pay for the drinks you invited us to tonight?"

I paid for it from my own pocket.

"What if you didn't have a deep-enough pocket?"

Then I got it. His role created expectations. Occasionally or perhaps often, he had to provide hospitality or more—help or support or subsistence. Where should he come up with the resources? Unsaid was "without being corrupt."

Neither he nor anyone else at the South Sudan workshop was saying, "In our culture it's okay to put yourself and your family above your obligations to serve in the public interest." Rather, his question described a cultural conflict. Public servants have a role-related obligation to be impartial and not corrupt. They may also experience a kinship-related obligation to favor family and friends, even when it entails corruption.

It is noteworthy that even in settings that experience systemic corruption, citizens and public officials routinely scorn bribery and affirm values of impartial public service. A study of villages in Kerala and Madhya Pradesh, India, concluded that "corruption is not accepted by most people in the survey; most respondents favor a rule-governed bureaucracy within a democratic setting, regardless of whether the society is plagued by corruption or not."[34] Half of Mexicans surveyed admitted to having been asked to pay a bribe, and almost four-fifths agreed that "politicians are corrupt." But 87 percent said politicians should be held accountable, and 80 percent "believed that citizens should obey the law without exception."[35]

The head of prisons confronted competing cultural norms, which might tempt him to take actions others, and importantly he himself, perceived to be corrupt. Even when officials and citizens value impartiality in public service, strong ties to kin and clan lead to pressures for favoritism. Three anthropologists documented conflicts between well-known official norms and "practical norms" in Niger, where the latter often result in actions that the people performing them know are "corrupt." (See Box 9.1.)

One approach is somehow to try to change South Sudan's culture, so that (for example) the strength of family ties is attenuated, collectivism is loosened, power distance is reduced, and an overarching identity can overcome cultural diversity. Another approach is to change the decision contexts faced by the head of prisons (and other officials), including their ability to convey favoritism and their calculations of the risks and rewards of doing so.

Corruption is a crime of calculation. As the auditor general of Uganda put it, "Someone will ask, 'Will it pay?' If it will, one will steal. If it won't pay, one

Box 9.1 Informal Norms in Human Resource Management in Niger

In Niger, public administration is riven with absenteeism, politicized allocation of posts, impunity ("untouchables"), influence peddling, kickbacks, bribes, extortion, and the abuse of power. "These deviations from the official norms cannot be attributed to a lack of knowledge of official standards. . . . Yet most officials continue to behave this way routinely. Everyone, or almost everyone, finds it more or less 'normal' not to respect the official standards on such occasions. These deviations from official standards have become 'habitual.'

"Based on this analysis, we can draw up a list of implicit, *de facto* practical norms . . . . These practical norms are of course never publicly stated as such, unlike official standards which are explicit in regulations, procedures and training . . . . These concern personnel management, and are similar to those in health and education." Here are some of them:

- Party activists and supporters must be rewarded with appointments to posts throughout the administration.
- Political affiliation is a major criterion in the assigning of posts.
- Political reasons are more important than the professional requirements of the job.
- The ability to obtain posts for protégés is a sign of social success.
- Posts are assessed in terms of the (legal or illegal) collateral financial benefits to which they provide access, or the resulting benefits for one's family.
- Any intervention to obtain a desired post is considered normal.
- A favor cannot be denied to a loved one or a powerful person.
- It is normal to present gifts to superiors to keep in their good graces.
- The rejection of an intervention is a sign of malice.
- It is normal to show leniency towards elders.
- The main reason to attend training is to receive per-diems
- Disciplining a subordinate leads to disapproval and problems that are best avoided.
- Fulfilling social obligations takes precedence over professional ones.
- One should be suspicious of colleagues or subordinates who are too active (hard-working).
- To delegate tasks is to attract problems.

Continued

Box 9.1 *Continued*

- Working in a team involves too many risks and constraints.
- Avoid conflict and don't interfere in the affairs of others.
- A good manager shares and redistributes resources.
- "Being at work" does not mean being on the job during official working hours.
- If you are absent, there is no need to plan for a replacement.
- It is normal to have two jobs, even if it is not officially permitted.
- To keep your own job, accept the assignment of a post recommended by an important person.

Source: Jean-Pierre Olivier de Sardan, Mahaman Tahirou Ali Bako, and Abdoutan Harouna, "Les Normes Pratiques en Vigueur dans les Secteurs de l'Éducation et la Santé au Niger: Une Base pour des Réformes Ancrées dans les Réalités?," *Etudes et Travaux du LASDEL* no.127, Niamey, Niger, Laboratoire d'Etudes et de Recherche sur les Dynamiques Sociales et le Développement Local, 2018, 5, 45–47.

won't steal. It should be too expensive to steal. This is why corruption is happening on a grand scale."[36] One might go further. The architect Frank Gehry said, "As an artist I have constraints—gravity is one of them." In designing public policy, *greed is like gravity*.

Taking this perspective on corruption leads to suppose what each person is doing is a self-interested calculation of benefits and costs, of risks and rewards. It focuses on the consequences of actions: the social benefits or costs, not just the personal ones. As Jean-Pierre Olivier de Sardan, Mahaman Tahirou Ali Bako, and Abdoutan Harouna point out, some corrupt behavior in health and education in Niger is "transgressive" and damaging, other forms relatively harmless—understanding the incentives and constraints officials and service providers face is crucial for reform.[37] In fighting corruption, the first task is to understand in context the various costs of corruption and of possible measures to reduce corruption—sometimes the latter aren't worth the trouble. Then, again in context, to experiment with structures, information, and incentives, hoping to shift the calculations of the corrupt and potentially corrupt. A lot of words, but notice what isn't there. This approach does not try to change people's values; it does not aspire to creating a new culture.

Peter Drucker has been quoted as saying, "Company cultures are like country cultures. Never try to change one. Try, instead, to work with what you've got."[38] That's excessive, but this statement isn't: we know little about designing public policies to change people's values and attitudes, except perhaps in the long run by influencing people's behavior.

Singapore is an excellent example. In the 1960s and 1970s, it moved from an equilibrium of corruption to one of remarkably good governance, without notably changing national cultural characteristics such as family ties, individualism, or power distance. Other valuable examples of reducing corruption are Colombia in the late 1990s, Georgia in 2004, the Philippines under Benigno Aquino III, Qatar, and Rwanda. A number of cities have also made impressive progress against corruption at various points in time, such as Bogotá and Medellín, Colombia; Campo Elias, Venezuela; Naga City, the Philippines; La Paz, Bolivia; and Mandaue, the Philippines. Craiova, Romania, and Martin, Slovak Republic, won the United Nations Public Service Awards in 2011 for their reforms against corruption. The reforms have sometimes suffered from backsliding,[39] but the progress made reveals the intersection between the careful analysis of corrupt systems (organizational structures, information, incentives, collective action problems, and so forth) and political acumen (not trying to do everything at once, building momentum, frying big fish, fostering collaboration with business and civil society, and so forth).[40]

The point is not that corruption is unconnected with cultural values and moral dilemmas—it is. Rather, it is that effective anti-corruption strategies do not need to rely on the daunting task of cultural change.

Cultures of Corruption

Let us now consider a second cultural conflict, in which people may pay bribes even when they loathe bribery. In countries experiencing systemic corruption, people may decry corruption in the morning, pay a bribe to get a needed service in the afternoon, and then in the evening complain that corruption has become part of their culture.

In Nigeria, noted the anthropologist Daniel Jordan Smith,

> people frequently condemn corruption and its consequences as immoral and socially ruinous, yet they also participate in seemingly contradictory behaviors that enable, encourage, and even glorify corruption. . . . In many instances, ordinary Nigerians see themselves as complicit in corruption, and indeed it is this awareness of collective responsibility for corruption

that fuels hopes for change, even as it paradoxically perpetuates cynicism and a sense of intractability.[41]

In India, the anthropologist Akhil Gupta found that

a highly placed official who fails to help a close relative or a fellow villager obtain a government position is often roundly criticized by people for not fulfilling his obligations to his kinsmen and village brothers. On the other hand, the same people often roundly condemn any official of another caste or village who has done precisely that as being "corrupt" and as guilty of "nepotism."[42]

In these situations, we may talk metaphorically of a culture of corruption as when "good people, trapped in a corrupt structure, become corrupted as they do their best within the given economic, legal, institutional structure."[43] In fact, in many cases where corruption becomes the expectation, people have excellent individual ethics. Given what everyone else is doing, it may be almost an imperative to bribe, to be dishonest, to cheat.

Do values therefore erode? Perhaps. Norms are shaped by corrupt equilibriums, as Cheyanne Scharbatke-Church and Diana Chigas note—and once in place, norms in turn influence future behavior, including in other settings. But are efforts to change cultural norms effective? Scharbatke-Church and Chigas shy away, noting that trying to influence norms can backfire; they leave the question to future research.[44]

Instead, consider that a corrupt equilibrium can be understood as an *n*-person prisoner's dilemma where many people wish they didn't have to participate but where individual, maximizing logic drives them to do so. Once corrupt behavior is embedded, each individual may have little choice but to go along. The logic of calculation and equilibrium suggest solutions that go beyond efforts to change a culture's norms and values.

The principles of change resemble other situations of collective action.[45] The principles include a variety of ways to "subvert" a corrupt equilibrium, including "frying big fish," taking two or three highly visible steps that people can perceive as progress, and reforming institutions to raise the risks and lower the rewards from corrupt behaviors.[46] The more general and "culture-free" literature on strategic change is also relevant.[47] (We will explore the related example of common-pool resources in the final chapter.)

Implications for Culture and Development

Around the world, "culture" is sometimes "blamed" for poverty or dictatorship, anomie or hyper-competitiveness, the subjugation of women or the inefficiency of agriculture. Correlations may well exist and so may theories that "explain" the deep roots of cultural patterns. A fatalistic inference may seem inescapable: "What can one do if culture is to blame?"[48] Or a utopian inference: "We must aim for a change of mentality, a cultural revolution, a transformation of values, a new basis for progressive politics, or an epistemology of the Global South."

Our reflections in this chapter suggest a different approach. First, we should examine the relevant concepts and measures and see if they are in fact valid and reliable across cultures. In the case of corruption, we saw how concepts and measures are contestable and inexact. And yet, across cultures people describe and decry similar acts as "corrupt." Across countries many measures of corruption are statistically coherent, and they are correlated with each other and with theoretically attractive precursors and consequences. Even though we found statistical connections between measures of corruption and measures of culture, we also saw again the common and discouraging challenges to cross-cultural empirical work: theory uncertainty, model uncertainty, and specification uncertainty, plus a small number of observations, a large number of possible causes and confounders, and limited data (especially over time). As a result, causal modeling linking culture to corruption is precarious.

Second, we should look for conflicting norms within given cultural settings, rather than at allegedly corrupt cultures. We examined family ties vs. impartial public service, and the dilemma posed in a corrupt equilibrium where citizens bribe even though they oppose bribery. Instead of trying to change cultural norms and values, we focused on ways to constrain the conflict of norms through redesigning the public servant's choices (structures, information flows, and incentives), thereby limiting the scope for corruption and nepotism. Beyond individual agents, we examined those corrupt equilibriums again in structural terms. How do systematically corrupted systems work, and how can they be undermined? We discovered that corruption can be related to many other problems of collective action—and that these other examples may suggest valuable, practical ideas for addressing our local, culturally imbued modes of corruption.

Third, insofar as cultures go, we can take them into account without trying to change them. We can ask how anti-corruption initiatives can take advantage of our cultural context. How they can emphasize our religion (all religions condemn bribery) and our relevant traditional values. Use our indigenous institutions to help design, implement, and monitor reforms. And restate the reforms we desire in language that appeals to our culture, not necessarily in the language of economics or Western philosophy or agencies of international development.

Finally, if we are outsiders we should begin with local people's complaints about corruption and related phenomena, including corruption they perceive in our institutions and "cultures." We should immerse ourselves in their outrage over corruption, their stories of dysfunction, and their desire to do better. And we should simultaneously recognize the contradictions in our own societies. Recall our own disappointing conformity to things we really don't admire, our own examples of stigma and self-stigma. We may thereby be able to think more boldly and practically, and act more humbly and humanely.

10

Culture and Development Reconsidered

When he finished his pathbreaking book on culture and development in Italy, Robert Putnam briefed an Italian minister of government. Putnam explained the deep roots of successful democracy and decentralization. The kinds of indigenous institutions and networks that particular districts possessed 150 years before almost perfectly predicted the performance of district governments after decentralization. Putnam went further, showing that some of the differences in "social capital" went back hundreds of years. The minister's first response was not appreciative. "Are you just telling me there's nothing we can do?"[1]

Overcoming cultural determinism may paradoxically involve facing up to cultural differences, even when they are embarrassing. In chapter 8 we encountered Bernard Lédéa Ouédraogo, who founded a new, culturally appropriate model of community development in West Africa. In his old government job, he was disillusioned by the dysfunctional response of local farmers to his high-minded efforts to develop them.

> The rural extension workers would arrive in a village, and the only concern of the officially organized farmers was to take advantage of the donkeys, bullocks, carts, hoes, and other materials we would make available to them. . . . It was normal that in such a situation the farmers had but one concern: prime the State "pump" for all it was worth and cheat the extension workers.

One could deny any problem with the local culture, blaming shortcomings instead on the government (always a promising culprit) or on the culturally inappropriate machinations of the market.

Or instead, one could ask how rural culture might be investigated, involved, and invigorated. This is what Ouédraogo did with his remarkable 6-S organization. As we saw in chapter 8, he built on local cultural strengths and indigenous networks, including age-group organizations and village elders.

The Culture and Development Manifesto. Robert Klitgaard, Oxford University Press (2021). © Oxford University Press.
DOI: 10.1093/oso/9780197517734.003.0010

It starts with what people *are* (based on a true appreciation of their African identity), what they *know* (respect for traditional knowledge and values, which implies the considerable effort necessary to become acquainted with them), their *know-how* (rediscovery of traditional techniques, some of which, for example in the field of water and soil conservation, have proven invaluable), and what they *wish to achieve* (which implies meaningful grassroots participation in defining the very objectives of the development process).[2]

Ouédraogo also had a clear-eyed view of their weaknesses, including substandard planning and accounting, a readiness for Big Men to take the financing for themselves, too little agricultural know-how in key domains, and "a cultural syndrome of distrust and lack of confidence." The point is that he and his colleagues built on cultural strengths and networks and took steps, through 6-S, to overcome weaknesses.

Or take another common phenomenon around the world: certain cultural groups lag in conventional measures of academic performance. One response is denial, especially when, lurking in the background, is an academic literature that connects academic performance, general intelligence, and heredity. Instead, it is easier just to say: "The measures are meaningless and biased against those cultural groups. Don't ever mention 'cultural deficits.'" Another response is to blame teachers and administrators or books and syllabi. The Pygmalion effect asserts that if teachers believe that students from such-and-such cultural group will learn less, then teachers will behave differently and their belief will be self-fulfilling. "The educational system is biased against that group."

Instead, one could investigate what cultural differences are relevant to learning and how they could be taken into account in pedagogy. This is what the Kamehameha Elementary Education Program (KEEP) in Hawai'i did. As we saw in chapter 8, anthropologists studied Hawaiian children and their families. They noted that when children were singled out at home, it was perceived as a scolding. Perhaps this was the reason why, in the classroom, Hawaiian children tended to freeze when called upon individually to read or recite. There were educational implications for other cultural behaviors, from group play to noisiness, from learning from stories to benefiting from examples from their indigenous worlds. KEEP changed the pedagogy for Hawaiian students, and the results were fewer dropouts, more student engagement and satisfaction, and higher achievement test scores.

Tailoring programs and policies to cultures obviously demands knowing about those cultures, in two senses. We need some sort of theoretical framework to lay out the possible interactions between cultures and policies. And we need some sort of data for the specific cultural setting, which would enable the concrete particulars of the interactions to be assessed and addressed.

Both steps are scary. First and foremost come the possibilities of misuse. Of dreaded words like reification, objectification, essentialism, cultural determinism. Of the loathed association between cultural "traits" and genetic ones. Of creating a kind of cultural apartheid. Of being a defeatist trait-taker instead of a revolutionary trait-maker. "You're condemning people from that culture to remain . . ."

A second scary thing, at least metaphorically, is the sheer scientific difficulty of modeling the culture by policy interactions and then estimating them in practice. Marcel Mauss expressed the ultimate in that modeling dream when he talked of capturing a culture's every dimension: no ethnography would be satisfactory, he said, without having included them all. There will always be that call for more factors, levels, nuances. As one recent critique of culture and poverty said,

> further theoretical development may be facilitated by a concern for systematically disentangling social psychological processes (often focused on perceptions) from cultural processes that involve intersubjectivity and shared meaning-making (e.g. symbolic boundaries, classification systems, and repertoires), in their interaction and articulation with social and institutional processes. These various levels should be examined in their interaction with access to a range of social, material, and other resources that act as determinants of poverty and inequality. . . . To consider a part of the equation will by definition result in an inadequate (because incomplete) understanding of crucial causal pathways.[3]

These scholars do not cite a prototype of such work. (And by the way, neither Mauss nor his students ever produced one of his sought-after depictions of *le fait social total*.)

Better, then—conclude many people interested in culture—to leave that scientific agenda aside, indeed to question its premises and authority. Culture isn't a bunch of "factors." It's not a matrix of measures. Yes, there's may be a dynamic, complex system here, but please don't even begin down the path of cultural "variables." As Marc-Éric Gruénais and Fatoumata Ouattara put it: "Anthropology makes fun of models of public health with their boxes and arrows that mix such massive, imprecise, and undefined variables as 'socio-cultural environment,' 'ethnic group,' 'socioeconomic status,' 'psycho-social factors,' etc. with risk factors measured down to the millimeter (insulin level, viral load, etc.)."[4]

We must do better. The realities of underdevelopment are harsh and galling. Current strategies are not working well enough or fast enough. We need more analysis of those culture by policy interactions, more experimentation with ways to enable local people to profit from international knowledge (such as it is), and to combine it creatively with their knowledge and know-how.

From Social Science to Soil Science?

I find a metaphor of Robert Putnam's useful. He refers to local cultural conditions as the *symbolic soil* in which development takes place.[5] Policies and projects may work better or worse, depending in part on these soil conditions; and if we understood the soil conditions better, we might decide to design a different policy or project.

Soil scientists analyze soils, using partial and incomplete measures.[6] They listen carefully to local farmers about their land and farming practices. Beyond describing differences in soil conditions, soil scientists have theories, models, and rules of thumb describing the interactions among types of soils, types of crops, and types of soil treatments. Soil scientists seem like trait-takers when they ask, "In this soil, what crops will grow best, given other factors like climate?" But they also ask questions like trait-makers: "In order to grow such-and-such a desired crop here, what changes can be made to the soil itself, such as irrigation, fertilizer, cross-cropping, shade, and so forth?"

Could anthropologists and other social scientists aspire to become more like soil scientists? We, too, might seek to provide *partial and incomplete* measures of local cultural conditions in order to *help local people* make better decisions. We, too, would listen to locals, recognizing that they know much more about their local conditions and practices than we ever can, that our comparative and theoretical science may at best provide new insights for local people to consider. As in the case of soil science, one idea is to choose appropriate "crops" to take advantage of given "soils"—in this case, selecting policies and projects to take advantage of local cultural strengths and minimize their weaknesses, given other aspects of the task environment. And as in the case of soil science, social science could also help local people consider how to change those cultural conditions, if they so desired.

Becoming more like soil scientists is at once bold and humble. The boldness comes from taking social science seriously and trying to apply it. As with soil scientists, the aim should be to help local people make their own decisions with the aid of both local and cross-cultural knowledge.

Humbly, the soil science analogy eschews Mauss's goal of "representing a culture" through social scientific research. The analogy may also reinforce the modest virtues of getting our hands dirty and keeping our feet on the ground.

Guided by the soil science metaphor, we should try to understand what classifications of cultural "soil conditions" might prove useful for specific issues and perhaps in specific settings. The impossibility of a perfect multivariate, dynamic model for all issues and all cultures need not paralyze us. Soil scientists also rely on experts from other disciplines—horticulturalists, chemists, extension workers, geographers, and so forth. So, too, applied cultural studies should be eclectic, always using whatever intellectual tools might be available to help assess local conditions. The appropriate disciplines may well depend on whether the issue is rural health clinics, credit and savings programs, producers' cooperatives, common-pool resources of various kinds, pedagogies, economic policies, and so forth. Some soil scientists specialize in particular crops or particular soil treatments. So, too, may the study of cultural settings eventually involve experts in particular kinds of settings and particular types of policy interventions, including cultural change.

Raising the possibility of intentional cultural change is scary—even with the proviso that local people should be the ones who decide. Cultural change is more problematic than soil treatment. Nonetheless, the soil science metaphor provides a useful guideline: the scientist's comparative and theoretical perspectives may be able to supplement local knowledge about soil conditions and soil-by-crop interactions, and decisions about change should rely on the locals.

An Example: Common-Pool Resources

Consider the work of Elinor Ostrom in Nepal. Local groups there faced challenges that were at once local (and intensely cultural) and generic (and appreciable through a variety of analytical models): the management of common-pool resources (also called common-property resources).

One example of a common-pool resource is a local forest. If a community manages the forest with an eye to the long-term welfare of all, community members will limit how many trees are cut in any period of time. And more of course: the management of a forest includes which trees are cut, how density is managed, what to do about diseases and pests, and other dimensions of forest health. But consider the potential for overcutting. Each individual profits personally (economists say "privately") from cutting down one tree more than their allotment, and the costs to the ecology of the forest, and therefore to the community, from one more harvested tree are small. But if everyone follows the individualistic, private logic of maximization, soon the forest is overcut. It takes a village, as they say—but how to organize the collective management of this common-property good?

Similar questions arose in the management of their local irrigation systems. Nepalis were aware of chronic tensions. They recognized in principle that sharing the water and managing the system would increase their total production. But they also were aware of the personal advantages of not sharing. Especially the farmers located upstream had opportunities to take more water than their allotment, which would mean less water for those downstream and lower overall production.

Imagine the difficult social scientific questions that arise. Estimate the optimal forest size, the optimal distribution of irrigation water: in principle, straightforward but in practice many complexities emerge. Given those estimates, economists and engineers can trot out models of the monitoring and incentives needed for optimal management. But let's focus on the "cultural" and political practicalities of managing a common-property resource. Who is going to determine and then legitimize "optimality" for the local forest or irrigation system? And who is going to implement the monitoring? How and how well? With what incentives and penalties for the enforcers and incentive-givers? With what cultural legitimacy? Determined through what local process? What if corruption and mismanagement occur?

Instead of avoiding these daunting questions as too hard, with too much potential for misuse, Ostrom was bold and humble in addressing them with the Nepalis.

Bold

She was bold in her confidence that learning about the economics of common-pool resources would help the Nepalis improve their own perceptions of the challenges and opportunities. Using knowledge from around the world, she helped farmers understand five kinds of property rights which often form "bundles": access, withdrawal, management, exclusion, and alienation. She shared her research on seven types of rules used in common-property resources: boundary, position, choice, information, scope, aggregation, and payoff.[7]

Humble

Ostrom was also humble. She appreciated in her heart as well as her head that the Nepalis were sovereign. They were wise in ways and domains that she was not. "She was really a field worker," wrote Prachanda Pradhan. "She strongly believed that we learn from the farmers and we have to give to the farmers what we have learnt; so, she propagated the idea 'from farmer to farmer.'"[8]

She had the anthropologist's humility in the face of diversity. When she revisited Nepal after winning the Nobel Prize in Economic Sciences, she was taken aback by people now asking her for "the" answer. She demurred. "Knowledge is not just about an answer," she told an interviewer, "it is about knowledge itself or about the processes. Sometimes complex processes are interactive and you need to know about the processes are different [*sic*] before you can judge what is happening."[9] As she emphasized in her Nobel lecture, "the application of empirical studies to the policy world leads one to stress the importance of fitting institutional rules to a specific social-ecological setting. 'One-size-fits-all' policies are not effective."[10]

> Achieving a higher standard of living without losing some of the strong capabilities of self-governance is a major challenge. To do so, however, requires listening to farmers in the first place and gaining information about their needs, their property rights, their ways of governing irrigation, and facilitating their plans for ways of managing improved physical capital. . . . And, if they have managed their own system in the past, they know what kind of property rights and duties have been established in the past that need to be taken into account in any effort to "modernize" a system.[11]

The combination of theoretical knowledge and careful listening led Ostrom to identify local conditions that were most conducive to effective community management:

- users have common interests;
- they place a high value on the resource far into the future;
- users support effective monitoring;
- accurate information is valued and easily communicated; and
- it is feasible to establish binding and enforceable regulations.[12]

Ostrom didn't do all this to *derive a solution*. Instead, she and the farmers worked together (with others) to create culturally attuned designs and learning-based implementation.[13] I want to underscore three things Ostrom and her colleagues could provide for the Nepali farmers.

1. Data

First, data. She could show them, with information that complemented their local knowledge, features of local forest ecology and farming systems that matter for its sustainable management—and she could put those features in a comparative context. These data helped farmers "locate" their challenges compared with other forests and irrigation systems. She and her colleagues screened over 500 case studies from around the world to create a data base of forty-four inshore fishing groups and forty-seven irrigation systems—data that included the actors, their strategies, the condition of the resource, and the rules in use. She created "a structured database called the Nepal Irrigation Institutions and Systems (NIIS) Database. We shared the design of this database with a number of colleagues who are deeply familiar with irrigation, and began to code the 135 case studies that we had collected from our trips to Nepal and from the published literature." Later she and her colleagues filled in missing data and added eighty more Farmer Managed Irrigation Systems (FMIS) to the data set.[14]

She could help farmers assess their management systems using quantitative data. For example, regarding irrigation systems, Ostrom and her colleagues assessed three performance measures: (1) their physical condition, (2) the quantity of water available to farmers at the tail end of a system at different seasons of the year, and (3) the agricultural productivity of the systems. After controlling for environmental differences among systems, she and her colleagues showed that irrigation systems governed by the farmers

themselves performed significantly better than government-managed systems on all three performance measures. (These findings made a difference
not only to the farmers but also to the Nepali government and international
development agencies.)

2. Case Studies of Success

Second, she could share with Nepalis specific examples from other countries of local people successfully designing and managing sustainable forest
policies and irrigation systems. There were also success stories from Nepal.
"Look at what these farmers did and how, and how much better their results
became. What do you think about that?"

3. Frameworks and Checklists

Third, she could in creative ways teach them about the economics of
common-pool resources. The simplifications and abstraction of an analytical
framework can help locals see dimensions that might be hidden. A model
can enable them to step back from their locally intense constructions of the
problems and opportunities. "You mean this problem isn't just of our particular families in our unique context? Of our culture and history and politics?
Or of Nepalis?"

These inputs—data, case studies, and frameworks—were then
supplemented with a checklist of design principles (see Table 10.1).[15]

And note how humbly she shared this knowledge. Ostrom had confidence
in the abilities of Nepalis, thus informed and inspired, to come up with creative and practical ideas. With specifics such as where to start and how. Her
"lessons" were not "here's the expert diagnosis, do this." Rather, she may have
hoped that farmers would respond this way:

> We're not alone in these challenges. Others have succeeded in meeting
> them. What they did, and some of the analytical principles we've learned,
> can help us rethink what we're doing and how we might do better. Data can
> help us monitor our progress. *We* are the key to doing better—not govern-
> ment, not international agencies, not even Elinor Ostrom.

And then, boldly and humbly, Ostrom worked with farmer groups over
time. She helped them install and improve their monitoring systems and incentive structures.

Table 10.1 Design Principles for Managing Common-Pool Resources

---

1A. User boundaries: Clear and locally understood boundaries between legitimate users and nonusers are present.

1B. Resource boundaries: Clear boundaries that separate a specific common-pool resource from a larger social-ecological system are present.

2A. Congruence with local conditions: Appropriation and provision rules are congruent with local social and environmental conditions.

2B. Appropriation and provision: Appropriation rules are congruent with provision rules; the distribution of costs is proportional to the distribution of benefits.

3. Collective-choice arrangements: Most individuals affected by a resource regime are authorized to participate in making and modifying its rules.

4A. Monitoring users: Individuals who are accountable to or are the users monitor the appropriation and provision levels of the users.

4B. Monitoring the resource: Individuals who are accountable to or are the users monitor the condition of the resource.

5. Graduated sanctions: Sanctions for rule violations start very low but become stronger if a user repeatedly violates a rule.

6. Conflict-resolution mechanisms: Rapid, low-cost, local arenas exist for resolving conflicts among users or with officials.

7. Minimal recognition of rights: The rights of local users to make their own rules are recognized by the government.

8. Nested enterprises: When a common-pool resource is closely connected to a larger social-ecological system, governance activities are organized in multiple nested layers.

Source: Michael Cox, Gwen Arnold, and Sergio Villamayor-Tomás. "A Review of Design Principles for Community-Based Natural Resource Management." *Ecology and Society* 15, no. 4 (2010): 38.

In her Nobel Prize lecture, Ostrom provided a generalization that most anthropologists would immediately recognize and approve: "Thus, it is not the general type of forest governance that is crucial in explaining forest conditions; rather, it is how a particular governance arrangement fits the local ecology, how specific rules are developed and adapted over time, and whether users consider the system to be legitimate and equitable." Notice how much further she went than just acknowledging those contingencies. She helped gather and assemble new data, found and publicized success stories, carefully studied the economic and ecological properties of common-pool resources, and created checklists and frameworks to distill things in usable form. And what she did and how made a profound difference to farmers in Nepal and, through her publications, around the world.

At the end of her Nobel lecture, Ostrom said there is more to learn:

We thus face the tough task of further developing our theories to help understand and predict when those involved in a common-pool resource dilemma will be able to self-organize and how various aspects of the broad context they face affect their strategies, the short-term success of their efforts, and the long-term robustness of their initial achievements. We need to develop a better theoretical understanding of human behavior as well as of the impact of the diverse contexts that humans face. (429)

What an invitation to the sorts of knowledge anthropologists, working with others, might provide—and how they might humbly but boldly do so.

Rethinking "Development"

Tania Murray Li distinguished three ways for anthropologists to engage with development.

1. Programming: working on interventions to improve social, economic, ecological, or other processes.
2. Critical engagement with programming. Being that person who continues to ask: What are the goals? Do we have the right treatments (policies, programs, projects . . .)? How are things being implemented, and what are the results?
3. Basic research: in her words, "the attempt to understand the world as it is, in all its diversity, complexity and flux."[16]

Li notes that each role is valuable; each also has its own dangers (even its own hubris). She also observes that, just as people and groups can apportion many identities, so anthropologists (and others) can move across the boundaries of the three roles.

Consider her first heading. Throughout this book, from the finance minister Don Fernando to the Burkinabe development expert Bernard Lédéa Ouédraogo, we have contemplated interactions between policy choices and cultural settings. Which, if ignored, could lead to failures. And which, we hoped, if correctly appreciated, could lead to better policies (programs, projects, designs, treatments . . .), as in the examples of chapter 8.

Now, let's expand our vision and go to Li's second and third categories, critical and basic research. In a fascinating paper, Li and James Ferguson note a worldwide phenomenon: more and more people lack "proper jobs."[17] They propose a kind of global ethnographic effort to get answers to ninety questions, which fall under these five categories: "What is and is not changing about work? What are the uses and meanings of land? How else—besides selling their labour or working the land—do people access livelihood resources? What are the emerging forms of social membership? How do people mobilize politically to make effective demands or to pursue systemic change?" (18–19). Reading through their queries is fascinating, because it reminds one of how little one knows about the answers to particular questions and forces one to ponder the linkages among them.

How to get the answers? And what to do with them if they suddenly appeared? The authors do not elaborate; their point is that we should begin with facts gathered across countries and cultures. But their paper concludes hopefully: "Grids of difference and similarity organized around a common set of questions are, at one level, descriptive devices. But if the questions we have posed are the right ones, they could contribute to a renewed global political-economic analysis of lives and livelihoods—one more adequate to our times than the one that begins, and too often ends, with the absence or presence of the 'proper job'" (20).

I agree. Thoroughly listing all the facts we would like to know is a useful discipline at the beginning of any research program. It helps us avoid a common syndrome, where we design our research around the data (or an answer) we already have rather than what (for various reasons) we wish we knew. Discussing with others the list of desired facts makes us aware of blind spots, presuppositions, *evidences invisibles*. And this, in turn, helps us together rethink what the goals and alternatives are and might be.

While looking for patterns, we should also examine the apparent exceptions. Do some countries or cultural groups "do better" than others in transforming jobs, alleviating employment shortcomings, enabling labor mobility, advancing the rights of various kinds of workers?[18] In these examples of "success"—as always, a contestable concept—what policies changed? What politics were involved? What were the roles of government, business, labor organizations, civil society, and political groups? And so forth. In carrying out such case studies of (relative) success, anthropologists have special skills in devising questions and gathering information.

The abiding point here is that we note the possibility of both big think and little think—indeed, of links among Li's three categories of "programming," critique, and basic research. What are the global phenomena of insufficient proper jobs? And how do they manifest themselves, here, there, with these people, with those other people? How does this knowledge help us rethink our goals and our alternatives? And how does stirring this pot of facts and issues help us "understand the world as it is, in all its diversity, complexity and flux"?

Anthropologists rightly complain that governments in their everyday work sideline big questions of constitutional arrangements, economic rights, cultural change, the patriarchy, and the like: "they are beyond this project's pay grade." Just as most business decisions take market conditions and legal restrictions as givens, so do "development projects" work within the status quo, even when change is the goal. It's important to note this limitation; might it also be important to go beyond it? Let's not just criticize others for failing to address, for example, "the conditions that position some groups to accumulate while others are impoverished" or for not providing "critical scrutiny of relations of production and appropriation"—let's show them how to do better.[19]

What I have in mind is cultural critique that lays out the deeper issues, reconsiders the goals of projects and business decisions accordingly, imagines different alternative courses of action, analyzes their effectiveness and costs and risks, and considers ways to share this knowledge to help foster a new politics and new channels of action. Invited to do so, encouraged to do so, perhaps anthropologists might undertake bold and humble research with their special knowledge-gathering techniques, which would help us rethink the ends and means of what we do.

What I'm suggesting here is programming with critique and creativity. A process that brings together outside and inside knowledge, in ways that kindle problem-solving and possibly partnerships. Beyond the important task of identifying how cultural features interact with particular projects, we're seeking new ways to think about goals (and risks), new kinds of alternatives, new and perhaps métisse ways to implement, and, as a result, new kinds of politics.

In this vein, let's turn to process. How might we marshal and share cultural (and other forms of) knowledge in ways that catalyze creativity?

Convening

The historian JoAnna Poblete studied a promising program for protecting local fisheries in American Sāmoa.[20] As in many poor countries, community fisheries were under pressure, to the point of collapse.[21] According to a 2000 report in American Sāmoa, "harvested species such as giant clams and parrotfish are overfished, and there is heavy fishing pressure on surgeonfish. Fewer and/or smaller groupers, snappers, and jacks are seen. Most village fishermen and elders believe that numbers of fish and shellfish have also declined." But five years after the start of the Community-Based Fisheries Management Program, an evaluation found that "the biomass status of the American Sāmoa bottomfish complex in 2005 was healthy" (116–117).

What led to this success, Poblete shows, was the ingenious and persistent combining of local knowledge and cultural appropriateness with outside resources and expertise. A key to

> the success of marine programs in American Sāmoa revolves around understanding and incorporating aspects of *fa'a Sāmoa* (the Sāmoan way of life). The inclusion of Sāmoan traditions and beliefs, such as *vā* (social relations) and *vā fealoa'i* (social respect), in the process of creating rules and procedures have enabled the successful implementation of American-style industry, government, and environmental expectations and policies in the region. (136)

As we saw in the 6-S organization in West Africa: "The underlying idea is to analyze a situation by comparing the views of all the members of the community as well as the external actors to identify (jointly) the reasons why existing organizations have seized up, and to support (without any preconceived design) the measures and reforms that the group deems both feasible and desirable."[22]

What I call *convening* brings together these capabilities in a safe space through a pragmatic process. Those convened have different if overlapping objectives, different if overlapping capabilities, and different if overlapping information about the state of the world and about if-then relationships. They are not fully aware of each other's objectives, capabilities, or information; they do not fully understand their strategic interrelations. Convening brings together their strengths and inspires them to address their challenges with new information, examples, and frameworks.

The kinds of convening recommended here provides participants with the following:

1. Data, especially data that help people "get on the same page" about the contexts and the challenges. Data-rich discussions help build trust, particularly about controversial issues.
2. An example of success on a similar problem in another setting, emphasizing what was done and how.
3. A framework for understanding the policy issues and the role of cultural factors in addressing alternatives. The framework or checklist conveys principles and often provides participants with a new way of conceptualizing the policy problem.
4. An imaginary news story of success five years from now. Participants read the news story aloud, then ponder together what steps might lead from now to then. The imaginary news story stimulates creative problem-solving.

In a convening, the intellectual problem of culture and development is transformed. The challenge is not to apply some complete culture by policy by outcomes model to the local situation; not to carry out a detailed ethnographic study; certainly not to be the outside expert who does the diagnosis and pronounces what should be done. The agenda is instead how to discover, how to be more creative about, the problems on the ground, the objectives, the alternatives, and the constraints—and to do so together. On this view, policy analysis (including cultural aspects) provides not so much a set of answers that decision-makers or citizens should adopt and bureaucrats should implement, but instead data, outside examples, and frameworks that help locals enrich their appreciation of alternatives and consequences.[23]

Dream Boldly

Might such an approach help overcome the warranted reluctance of many anthropologists to engage with development policies and projects? They worry (with some reason) that standard ways of applying anthropology to development means the following:

- That you have to be part of a "technified," partial "theory of change" that ignores lofty ideals, deep political causes, and on-the-ground realities.

- That you have to "learn about the people," then report on them in ways that serve power structures and limited-budget, limited-imagination endeavors.
- That you have to be complicit with blaming the victims for "failures." The victims can be countries as well as local communities: they are conveniently labeled corrupt, inefficient, ignorant.

Applying cultural knowledge to development activities is felt to be selling out. Sympathize with Tania Murray Li's horror at participating in a discussion of a forestry project in which an Indonesian official blithely suggested assassinating ten mobsters who were illegally logging (all of whom happened to be Chinese-Indonesians, which the official was not).[24] Or with Jean-Pierre Olivier de Sardan's confronting "traveling projects," which arrive from development agencies with a kind of blueprint (maybe with some tinkering based on a survey and a focus group), and which are unable to see what he, as an anthropologist, perceives: the steadfast resistance of locals seeking both good ends (equality) and bad ones (corruption), and therefore the to-him-predictable project failures.[25] Or with Marc-Éric Gruénais' conviction that what (national and international) development agencies need simply doesn't fit with what anthropologists can or should provide.[26]

Consider, too, the Swiss anthropologist Annick Tonti's remark that the culture she didn't understand as an anthropologist in a development project wasn't the locals. "I realized that I had no difficulties in communicating with the Bangladeshis, but that I had great difficulties in speaking with the economists, with whom I had to work in that very office. I wasn't really able to communicate with the technicians or engineers, who were involved in our different projects. Perhaps worst of all, I had no idea about development management."[27]

But as we have seen, something different could and should be on offer:

- Applications where a subtle appreciation of cultural texts leads to fewer cultural misunderstandings. Serves as an antidote to poisonous texts in negotiations. Helps unpack different possibilities for "taking indigenous organizations and networks into account."
- Theory-light, nonquantitative, but still scientific ways to adjust to cultural diversity. In the design of stoves and road signs and housing for the poorest. In agroforestry. In tailoring pedagogies to local cultural

knowledge and learning styles. In helping Indigenous nations align their governance and policies to their traditions. In collecting data relatively quickly and using checklists in ways that enable rather than brand or condemn.

- Ways to partner with local organizations that respect their autonomy and strengths and also work with them on their weaknesses, which leads to their making better choices, as in the 6-S initiative in West Africa.
- And, in my dream world, using cultural knowledge as part of a new paradigm of policy analysis and evaluation. One that goes beyond "local participation" and never utters "buy-in." One that combines the best of international knowledge and local knowledge, with the goal of catalyzing creativity and problem-solving.

In this chapter, we saw an example of that dream with Elinor Ostrom and the management of common-pool resources in Nepal. She combined (a) quantitative data, case studies, and analytical models; and (b) the anthropologist's traditional virtues of working with local people with acumen and respect. The metaphor is soil science, as opposed to social science.[28]

That's my dream for policy analysis as well as for the application of anthropological wisdom. And for other dreamers out there, those who long to eschew "development" for a whole different paradigm. Who would love to help launch a new politics, or several. Or to enable a "pluriverse," with epistemologies from the Global South, with knowledge born in opposition and cultural mosaics. For you, may I suggest reaffirming and applying several classical methods of anthropology?

1. Help us countenance diverse ways of life as ways to "decenter" dominant paradigms. In James Ferguson's words, "to see in the noncapitalist social forms that anthropologists have so often studied not only historical data but concrete forms of political inspiration."[29] We may thereby more readily see the shallowness of "development."[30] To understand how it may be, in the trope of Marshall Sahlins, that hunters and gatherers "have affluent economies, their absolute poverty notwithstanding."[31]

2. Combine theoretical explorations with detailed local description. As Clifford Geertz emphasized, "the characteristic intellectual movement" of anthropology can be, should be, "a constant dialectical tacking between the most local of local detail and the most global of global structure in such a way as to bring them into simultaneous view."[32]

3. Carry out more studies of (relative) "success" at the local level, as recommended by Jean-Pierre Olivier de Sardan, Mahaman Tahirou Ali Bako, and Abdoutan Harouna:

> The research we have carried out over the last 20 years at the heart of the health and education systems in Niger have led us to encounter various reformatory professionals working on the frontline and providing services to users. These "admirable exceptions" attempt to improve the everyday operation of schools and health centres without resources, publicity or support, and sometimes even against the wishes of their superiors. They invent local solutions. They establish new practical norms or adapt those already in place. They do not adhere rigorously to the wide range of official norms in force. Their "good practice" is not the good practice of the "best students" of the international organizations, instead it involves innovations and improvements that are primarily adapted to the real working contexts and remain invisible to the experts in most cases. In our view, making them visible, documenting these multiple, unobtrusive reforms, is a priority task for anthropological research.[33]

4. Investigate ethnographically radical reformulations of development. For example, for those of us who dream of a new politics based on different bases for sharing other than private property rights and social welfare programs, have a careful look at the so-called Islamic State and at high-fervor communist experiments. For those of us who dream of different systems of education other than those based on Western or Sinic academic merit, review what happened during the Cultural Revolution in China.[34] For those of us who advocate revolutionary efforts to dismantle race and caste, judiciously analyze the outcomes of ethnic policies in the Soviet Union and preferential treatment in India and Malaysia.

5. Critically analyze contemporary cultural anthropology's oppositional texts and dreams. By analogy: classic works of anthropology have been "deconstructed," revealing the rhetorical techniques used to gain authority, the hidden assumptions (often sexist and culturalist despite all their purported liberalism), and the weaknesses of empirical argument.[35] More than three decades ago, James Clifford noted that "the stance of the ethnographer who speaks as an insider on behalf of his or her people is a familiar one; it is a stock role of the ethnographic

liberal."[36] How about, today, deconstructing the stock role of the ethnographic radical? Unpack the monolithic renderings of "dominant paradigms" and "governmentality" in contrast to infinitely varied local realities. Speculate about the sources and meanings of being "at once cynical about the 'situation of social action' and utopian about the 'ends of social action.' "[37]

What Manifesto?

This book is a manifesto for doing better in development by taking culture into account. The word "manifesto" may suggest a slap in the face: its etymology combines the hand (*manus*) and offense (*fendere*). Manifestos are often defined by what they decry, a quality Mary Ann Caws called their "againstness." A manifesto, she says, "is peculiar and angry, quirky, or downright crazed. Always opposed to something, particular or general, it has not only to be striking but to stand up straight."[38] And manifestos can be rude. The "Dada Cannibalistic Manifesto" (1920) began, "You are all accused. Stand up."[39]

Not my message here (and you may be seated). Nor do I want to hector. Lee Scrivner concluded his "manifesto on manifestos" with a persuasive warning: "After reviewing these most recent manifestos, one feels that erasure is the best antidote for them. And with such conclusions, I feel that I can only advise such a rule of thumb for manifestos in general; they should never explicitly or implicitly advise others on what they should or shouldn't do, say or believe."[40]

Let's rather focus on inspiration and hope. The Canadian photographer Freeman Patterson begins his art statement this way:

> Every artist is, first of all, a craftperson thoroughly knowledgeable about the materials, tools, and techniques of his or her particular medium and skilled in using many of them.
>
> However, in my view, no amount of technical knowledge and competence is, of itself, sufficient to make a craftperson into an artist. That requires caring—passionate caring about ultimate things.[41]

Or consider the "Metamodernist Manifesto."[42] "We see this manifesto as a kind of informed naivety, a pragmatic idealism, a moderate fanaticism, oscillating between sincerity and irony, deconstruction and construction, apathy and affect, attempting to attain some sort of transcendent position, *as if* such a thing were within our grasp."[43]

In a similar spirit, this culture and development manifesto is not advising anthropologists to be economists, nor economists to be anthropologists. It is not (at least, not primarily) saying "be interdisciplinary." It is proposing—and I hope illustrating—how we all might become even more engaged, more constructive, bolder, humbler. Technically equipped and passionately caring. And "pragmatically idealistic."

This manifesto shows how we can look at the intersections among cultural settings, local choices, and development outcomes. Yes, as social scientists, and also in the hands-on and helpful manner of soil scientists. It's not enough simply to aver that "culture matters." At the end of a long review of the literature on culture and development, a distinguished economist declares:

> A first and very important conclusion is that taking culture on board means first of all to take into account the effects of different cultures when designing development policies. One should take cultures as given and see what are the best development policies given the prevailing culture. Particular policies or institutional reforms must be tailored to fit the existing cultural environment. This is how they work best.[44]

Despite a barrage of cross-references for virtually every assertion in the body of his remarkably thorough review, in this "policy conclusion" the author provides no examples of such tailoring. He's not alone. Throughout the book, we've seen many instances of saying that culture matters—and in effect leaving it there. The manifesto says we should do much more: show how to assess differing cultural strengths and then take advantage of them, with the help of theoretical frameworks and real-world examples.

The culture and development manifesto declares the importance of identifying success stories by combining quantitative methods to find them and qualitative methods to understand their details—and then sharing the stories in ways that people can see *how*, not just *that*, progress occurred. The resulting case studies can remind us of vital though often overlooked dimensions, including cultural settings. They can teach us, as ethnographies also can, about the importance of context, about the yin and yang of similarity and difference. And they can inspire our imaginations: "I never would have thought of doing that," or "I love the way they interpreted this."

A good manifesto expresses hope—in this instance, that convening new combinations of local knowledge and international knowledge by sharing data, examples of surprising success, and checklists can help us reframe what we're trying to do and how.

We can express that hope, because we've seen it work.

Notes

Chapter 1

1. In flights of theorizing, "culture" can encompass everything. "From the social work perspective, culture is far more than one or more dominant set of rules or ways of guiding society. Within social work, culture is viewed as a fundamental aspect of every relationship or system, at every social level. In other words, culture is the 'ideas, images, and meanings' as well as 'customs, habits, skills, technology, arts, values, ideology, science and . . . behavior of a group of people in a specific time period.'" Lois H. Silverman, *The Social Work of Museums* (Oxford and New York: Routledge, 2010), 37–38.

2. William Graham Sumner, *Folkways: A Study of the Sociological Importance of Usages, Manners, Customs, Mores, and Morals* (Boston: Ginn, 1899), iv.

3. Victor C. de Munck and Giovanni Bennardo, "Disciplining Culture: A Sociocognitive Approach," *Current Anthropology* 60, no. 2 (2019): 174, https://doi.org/10.1086/702470.

4. Silvia Marcos, "We Come to Ask for Justice, Not Crumbs," in *Indigenous Peoples and the Modern State*, ed. Duane Champagne, Karen Jo Torjesen, and Susan Steiner (Walnut Creek, CA: AltaMira Press, 2005), 101, translation by Marcos. "Being an Indian," Marcos noted, "showing the signs of this identity (that is, speaking an indigenous language and acting following Indian customs) was—and to a large extent still is—a sign of 'backwardness' and 'ignorance' and a reason for shame" (97).

5. Jean-Emmanuel Pondi, *Repenser le Développement à Partir de l'Afrique* (Yaoundé: Éditions Afrédit, 2011), book jacket. Translations here and elsewhere are mine unless otherwise noted.

6. Thandika Mkanwilli, "Running While Others Walk: Knowledge and the Challenge of Africa's Development," *African Development* 36, no. 2 (2011): 7, 6, 9.

7. James Ferguson, *The Anti-Politics Machine: "Development," Depoliticization, and Bureaucratic Power in Lesotho* (Minneapolis and London: University of Minnesota Press, 1994), 284.

8. Jean-Philippe Venot and Gert Jan Veldwisch, "Sociotechnical Myths in Development," *Anthropologie et Développment* 46–47 (2017): 17.

9. "The extraordinary thing about Developmentspeak is that it is simultaneously descriptive and normative, concrete and yet aspirational, intuitive and clunkily pedestrian, capable of expressing the most deeply held convictions or of being simply 'full of sound and fury, signifying nothing.' This very elasticity makes it almost the ideal postmodern medium, even as it embodies a modernizing agenda." Andrea Cornwall and Deborah Eade, eds. *Deconstructing Development Discourse: Buzzwords and Fuzzwords*

(Rugby, UK: Practical Action, 2010), ix. A companion volume on *Deconstructing Deconstructionist Discourse* might document, with many of the same pejorative adjectives, something called Postmodernspeak, with its bricolage, commoning/uncommoning, decentering, decolonial feminism, discourses, governmentality, hegemony, imbrication, mestizaje, narratives, pluriverse, scientism, even texts.

10. Arturo Escobar, *Encountering Development: The Making and Unmaking of the Third World* (Princeton, NJ: Princeton University Press, 2012).

11. In a remarkable mashup of metaphors, the editors of a 2010 volume entitled *Reconsidering Culture and Poverty* put it this way: "Culture was a 'third rail' in scholarship on poverty for so long that it became essentially a black box, one now ripe for reopening." Mario Luis Small, David J. Harding, and Michèle Lamont, "Reconsidering Culture and Poverty," *The Annals of the American Academy of Political and Social Science* 629 (May 2010): 10.

12. Felix Giuliagno, "Nobel Prize Winner Angus Deaton Shares 3 Big Ideas," *Financial Times*, October 12, 2015, http://www.ft.com/intl/cms/s/0/b60c2e76-70f0-11e5-ad6d-f4ed76f0900a.html#axzz423eMMu8n.

13. Tania Murray Li, *Land's End: Capitalist Relations on an Indigenous Frontier* (Durham, NC: Duke University Press, 2014), 179. "Among the many elements I have identified, three were especially important: the experience of social stigma, livelihood insecurity, and a desire for access to the roads and schools highlanders associated with a modern village life" (57).

14. Tania Murray Li, "After Development: Surplus Labor and the Politics of Entitlement." *Development and Change* 48, no. 6 (Nov. 2017): 1247, https://doi.org/10.1111./dech.12344.

15. Arjun Appadurai, *The Future as Cultural Fact: Essays on the Global Condition* (London: Verso, 2013), 292.

16. Tshering Tobgay, "The First Ten Years of Democracy: Reflections from Bhutan," lecture at Oxford University, January 9, 2019, https://www.youtube.com/watch?v=HSrJGjkgaPg @52:27, @55:25.

17. Mkandawire, "Running While Others Walk," 13.

18. Ferguson, *The Anti-Politics Machine*, 186, 187, 187–188.

Chapter 2

1. Portions of the following are adapted from *Tropical Gangsters* (New York: Basic Books, 1990) and *Tropical Gangsters II: Adventures in Development in the World's Poorest Places* (Amazon KDP Books, 2013).

2. Private land registration, often institutionally and politically difficult, pays productivity and income dividends because more secure tenure leads to more investment. Steven Lawry, Cyrus Samii, Ruth Hall, Aaron Leopold, Donna Hornby, and Farai Mtero, "The Impact of Land Property Rights Interventions on Investment and Agricultural Productivity in Developing Countries: A Systematic Review," *Journal of Development Effectiveness* 9, no. 1 (January 2017): 61–68. See also Timothy

Besley and Maitreesh Ghatak, "Property Rights and Economic Development," in *Handbook of Development Economics*, vol. 5, ed. Dani Rodrik and Mark Rosenzweig (Amsterdam: Elsevier, 2010), 4525–4595.

3. Claude Ake, "Building on the Indigenous," in United Nations Economic Commission for Africa, *International Conference on Popular Participation in the Recovery and Development Process in Africa* (Addis Ababa: United Nations Economic Commission for Africa, 1990), 19. Ake concluded that "building on the indigenous is the necessary condition for self-reliant development to which there is now no alternative. The evidence is in: dependent development has failed. . . . To all appearances, the failure is irreversible" (21).

4. Piet Buijsrogge, *Initiatives Paysannes en Afrique de L'Ouest* (Paris: L'Harmattan, 1989), 25.

5. Carlos Fuentes, "La Socialización de la Política desde Abajo," *Ventana* (Nicaragua), no. 446 (November 12, 1990): 8–9.

6. Boaventura de Sousa Santos, *The End of the Cognitive Empire: The Coming of Age of Epistemologies of the South* (Durham and London: Duke University Press, 2018), 3, 8.

7. T. Scarlett Epstein, "How Can Ethnology Help to Promote Third World Development?," in *Ethnologische Beiträge zur Entwicklungspolitik 2*, ed. Frank Bliss and Michael Schönhuth (Bonn: Politischer Arbeitskreis Schulen, 1990), 3.

Chapter 3

1. Balandier recounted his crucial encounter with Camus, whom *he* compared to Bogart (151). Balandier was eager for Camus's opinion of his new novel. "The judgment that most perturbed me was that of Albert Camus. I invited him to dinner, along with Leiris, in the Latin Quarter. He spoke to me little of my book, incited me to continue, to surmount the redoubtable obstacle of the second try, after which he added indifferently, 'It's not the kind of work I would loan to my wife.' I was left stupefied." Balandier did make a second try at a novel—about Africa—but it was rejected, and soon he was in Africa doing anthropology. Georges Balandier, *Histoire d'Autres* (Paris: Stock, 1977), 154.

2. Georges Balandier, ed. *Étude Comparée des Motivations et Stimulations Économiques en Milieu Coutumier et en Milieu "Moderniste" dans le Cadre des Pays Dits "Sous-développés."* Bureau International de Recherche sur les Sociales du Progrès Technique (BIRISPT)/6-/IS.1/54 (Paris: Conseil International des Sciences Sociales, 1954). Balandier was the rapporteur.

3. Gillian Tett, *The Silo Effect: The Peril of Expertise and the Promise of Breaking Down Barriers* (New York: Simon & Schuster, 2015), 48.

4. Pierre Bourdieu, *The Social Structures of the Economy*, trans. Chris Turner (Cambridge, MA: Polity Press, 2005), 4, 5, 7.

5. Bourdieu, *The Social Structures of the Economy*, 223, 228, 6.

6. Bourdieu, *The Social Structures of the Economy*, 209.

7. Bourdieu, *The Social Structures of the Economy*, 2.

8. Francis Fukuyama, "Social Capital and Development: The Coming Agenda," *SAIS Review* 22, no. 1 (Winter–Spring 2002): 27, 23–37.

9. David B. Kronenfeld, *Culture as a System: How We Know the Meaning and Significance of What We Do and Say* (London and New York: Routledge, 2018), 5. "Culture here is a system of concepts, structures, and relations that groups of people use to organize and interpret their experienced worlds—including their behavior, their relationships, and the personalities, apparent beliefs, values, and so forth of others" (4).

10. Interviewed in Thomas A. Bass, *Camping with the Prince and Other Tales of Science in Africa* (Boston: Houghton Mifflin, 1990), 57–59.

11. Jean-Pierre Olivier de Sardan, *Anthropology and Development: Understanding Contemporary Social Change*, trans. Antoinette Tidjani Alou (London and New York: Zed Books, 2005), 204.

12. Ali A. Mazrui, *Cultural Forces in World Politics* (London: James Currey, 1990), 1, 4.

13. Daniel Etounga-Manguelle, *L'Afrique: A-t-elle Besoin d'un Programme d'Adjustement Culturel?* (Ivry-sur-Seine: Éditions Nouvelles du Sud, 1990), 82.

14. Daniel Etounga-Manguelle, *Vers Une Société Responsable: Le Cas de l'Afrique* (Paris: L'Harmattan, 2009), 12.

15. Axelle Kabou, *Et Si L'Afrique Refusait le Développement?* (Paris: L'Harmattan, 1991).

16. Vernon W. Ruttan, "What Happened to Political Development?," *Economic Development and Cultural Change* 39, no. 2 (Jan. 1991): 276. In contrast to political science, Ruttan says, where such statements are common, "it would be hard to find a leading scholar in the field of development economics who would commit himself or herself in print to the proposition that 'in terms of explaining different patterns of political and economic development . . . a central variable is culture—the subjective attitudes, beliefs, and values prevalent among the dominant groups in the society'" (276, citing Samuel Huntington).

17. Takeo Doi, *The Anatomy of Dependence* (Tokyo: Kodansha International, 1973).

18. Richard Lynn and Susan Hampson, "The Rise of National Intelligence: Evidence from Britain, Japan and the U.S.A.," *Personality and Individual Differences* 7, no. 1 (1986): 30, https://doi.org/10.1016/0191-8869(86)90104-2. See also Garrett Jones, *Hive Mind: How Your Nation's IQ Matters So Much More Than Your Own* (Stanford: Stanford University Press, 2015).

19. Enrico Spolaore and Romain Wacziarg, "Long-term Barriers to Economic Development," in *Handbook of Economic Growth*, ed. Philippe Aghion and Steven N. Durlauf (Amsterdam: Elsevier, 2014), 121–176. A classic debater's brief is provided by Albert O. Hirschman, "Obstacles to Development: A Classification and a Quasi-vanishing Act," *Economic Development and Cultural Change* 13, no. 4 (July 1965), Part 1: 385–393.

20. Joyee Deb, "Cooperation and Community Responsibility," *Journal of Political Economy* 128, no. 5 (May 2020): 1976–2009, https://doi.org/10.1086/705671; Richard A. Posner, "A Theory of Primitive Society, with Special Reference to Law," *The Journal of Law & Economics* 23, no. 1 (Apr. 1980): 1–53, https://chicagounbound.uchicago.edu/jle/vol23/iss1/2.

21. Li, *Land's End*, 15.

22. Cited by Helen Tilley, *Africa as a Living Laboratory: Empire, Development, and the Problem of Scientific Knowledge, 1870–1950* (Chicago: University of Chicago Press, 2011), 268.

23. Dele Olowu, "African Economic Performance: Current Programs and Future Failures," in *The Failure of the Centralized State: Institutions and Self-Governance in Africa*, ed. James S. Wunsch and Dele Olowu (Boulder, CO: Westview, 1990), 117.

24. Gustavo Canavire-Bacarreza, Jorge Martínez-Vázquez, and Bauyrzhan Yedgenov, "Identifying and Disentangling the Impact of Fiscal Decentralization on Economic Growth" (Working Paper 19–03, International Center for Public Policy, Atlanta: Georgia State University, 2019).

25. Robert Klitgaard, *Adjusting to Reality: Beyond "State vs. Market" in Economic Development* (San Francisco: ICS Press and International Center for Economic Growth), chap. 9.

26. Robert D. Putnam, Robert Leonardi, and Raffaela Nanetti, *Making Democracy Work: Civic Traditions in Modern Italy* (Princeton, NJ: Princeton University Press, 1994).

27. Christiaan Grootaert and Thierry van Bastelaer, "Conclusion: Measuring Impact and Drawing Policy Conclusions," in *The Role of Social Capital in Development*, ed. Christiaan Grootaert and Thierry van Bastelaer (Cambridge: Cambridge University Press, 2002), 348.

28. For example, in his "provisional notes" on social capital, Bourdieu wrote:

   > Social capital is the set of current or potential resources that are linked to the possession of a sustainable network of more or less institutionalized relationships of mutual acquaintance and recognition; or, in other words, belonging to a group as a set of agents who are not only endowed with common properties (likely to be perceived by the observer, by others or by themselves) but are also united by permanent and useful links.

   Pierre Bourdieu, "Le Capital Social: Notes Provisoires," *Actes de la Recherche en Sciences Sociales*, no. 31 (Jan. 1980): 1.

29. Frances Cleaver, "The Inequality of Social Capital and the Reproduction of Chronic Poverty," *World Development* 33, no. 6 (Jun 2005): 895.

30. Katherine N. Rankin, "Social Capital, Microfinance, and the Politics of Development," *Feminist Economics* 8, no. 1 (Jan. 2002): 1–24.

31. Anthony Bebbington, "Social Capital and Development Studies, II: Can Bourdieu Travel to Policy?," *Progress in Development Studies* 7, no. 2 (2007): 160.

32. Joseph Henrich, *The Secret of Our Success: How Culture Is Driving Human Evolution, Domesticating Our Species, and Making Us Smarter* (Princeton, NJ and Oxford: Princeton University Press, 2016).

33. David Morawetz, *Why the Emperor's Clothes Are Not Made in Colombia: A Case Study in Latin American and East Asian Manufactured Exports* (New York: Oxford University Press, 1981), chap. 7.

34. Thomas Sowell, *Migrations and Cultures: A World View* (New York: Basic Books, 1997).

35. David L. Szanton, *Estancia in Transition: Economic Growth in a Rural Philippine Community* (Manila: Ateneo de Manila University Press, 1971).

36. Personal communication, 1993. See also his "Contingent Moralities: Social and Economic Investment in a Philippine Fishing Town," in *Market Cultures: Society and Morality in the New Asian Capitalisms*, ed. Robert W. Hefner (Oxford and New York: Routledge, 2018), 257–267.

37. Sarah Percy, "What Makes a Norm Robust: The Norm Against Female Combat," *Journal of Global Security Studies* 4, no. 1 (Jan. 2019): 123–138.

38. Henrich, *The Secret of Our Success*, 328.

39. Polly Hill, *Development Economics on Trial: The Anthropological Case for a Prosecution* (Cambridge: Cambridge University Press, 1986), xi.

40. Jean-Pierre Olivier de Sardan, "La Manne, les Normes et les Soupçons: Les Contradictions de L'aide Vue d'en Bas," *Revue Tiers Monde* 219, no. 3 (2014): 50, https://doi.org/10.3917/rtm.219.0197.

41. Tania Murray Li, *The Will to Improve: Governability, Development, and the Practice of Politics* (Durham, NC: Duke University Press, 2007), 3–4.

42. Tim Ingold, *Anthropology: Why It Matters* (Cambridge, UK: Polity Press, 2018).

43. Robert M. Wulff and Shirley J. Fiske, "Introduction," in *Anthropological Praxis: Translating Knowledge into Action*, ed. Robert M. Wulff and Shirley J. Fiske (Boulder, CO: Westview, 1987), 10.

44. John van Willigen, Barbara Rylko-Bauer, and Ann McElroy, "Preface," in *Making Our Research Useful: Case Studies in the Utilization of Anthropological Knowledge*, ed. John van Willigen, Barbara Rylko-Bauer, and Ann McElroy (Boulder, CO: Westview, 1989), xi.

45. Roger Bastide, *Anthropologie Appliquée* (Paris: Payot, 1971), 142.

46. Gustaaf Houtman, "Interview with Maurice Bloch," *Anthropology Today* 4, no. 1 (1988): 19.

47. Robert Borofsky, *An Anthropology of Anthropology* (Kailua, HI: Center for Public Anthropology, 2019), 1. Open access: https://books.publicanthropology.org/an-anthropology-of-anthropology.pdf.

Chapter 4

1. Marcel Mauss, *Manuel d'Ethnographie* (Paris: Payot, 1947).

2. Cited in Tilley, *Africa as a Living Laboratory*, 270, 268, 269.

3. Horowitz, "Development Anthropology in the United States," 193.

4. Marvin Harris, *Cultural Materialism: The Struggle for a Science of Culture* (New York: Vintage, 1980), 235.

5. George E. Marcus and Michael M. J. Fischer, *Anthropology as Cultural Critique: An Experimental Moment in the Human Sciences* (Chicago: University of Chicago Press, 1986), 19.

6. Katy Gardner and David Lewis, *Anthropology and Development: Challenges for the Twenty-First Century* (London: Pluto Press, 2015), 91.

7. "Most leading departments of anthropology in the United States provide no formal (and very little informal) training in fieldwork methods. . . . Preparation for anthropologists, in Britain at least, . . . has too easily relied on the notion of 'instinct,' ideally detached interaction but in practice an open-ended approach."

Judith Okely, *Anthropological Practice: Fieldwork and the Ethnographic Method* (London: Bloomsbury Academic, 2013), 4, 6.

8. "The veterans boasted that they had gone into the field without any guidance or, at best, with risible and conflicting pieces of advice on matters of etiquette. The great ethnographer, Edward Evans-Pritchard, claimed that he was told by his supervisor Charles Seligman to keep his hands off the local girls, while Malinowski advised him to take a native mistress as soon as possible." Adam Kuper, "Anthropology and Anthropologists Forty Years On," *Anthropology of This Century* no. 11 (Oct. 2014), http://aotcpress.com/articles/anthropology-anthropologists-forty-years/.

9. Okely, *Anthropological Practice*, 3.

10. Clifford Geertz, *The Interpretation of Cultures* (New York: Basic Books, 1973), 22, 23.

11. "I like the way Indians look, the way they walk, the polite 'buenas tardes' they fling one on the trail; their dignity I like, their utter lack of pretense, their disregard of clocks, the tilt of their sombreros, and the fling of the sarape across the shoulder. Above all I like their magnificent inertia, against which neither Spain nor Europe nor western civilization has prevailed." Stuart Chase, *Mexico: A Tale of Two Civilizations* (New York: Macmillan, 1931), 304.

12. "They [peasants] do not reject the idea of planning as wicked: they simply do not have the category. . . . To plan a future state of affairs which is radically different from the present is to us quite rational. But those who think in terms of the round of time see such changes as coming from mystical forces like fate, or luck, or witchcraft or acts of God, and to plan for such events makes nonsense." F. G. Bailey, "The Peasant View of a Bad Life," in *Peasants and Peasant Societies*, ed. Teodor Shann (Middlesex: Penguin, 1971), 315, 316.

13. Sherry B. Ortner, "Dark Anthropology and Its Others: Theory Since the 80s," *HAU: Journal of Ethnographic Theory* 6, no. 1 (2016): 47–73.

14. Boaventura de Sousa Santos and César A. Rodríguez-Garavito, "Introduction: Expanding the Economic Canon and Searching for Alternatives to Neoliberal Globalization," in *Another Production Is Possible: Beyond the Capitalist Canon*, ed. Boaventura de Sousa Santos (London and New York: Verso, 2006), xxiii.

15. Aimee Meredith Cox, *Shapeshifters: Black Girls and the Choreography of Citizenship* (Durham, NC: Duke University Press, 2015).

16. Sherry B. Ortner, "Practicing Engaged Anthropology," *Anthropology of This Century* 25 (May 2019): no page numbers in the online version, http://aotcpress.com/ar-ticles/practicing-engaged-anthropology/; referring to Anna Lowenhaupt Tsing, *The Mushroom at the End of the World: On the Possibility of Life in Capitalist Ruins* (Princeton, NJ: Princeton University Press, 2015).

17. Marc-Éric Gruénais and Fatoumata Ouattara, "De L'Anthropologie dans un Projet de Santé Maternelle," in *Accompagner les Femmes à la Maternité au Burkina Faso: Anthropologie et Santé Publique dans un Projet D'Amélioration des Soins Obstétricaux*, ed. Fatoumata Ouattara, Marc-Éric Gruénais, Fabienne Richard, and Charlemagne Ouédraogo (Paris: L'Harmattan, 2016), 32–33.

18. Arturo Escobar, *Designs for the Pluriverse: Radical Interdependence, Autonomy, and the Making of Worlds* (Durham and London: Duke University Press, 2018), 6, 221, 224.

19. Edward F. Fischer, *The Good Life: Aspiration, Dignity, and the Anthropology of Wellbeing* (Stanford: Stanford University Press, 2014), 19.

20. Jonas L. Tinius and Johannes Lenhard, "'Economy, Happiness, and the Good Life:' An Interview with Edward F. Fischer," *King's Review*, December, 26, 2017, https://www.kingsreview.co.uk/27dec_jl_.

21. Ulf Hannerz, *Anthropology's World: Life in a Twenty-First Century Discipline* (London: Pluto Press, 2010), 49.

22. Jonathan Lanman, Hugh Turpin, and Samuel Ward, "Causes, Effects, and the 'Mush' of Culture," *Current Anthropology* 60, no. 2 (Apr. 2019): 188.

23. James Ferguson and Tania Murray Li, "Beyond the "Proper Job": Political-Economic Analysis after the Century of Labouring Man" (PLAAS Working Paper 51, Cape Town: University of the Western Cape, April 2018), 4.

24. Marcel Mauss, "Divisions et Proportions des Divisions de la Sociologie," *Année Sociologique*, Nouvelle Serie, vol. 2 (1927), in Mauss, *Oeuvres*, Vol. 3, edited by Victor Karkady (Paris: Éditions de Minuit, 1969), 239, 242, 243–244.

25. Maarja Kaaristo and Maurice Bloch, "The Reluctant Anthropologist. An Interview with Maurice Bloch." *Eurozine*, February 28, 2008, https://www.researchgate.net/publication/273451893_The_Reluctant_Anthropologist_An_Interview_with_Maurice_Bloch.

26. James Ferguson, *The Anti-Politics Machine: "Development," Depoliticization, and Bureaucratic Power in Lesotho* (Minneapolis and London: University of Minnesota Press, 1994).

27. Escobar, *Encountering Development*.

28. Among other of his works, see Jean-Pierre Olivier de Sardan, "La Manne, les Normes et les Soupçons: Les Contradictions de L'aide Vue d'en Bas," *Revue Tiers Monde* 219, no. 3 (2014): 197–215.

29. Tania Murray Li, *The Will to Improve: Governability, Development, and the Practice of Politics* (Durham, NC: Duke University Press, 2007).

30. Annick Tonti, "The Model of Swiss Development Cooperation," in *The Socio-Cultural Dimension in Development: The Contribution of Sociologists and Social Anthropologists to the Work of Development Agencies*, ed. Michael Schönhuth. Sonderpublikation der GTZ, no. 249 (Eschborn, Germany: Deutsche Gesellschaft für Technische, 1991), 54.

31. Gérard Lenclud, "La Question de L'application dans la Tradition Anthropologique Française," in *Les Applications de L'anthropologie: Un Essai de Réflexion Collective depuis la France*, ed. Jean-François Baré (Paris: Éditions Karthala, 1995), 84.

32. Mondher Kilani, "Anthropologie du Développement ou Développement de L'anthropologie? Quelques Réflexions Critiques," in *La Culture, Otage du Développement?* ed. Gilbert Rist (Paris: L'Harmattan, 1994), 20.

33. Thierry Berche, *Anthropologie et Santé Publique en Pays Dogon* (Paris: Karthala, 1998), 34.

34. Marc-Éric Gruénais, "L'anthropologie Sociale: Est-elle Inapplicable?," *Bulletin de l'APAD* (2012): 34–36, https://journals.openedition.org/apad/4109.

35. Clifford Geertz, "Distinguished Lecture: Anti Anti-Relativism," *American Anthropologist* 86, no. 2 (1984): 276, 275.

36. Michael M. Horowitz, "Development Anthropology in the United States," in *Ethnologische Beiträge zur Entwicklungspolitik 2,* ed. Frank Bliss and Michael Schönhuth (Bonn: Politischer Arbeitskreis Schulen, 1990), 190–191.

37. Hill, *Development Economics on Trial,* 66. Economists, too, have their envies: those chaps with the "dirty ankles" (in the anthropologist Parker Shipton's phrase) *know* in ways that we don't. "It is the insistence on descriptive realism that makes the use of these ethnographic studies so potentially attractive. . . . Relatively few economists have been willing to make the investment in time needed to generate the information to assure a reasonably adequate understanding of even economic relations at the village or community level." Vernon W. Ruttan, "Cultural Endowments and Economic Development: What Can We Learn from Anthropology?," *Economic Development and Cultural Change* 36, no. S3 (1988): S257.

38. Olivier de Sardan, *Anthropology and Development,* 204. <AQ: Anthropology or Culture?>

39. Sol Tax, *Penny Capitalism: A Guatemalan Indian Community* (Washington, DC: Smithsonian Institute of Social Anthropology, 1953), iv.

40. Renato Rosaldo, *Culture and Truth: The Remaking of Social Analysis* (Boston: Beacon, 1989), 33.

41. C. P. Snow, *The Two Cultures.* With an Introduction by Stefan Collini (Cambridge and New York: Cambridge University Press, 1998).

42. Henri Hubert and Marcel Mauss, "Introduction à L'Analyse de Quelques Phénomènes Religieux," in Mauss, *Oeuvres,* edited by Victor Karady, vol. 1 (Paris: Éditions de Minuit, 1968 [1906]), 37–8.

43. Georges Balandier, *L'Anthropologie Apliquée aux Problèmes des Pays Sous-Developpés,* Fasc. I and II, prepared for a course at Institut d'Études Politiques, Université de Paris (Paris: Les Cours de Droit, 1954–1955).

44. Henrich, *The Secret of Our Success.*

45. Steven Seidman, "Substantive Debates: Moral Order and Social Crisis—Perspectives on Modern Culture," in *Culture and Society: Contemporary Debates,* ed. Jeffrey C. Alexander and Steven Seidman (Cambridge: Cambridge University Press, 1990), 234.

46. Karen Ho and Jill R. Cavanaugh, "What Happened to Social Facts? Introduction," *American Anthropologist* 121, no. 1 (Feb. 2019): 160. They elaborate: "In particular, we want to recognize the trenchant research, especially from minority, feminist, and postcolonial critiques, that has transformed the social sciences and humanities and that has demonstrated that power, hierarchy, and location centrally shape what gets represented as rational, unencumbered knowledge" (161).

47. James R. Veteto and Joshua Lockyear, "Applying Anthropology to What? Tactical/ Ethical Decisions in an Age of Global Neoliberal Imperialism," *Journal of Political Ecology* 22, no. 1 (2015): 361.

48. "Summing up, don't let cultures be put in boxes or cages, or be drawn on a map," concluded Pia Stalder. "Cultures only exist through interactive games among individuals. It is necessary to 'learn not to think in terms of differences or

categories' because the cartographic vision makes no sense and has no reason to exist." Pia Stalder, "Management Interculturel: Entre Théorie et Anarchie," in *Le Défi Interculturel: Enjeux et Perspectives pour Entreprendre*, ed. Pierre-Robert Cloet (Paris: Editions L'Harmattan, 2017), 9 of conference draft, https://www.fredericmaillard.com/wp-content/uploads/2015/09/150909_Article_Stalder.pdf.

49. On the marginality of cultural anthropology as a field of study, see Hannerz, *Anthropology's World*, chapter 3.

50. Hannerz, *Anthropology's World*, 167.

51. Morris Freilich, "Is Culture Still Relevant?," in *The Relevance of Culture*, ed. Morris Freilich (New York: Bergin & Garvey, 1989), 5; Morris Freilich, ed. *Marginal Natives: Anthropology at Work* (New York and London: Harper & Row, 1970).

52. Marcus and Fischer, *Anthropology as Cultural Critique*, 130, 131.

53. Cuddihy, *The Ordeal of Civility: Freud, Marx, Lévy-Strauss, and the Jewish Struggle with Modernity*. Boston: Beacon, 1987 [1974], 152. Cuddihy writes that the Frankfurt Institute members—Adorno, Horkheimer, Marcuse—"are famous for their indignant repudiation of all sociology-of-knowledge attempts to relativize their radicalism by exploring its possible connections with their cultural marginality and ethnicity." "Their target of their criticism," wrote H. D. Forbes of the Frankfurt group, in words that might equally apply to cultural anthropology, "was not the philosophical idea of a free and rational society, but the philistine complacency that views the events of this century as the realization of that ideal." H. D. Forbes, *Nationalism, Ethnocentrism, and Personality: Social Science and Critical Theory* (Chicago: University of Chicago Press, 1985), 191.

54. The hostility between anthropologists and policymakers may be greater still. Consider this outpouring by the French anthropologist Jean Copans, speaking of his dealings with French government: "The absence of policy, of cultural strategy, of technical directives, of purely administrative rationality . . . defies all good will. The technical and intellectual incompetence surpasses understanding. . . . The diplomatic tribalism, the ethos of the closed space par excellence . . . all of these constitute a coded universe where the distinction between appearance and reality has truly lost all sense. . . . [During my time in Africa] I remained super marginal [to the official culture]." Jean Copans, *La Longue Marche de la Modernité Africaine: Savoirs, Intellectuels, Démocratie* (Paris: Karthala, 1991), 52, 53n, 53.

55. For example, Shalom H. Schwartz and Anat Bardi, "Value Hierarchies Across Cultures: Taking a Similarities Perspective" *Journal of Cross-Cultural Psychology*, 32, no. 3 (2001): 268–290; Anna K. Döring et al., "Cross-cultural Evidence of Value Structures and Priorities in Childhood," *British Journal of Psychology* 106, no. 4 (2015): 675–699.

56. Stanley Cavell, *Must We Mean What We Say?* (Cambridge: Cambridge University Press, 1976).

57. Copans, *La Longue Marche de la Modernité Africaine*, 72, 69.

58. Nancy Postero and Eli Elinoff, "Introduction: A Return to Politics," *Anthropological Theory* 19, no. 1 (Mar. 2019): 3.

Chapter 5

1. A. L. Kroeber and Clyde Kluckhohn, with the assistance of Wayne Untereiner and Alfred G. Meyer, *Culture: A Critical Review of Concepts and Definitions. Papers of the Peabody Museum of American Archaeology and Ethnology* 47, no. 1 (Cambridge, MA: Harvard University, 1952), http://www.pseudology.org/psyhology/culturecriticalreview1952a.pdf.

2. "UNESCO Universal Declaration on Cultural Diversity," adopted by the 31st Session of the General Conference of UNESCO (Paris: UNESCO, 2002), 12.

3. Stelios Michalopoulos and Elias Papaioannou, "National Institutions and Subnational Development in Africa," *Quarterly Journal of Economics* 129, no. 1 (Feb. 2014): 151–213, https://doi.org/10.1093/qje/qjt029.

4. I cannot resist this complexification from Kroeber and Kluckhohn's monograph. Not only do they proffer 164 definitions of culture, but they also confess that "the 'whole' culture is a composite of varying and overlapping subcultures. Sub-cultures may be regional, economic, status, occupational, clique groups—or varying combinations of these factors. Some sub-cultures seem to be primarily traceable to the temperamental similarities of the participating individuals," Kroeber and Kluckhohn, *Culture*, 157.

5. Mary Douglas and Aaron Wildavsky, *Risk and Culture* (Berkeley and Los Angeles: University of California Press, 1982).

6. For an endearing autobiographical account of her grid-group theory (and its development in collaboration with Wildavsky), see Mary Douglas, "A History of Grid and Group Cultural Theory," Toronto, Canada: University of Toronto, 2007, https://semioticon.com/sio/files/douglas-et-al/douglas1.pdf.

7. For some applications of grid-group theory, see Richard J. Ellis and Michael Thompson, eds. *Culture Matters* (Boulder, CO: Westview, 1997).

8. Alberto Alesina and Paola Giuliano, "Culture and Institutions," *Journal of Economic Literature* 53, no. 4 (Dec. 2015): 898–944, and the references therein.

9. Luigi Guiso, Helios Herrera, and Massimo Morelli, "Cultural Differences and Institutional Integration," *Journal of International Economics* 99, Suppl. 1 (2016): 1013–1036.

10. Luigi Guiso, Paola Sapienza, and Luigi Zingales, "Does Culture Affect Economic Outcomes?," *Journal of Economic Perspectives* 20, no. 2 (2006): 23.

11. Yuri Gorodnichenko and Gérard Roland, "Which Dimensions of Culture Matter for Long-Run Growth?," *American Economic Review* 101, no. 3 (2011): 492–498; Yuri Gorodnichenko and Gerard Roland, "Culture, Institutions, and the Wealth of Nations," *Review of Economics and Statistics* 99, no. 3 (July 2017): 402–416; Hazel R. Markus and Shinobu Kitayama, "Culture and the Self: Implications for Cognition, Emotion, and Motivation," *Psychological Review* 98, no. 2 (Apr. 1991): 224–253. Hazel R. Markus and Alana Conner, *Clash!: 8 Cultural Conflicts That Make Us Who We Are* (New York: Penguin, 2013).

12. See Geert Hofstede's website at https://geerthofstede.com/landing-page/national-culture.html.

13. See Geert Hofstede's website at https://geerthofstede.com/landing-page/national-culture.html.

14. See the World Value Survey's website http://www.worldvaluessurvey.org/WVSContents.jsp?CMSID=Findings. The analysis is a statistical updating of Ronald Inglehart and Wayne E. Baker, "Modernization, Cultural Change, and the Persistence of Traditional Values," *American Sociological Review* 65, no. 1 (Feb. 2000): 19–51.

15. Ronald F. Inglehart, *Cultural Evolution: People's Motivations Are Changing, and Reshaping the World* (Cambridge and New York: Cambridge University Press, 2018), 49–51.

16. For example, Daniel Fehder, Michael Porter, and Scott Stern, "The Empirics of Social Progress: The Interplay between Subjective Well-Being and Societal Performance," *American Economic Review Papers and Proceedings* 108 (May 2018): 477–482; Charles I. Jones and Peter J. Klenow, "Beyond GDP? Welfare Across Countries and Time," *American Economic Review* 106, no. 9 (Sept. 2016): 2426–2457.

17. For political rights and civil liberties, Freedom House, *Freedom in the World 2020: A Leaderless Struggle for Democracy* (Washington, DC: Freedom House, 2020), https://freedomhouse.org/report/freedom-world/2020/leaderless-struggle-democracy. For rule of law, World Justice Project, *The World Justice Project Rule of Law Index® 2020*, Washington, DC, World Justice Project, 2020, https://worldjusticeproject.org/sites/default/files/documents/WJP-ROLI-2020-Online_0.pdf.

18. The data on DALY per capita are from World Health Organization, *Global Health Estimates 2016: Disease Burden by Cause, Age, Sex, by Country and by Region, 2000–2016* (Geneva: WHO, 2018). See also Simon I. Hay et al., "Global, Regional, and National Disability-Adjusted Life-Years (DALYs) for 333 Diseases and Injuries and Healthy Life Expectancy (HALE) for 195 Countries and Territories, 1990–2016: A Systematic Analysis for the Global Burden of Disease Study 2016," *The Lancet* 390, no. 10100 (Sept. 2017): 1260–1344, https://doi.org/10.1016/S0140-6736(17)32130-X.

19. John F. Helliwell, Richard Layard, Jeffrey Sachs, and Jan-Emmanuel De Neve, eds. *World Happiness Report 2020* (New York: Sustainable Development Solutions Network, 2020), https://worldhappiness.report/ed/2020/.

20. I cannot resist including this remark by the historian Tadashi Aruga: "Thus 'wish to enjoy happiness' [*kôfuku*] was [Fukuzawa Yukichi's 1866] translation. His translation contributed to popularizing the word *kôfuku* in Meiji Japan. Publicists for the freedom and people's rights movement often spoke of the right to preserve or enjoy happiness without being harassed by the government. Although they did not employ a Japanese word equivalent to 'pursuit' either, they understood the meaning of this right better than Fukuzawa had done in 1866." Tadashi Aruga, "The Declaration of Independence in Japan: Translation and Transplantation, 1854–1997," *The Journal of American History* 85, no. 4 (Mar. 1999): 1409–1431, http://chnm.gmu.edu/declaration/.

21. Joaquim Oltra, "Jefferson's Declaration of Independence in the Spanish Political Tradition," *The Journal of American History* 85, no. 4 (Mar. 1999): 1370–1379, http://chnm.gmu.edu/declaration/oltra.html.

22. The 2018 data for GDP per capita, adjusted for purchasing power parity, come from the World Bank: https://data.worldbank.org/indicator/NY.GDP.PCAP. PP.CD?view=map. "Liberty" is the sum of Freedom House's measures of political rights and civil liberties (endnote 151), inverted so that higher numbers are better.

23. Inglehart, *Cultural Evolution*, 3–4, 48–49.

24. Geert Hofstede, "Dimensionalizing Cultures: The Hofstede Model in Context," *Online Readings in Psychology and Culture* 2, no. 1 (2011): 8; Henri C. Santos, Michael E. W. Varnum, and Igor Grossmann, "Global Increases in Individualism," *Psychological Science* 28, no. 9 (Sept. 2017): 1228–1239.

25. Liza G. Steele and Scott M. Lynch, "The Pursuit of Happiness in China: Individualism, Collectivism, and Subjective Well-Being During China's Economic and Social Transformation," *Social Indicators Research* 114, no. 2 (Nov. 2013): 441–451.

26. This sentence draws on unpublished research by my doctoral student Zhijun Gao.

27. Alberto Alesina and Nicola Fuchs-Schündeln, "Good Bye Lenin (Or Not?)—The Effect of Communism on People's Preferences," *American Economic Review* 97, no. 9 (Sept. 2007): 1507–1528.

28. Göran Hydén, "Reciprocity and Governance in Africa," in *The Failure of the Centralized State: Institutions and Self-Governance in Africa*, ed. James S. Wunsch and Dele Olowu (New York and Abington, UK: Routledge, 2019), 253.

29. Gerard Roland concludes a remarkable empirical analysis of the "deep roots" of modern cultures forthrightly: "A major weakness of the current paper is that it does not have a theoretical model to formulate hypotheses about the relations between the different variables for which data were collected." Gerard Roland, "The Deep Historical Roots of Modern Culture: A Comparative Perspective," Keynote Lecture at 2nd World Congress in Comparative Economics, revised December 2019, 22. I am grateful to Prof. Roland for sharing this update.

30. Alesina and Giuliano, "Culture and Institutions"; Gorodnichenko and Roland, "Culture, Institutions, and the Wealth of Nations."

31. For example: "In other words reciprocity/trust and dependence/exploitation each can hold society together, although at quite different levels of efficiency and institutional performance. Once in either of these two settings, rational actors have an incentive to act consistently with its rules. History determines which of these two stable outcomes characterizes any given society. Historical turning points thus can have extremely long-lived consequences. History is not always efficient, in the sense of weeding out social practices that impede progress and encourage collective irrationality. Nor is this inertia somehow attributable to individual irrationality. On the contrary individuals responding rationally to the social context bequeathed to them by history reinforce the social pathologies." Robert D. Putnam, "Democracy, Development, and the Civic Community: Evidence from an Italian Experiment," in *Culture and Development in Africa*, ed. Ismail Serageldin and June Tabaroff (Washington, DC: World Bank, 1994), 71.

32. Harris, *Cultural Materialism*, 61–62.

33. Andreas P. Kyriacou, "Individualism-Collectivism, Governance and Economic Development," *European Journal of Political Economy* 42 (2016): 91. See also Gorodnichenko and Roland, "Culture, Institutions, and the Wealth of Nations."

34. Alberto Bisin and Thierry Verdier, "On the Joint Evolution of Culture and Institutions" (Working Paper no. 23375, National Bureau for Economic Research, April 2017; updated May 7, 2019), 16, https://s18798.pcdn.co/albertobisin/wp-content/uploads/sites/16384/2020/01/cirevision.pdf.

35. For example: "In general the joint evolution of culture and institutions is highly non-linear. This feature has a number of implications, including the non-ergodic character of the underlying dynamic processes between culture and institutions as well as complex phenomena like hysteresis and oscillations. In other words, the dynamics of culture and institutions are prone to display, for instance, sensitivity of equilibrium trajectories to initial conditions, existence of irreversibility and thresholds effects, and non-monotonicity of cultural and institutional changes over transition paths. From an empirical point of view, these phenomena appear consistent with the great diversity of development experiences encountered across the world." Bisin and Verdier, "On the Joint Evolution of Culture and Institutions," 44.

36. For example, Louis Putterman and David N. Weil, "Post-1500 Population Flows and the Long-Run Determinants of Economic Growth and Inequality," *Quarterly Journal of Economics* 125, no. 4 (Nov. 2010): 1627–1682; Oded Galor, *Unified Growth Theory* (Princeton, NJ: Princeton University Press, 2011); Areendam Chanda, C. Justin Cook, and Louis Putterman, "Persistence of Fortune: Accounting for Population Movements, There Was No Post-Columbian Reversal," *American Economic Journal: Macroeconomics* 6, no. 3 (July 2014): 1–28; Enrico Spolaore and Romain Wacziarg, "Ancestry, Language and Culture," in *The Palgrave Handbook of Economics and Language*, ed. Victor Ginsburgh and Schlmo Weber (London: Palgrave Macmillan, 2016), 174–211.

37. Enrico Spolaore and Romain Wacziarg, "How Deep Are the Roots of Economic Development?," *Journal of Economic Literature* 51, no. 2 (June 2013): 325–369.

38. Randy Thornhill and Corey L. Fincher, *The Parasite-Stress Theory of Value and Sociality: Infectious Disease, History, and Human Values Worldwide* (New York: Springer, 2014); Randy Thornhill and Corey L. Fincher, "The Parasite-Stress Theory of Sociality and the Behavioral Immune System," in *Evolutionary Perspectives in Social Psychology*, ed. Virgil Zeigler-Hill, Lisa L. M. Welling, and Todd K. Shackelford (Cham, Switzerland: Springer International, 2015), 419–437.

39. Christopher Eppig, Corey L. Fincher, and Randy Thornhill, "Parasite Prevalence and the Worldwide Distribution of Cognitive Ability," *Proceedings of the Royal Society B: Biological Sciences* 277 (Dec. 2010): 3801–3808, https://royalsocietypublishing.org/doi/full/10.1098/rspb.2010.0973.

40. Cody T. Ross and Peter J. Richerson, "New Frontiers in the Study of Human Cultural and Genetic Evolution," *Current Opinion in Genetics and Development* 29 (Dec. 2014): 103–109.

41. Jüri Allik and Robert McCrae, "Toward a Geography of Personality Traits: Patterns of Profiles across 36 Cultures," *Journal of Cross-Cultural Psychology* 35, no. 1 (2004): 13–28.

42. Kevin Laland, John Odling-Smee, and Sean Myles, "How Culture Shaped the Human Genome: Bringing Genetics and the Human Sciences Together," *Nature Reviews Genetics* 11, no. 2 (2010): 137–148; Samuel Bowles and Herbert J. Gintis, *A Cooperative Species: Human Reciprocity and Its Evolution* (Princeton, NJ: Princeton University Press, 2011).

43. Nicholas A. Christakis, *Blueprint: The Evolutionary Origins of a Good Society* (New York: Little, Brown Spark, 2019).

44. Anke Becker, Benjamin Enke, and Armin Falk, "Ancient Origins of the Global Variation in Economic Preferences," *American Economic Review Papers and Proceedings* 110 (May 2020): 319–323, https://doi.org/10.1257/pandp.20201071.

45. For example, Mats Söderbom and Francis Teal, with Markus Eberhardt, Simon Quinn, and Andrew Zeitlin, *Empirical Development Economics* (London and New York: Routledge, 2015).

46. Alan Barreca, Karen Clay, Olivier Deschenes, Michael Greenstone, and Joseph S. Shapiro, "Adapting to Climate Change: The Remarkable Decline in the U.S. Temperature-Mortality Relationship over the Twentieth Century," *Journal of Political Economy* 124, no. 1 (Feb. 2016): 105–159.

47. Tim Salimans, "Variable Selection and Functional Form Uncertainty in Cross-Country Growth Regressions," *Journal of Econometrics* 171, no. 2 (2012): 267–280.

48. Johannes W. Fedderke and Robert Klitgaard, "Economic Growth and Social Indicators: An Exploratory Analysis," *Journal of Comparative Policy Analysis* 8, no. 3 (Sept. 2006): 283–303. First published in 1998 in *Economic Development and Cultural Change* 46, no. 3: 455–489.

49. For example, Kristopher J. Preacher and Sonya K. Sterba, "Aptitude-by-Treatment Interactions in Research on Educational Interventions," *Exceptional Children* 85, no. 2 (2019): 248–264; A. Alexander Beaujean, "Identifying Cultural Effects in Psychological Treatments Using Aptitude-Treatment Interactions," in *Cultural Competence in Applied Psychology*, ed. Craig L. Frisby and William T. O'Donahue (New York: Springer, Cham, 2018), 473–497; Richard E. Snow, "Aptitude-Treatment Interaction as a Framework for Research on Individual Differences in Learning," in *Learning and Individual Differences: Advances in Theory and Research*, ed. Phillip L. Ackerman, Robert J. Sternberg, and Robert Glaser (New York: W. H. Freeman/Times Books/Henry Holt, 1989), 13–59.

50. George Psacharopoulos, *Higher Education in Developing Countries: A Cost-Benefit Analysis* (Washington, DC: World Bank, 1980), 58–59.

51. Gerard Roland, "Culture, Institutions, and Development," in *The Handbook of Economic Development and Institutions*, ed. Jean-Marie Baland, François Bourguignon, Jean-Philippe Platteau, and Thierry Verdier (Princeton, NJ: Princeton University Press, 2020), 414–448; the quotes are from pages 15 and 16 of this preprint from 2017, https://eml.berkeley.edu/~groland/pubs/Culturesurveyvf.pdf.

52. Monica Bell, Nathan Fosse, Michèle Lamont, and Eva Rosen, "Beyond the Culture of Poverty: Meaning-making among Low-income Population around Family, Neighborhood, and Work," in *The Blackwell Encyclopedia of Race, Ethnicity and*

Nationalism, ed. John Stone, Rutledge M. Dennis, Polly Rizova, and Anthony Smith (New York: Wiley, 2014).

53. "But how are researchers to achieve these aims, given the extravagant number of causes at work in cultural change? The size of social networks, the availability of resources, the difficulty of the task environment, the beliefs of the local polity—all of these and more besides will jointly determine the spread and stability of culture. Given this causal profusion, researchers require more than clearly articulated aspirations; they need principles and methods for determining what causal processes are likely to be salient in any given case, understanding the general applicability and dynamics of these processes, and aggregating these together to produce satisfying explanations." Andrew Buskell, "Looking for Middle Ground in Cultural Attraction Theory," *Evolutionary Anthropology* 28, no. 1 (2019): 14, https://doi.org/10.1002/evan.21762.

54. For example, Jacob Bien, Jonathan Taylor, and Robert Tibshirani, "A Lasso for Hierarchical Interactions," *The Annals of Statistics* 41, no. 3 (2013): 1111–1141, https://projecteuclid.org/euclid.aos/1371150895; Garitt L. Page, Fernando A. Quintana, and Gary L. Rosner, "Discovering Interactions Using Covariate Informed Random Partition Models," arXiv preprint, October 2018, https://arxiv.org/pdf/1810.00121.pdf.

55. Allen W. Rew, "The Link Between Advisory Work and Academic Research and Teaching: Perspectives from a Supplier Institution for Development Cooperation," in *The Socio-Cultural Dimension*, 47.

Chapter 6

1. David C. Rose, *Why Culture Matters Most* (New York: Oxford University Press, 2019).

2. Christakis, *Blueprint*.

3. For example, Spolaore and Wacziarg, "How Deep Are the Roots of Economic Development?"; and Thornhill and Fincher, *The Parasite-Stress Theory of Value and Sociality*.

4. Albert O. Hirschman, *Development Projects Observed* (Washington, DC: Brookings Institution, 1967), chap. 4.

5. Hirschman, *Development Projects Observed*, 130–131.

6. Bastide, *Anthropologie Appliquée*, 42.

7. Jonathan Rigg, "Grass-Roots Development in Rural Thailand: A Lost Cause?," *World Development* 19, nos. 2/3 (Feb./Mar. 1991): 204.

8. Rigg, "Grass-Roots Development," 202, 203.

9. David Gow, Christine Haugen, Alan Hoben, Michael Painter, Jerry VanSant, and Barbara Wyckoff-Baird, *Social Analysis for the Nineties: Case Studies and Proposed Guidelines* (Bethesda, MD: Development Alternatives,1989), 18.

10. Amy Chua, *World on Fire: How Exporting Free Market Democracy Breeds Ethnic Hatred and Global Instability* (New York: Doubleday, 2002).

11. Robert Horne, Lisa Graupner, Susie Frost, John Weinman, Siobhan Melanie Wright, and Matthew Hankins, "Medicine in a Multicultural Society: The Effects of Cultural

Backgrounds on Beliefs about Medication," *Social Science & Medicine* 59, no. 6 (2004): 1307. https://doi.org/10.1016/j.socscimed.2004.01.009.

12. Janya McCalman, Crystal Jongen, Roxanne Bainbridge, and Antonio Clifford, *Cultural Competence in Health: A Review of the Evidence* (Singapore: Springer, Singapore, 2017).

13. Judith Kleinfeld, "First Do No Harm: A Reply to Courtney Cazden," *Anthropology and Education Quarterly* 14, no. 4 (1983): 284.

14. John S. Zeuli and Robert E. Floden, "Cultural Incongruities and Inequities of Schooling: Implications for Practice from Ethnographic Research?," *Journal of Teacher Education* 38, no. 6 (Nov. 1987): 13.

15. Catherine Savage, Rawiri Hindle, Luanna Meyer, Anne Hynds, Wally Penetito, and Christine E. Sleeter, "Culturally Responsive Pedagogies in the Classroom: Indigenous Student Experiences across the Curriculum," *Asia-Pacific Journal of Teacher Education* 39, no. 3 (Aug. 2011): 194. https://doi.org/10.1080/1359866X.2011.588311.

16. "More practically, beyond a certain point, reifying culture to the status of an independent variable at the national (let alone 'civilizational') level proved to be neither intellectually interesting nor in any way useful for policy purposes; at best it might generate an opening for a more serious conversation about culture, but at worst it could reinforce unhelpful stereotypes and undermine the space for agency (e.g., political leadership, civic deliberation, individual and collective choice)." Michael Woolcock, "Culture, Politics, and Development," in *The Oxford Handbook of the Politics of Development*, ed. Carol Lancaster and Nicolas van de Walle (New York: Oxford University Press, 2018), 110.

17. Simon Harrigan, "Relief and an Understanding of Local Knowledge: The Case of Southern Sudan," in *Culture and Public Action*, ed. Vijayendra Rao and Michael Walton (Stanford: Stanford University Press, 2004), 307–327.

18. "These general strategic campaigns are on: General Reconciliation, General Inclusiveness or Participation, General Equity and Geographical Balance, General Appeal for All Refugees and IDPs [internally displaced people] to Return, General Cementing of Unity and General Mobilization and Organization."

19. Klitgaard, *Tropical Gangsters II*, chap. 16 at position 2185–2816. https://www.amazon.com/Tropical-Gangsters-II-Adventures-Development-ebook/dp/B00C9GEQ58

20. Markus and Conner, *Clash!*, 180–182.

21. Jean-Pierre Olivier de Sardan, Aïssa Diara, and Mahaman Mora, "Travelling Models and the Challenge of Pragmatic Contexts and Practical Norms: The Case of Maternal Health," *Health Research Policy and Systems* 15, Suppl. 1 (July 2017): 71–87. https://doi.org/10.1186/s12961-017-0213-9

Chapter 7

1. Deborah Tannen, *You Just Don't Understand: Women and Men in Conversation* (New York: William Morrow, 2001). In the Afterword, Tannen summarized: "report-talk is about *impersonal* information and rapport-talk is about *personal* information" (303).

2. Raymonde Carroll, *Cultural Misunderstandings: The French-American Experience*, trans. Carol Volk (Chicago: University of Chicago Press, 1988).

3. Fatoumata Ouattara, Héléne Sam Tiendrébéogo, Caroline Yaméogo, and Domenique Pobel, "Des Rencontres entre des Usager et des Personnels de Santé: L'Anthropologie entre Médiation et Production de Donnees," in *Accompagner les Femmes à la Maternité au Burkina Faso*, ed. Ouattara et al., 171–189.

4. The following account is based on Ouattara et al., "Des Rencontres." 172–179.

5. Meghan A. Bohren, et al., "How Women Are Treated During Facility-Based Childbirth in Four Countries: A Cross-Sectional Study with Labour Observations and Community-based Surveys," *The Lancet*, published online October 8, 2019, 1. https://doi.org/10.1016/ S0140-6736(19)31992-0.

6. Ouattara et al., "Des Rencontres," 187.

7. Fabienne Richard, Charlemagne Ouédraogo, Georges Rouamba, Bruno Dujardin, and Vincente De Brouwere, "Conclusion: Que Reste-t-il Quatre Ans Après la Fin du Projet Aquasou?," in *Accompagner les Femmes à la Maternité au Burkina Faso*, ed. Ouattara et al., 211.

8. Elisabeth Lasch-Quinn, *Race Experts: How Racial Etiquette, Sensitivity Training, and New Age Therapy Hijacked the Civil Rights Revolution* (New York: W. W. Norton, 2001).

9. James S. Wunsch and Dele Olowu, "The Failure of the Centralized African State," in *The Failure of the Centralized African State: Institutions and Self-Governance in Africa*, ed. James S. Wunsch and Dele Olowu (New York and Abington, UK: Routledge, 2019), 13–14.

10. Claudia Baez-Camargo and Lucy Koechlin, "Informal Governance: Comparative Perspectives on Co-optation, Control and Camouflage in Rwanda, Tanzania and Uganda," *International Development Policy/Revue Internationale de Politique de Développement* 10 (2018): 78–100. https://journals.openedition.org/poldev/2646

11. Michael Cernea, "Farmer Organizations and Institution Building for Sustainable Development," *Regional Development Dialogue* 8, no. 2 (Summer 1987); cited in Norman Uphoff, "Fitting Projects to People," in *Putting People First: Sociological Variables in Rural Development*, 2nd ed., ed. Michael M. Cernea (New York: Oxford University Press, 1991), 496.

12. Miriam Shakow, "The Rise and Fall of 'Civil Society' in Bolivia." *American Anthropologist*, published online July 11, 2019. https://doi.org/10.1111/aman.13266

13. Norman Uphoff, "Fitting Projects to People," 496–497, my emphasis. Uphoff cites as his source of evidence Milton J. Esman and Norman Uphoff, *Local Organizations: Intermediaries in Rural Development* (Ithaca, NY: Cornell University Press, 1984).

14. Avishay Braverman, J. Luis Guasch, Monika Huppi, and Lorenz Pohlmeier, "Promoting Rural Cooperatives in Developing Countries: The Case of Sub-Saharan Africa" (World Bank Discussion Papers WDP 121, Washington, DC, 1991). http:// documents.worldbank.org/curated/en/128481468768546748/Promoting-rural-cooperatives-in-developing-countries-the-case-of-sub-Saharan-Africa.

15. Norman Uphoff, "Why NGOs Are Not a Third Sector: A Sectoral Analysis with Some Thoughts on Accountability, Sustainability and Evaluation," in *Non-Governmental*

Organisations—Performance and Accountability: Beyond the Magic Bullet, ed. Michael Edwards and David Hulme (London: Earthscan, 1995), 21–22.

16. Charles Taylor, "The Politics of Recognition," in *Multiculturalism: Examining the Politics of Recognition*, ed. Amy Gutmann (Princeton, NJ: Princeton University Press, 1994), 25–73.

17. Cited in Bernard J. Lecomte, *Project Aid: Limitations and Alternatives* (Paris: Development Centre, OECD, 1986), 93.

18. Lecomte, *Project Aid*, p. 24. He cites sociologist Alfred Schwartz's characterization of the farmer in Côte d'Ivoire: "Readily on the defensive, he always looks very suspiciously at what is really behind the proposed innovation, and the real motives of its promoters. . . . Even when he appears to join in readily, he frequently does so only to gain time and defuse the initiative more effectively" (25).

19. Olivier de Sardan, "La Manne, les Normes et les Soupçons," 35.

20. Mamadou Dia, *Africa's Management in the 1990s and Beyond: Reconciling Indigenous and Transplanted Institutions* (Washington, DC: World Bank, 1996), 1.

21. Marie-Dominique Perrot, "À Propos du Culturalisme: Du Super-flou au Superflu?," in *La Culture, Otage du Développement?*, ed. Gilbert Rist (Paris: L'Harmattan, 1994), 46.

Chapter 8

1. Chittranjan N. Daftuar, "The Role of Human Factors Engineering in Underdeveloped Countries, with Special Reference to India," in *Ethnic Variables in Human Factors Engineering*, ed. Alphonse Chapanis (Baltimore: Johns Hopkins University Press, 1975), 95.

2. Daftuar, "The Role of Human Factors Engineering," 102–105.

3. Charles R. Brown, "Human Factors Problems in the Design and Evaluation of Key-entry Devices for the Japanese Language," in *Ethnic Variables*, 223.

4. Baruch Givoni, "Human Factors in Town Planning and Housing Design," in *Ethnic Variables*, 249–259.

5. M. Bayona-ba-Meya, ed., *Facteurs Culturels et Projets de Développement Rural en Afrique Centrale* (Paris: L'Harmattan, 1989).

6. Atul Gawande, *The Checklist Manifesto: How to Get Things Right* (New York: Macmillan, 2010).

7. Gerald F. Murray, "The Tree Gardens of Haiti: From Extraction to Domestication," in *Social Forestry: Communal and Private Management Strategies Compared*, ed. David Challinor and Margaret Hardt Frondorf (Washington, DC: Paul H. Nitze School of Advanced International Studies, Johns Hopkins University, 1991), 36.

8. G. F. Murray and M. E. Bannister, "Peasants, Agroforesters, and Anthropologists: A 20-year Venture in Income-generating Trees and Hedgerows in Haïti," *Agroforestry Systems* 61 (2004): 389.

9. Murray, "Tree Gardens," 40.

10. Gerald F. Murray, "A Haitian Peasant Tree Chronicle: Adaptive Evolution and Institutional Intrusion," in *Reasons for Hope: Instructive Experiences in Rural*

Development, ed. Anirudh Krishna, Norman Uphoff, and Milton J. Esman (West Hartford, CT: Kumarian Press, 1997), 243.

11. David Gow, Christine Haugen, Alan Hoben, Michael Painter, Jerry VanSant, and Barbara Wyckoff-Baird, *Social Analysis for the Nineties: Case Studies and Proposed Guidelines* (Bethesda, MD: Development Alternatives, 1989)..

12. Murray and Bannister, "Peasants, Agroforesters, and Anthropologists," 392.

13. Murray and Bannister, "Peasants, Agroforesters, and Anthropologists," 394.

14. Murray, "Tree Gardens," 37.

15. Murray and Bannister, "Peasants, Agroforesters, and Anthropologists," 394.

16. Murray, "Tree Gardens," 38.

17. Murray, "Tree Gardens," 43.

18. Karen Ann Watson-Gegeo and Steven T. Boggs, "From Verbal Play to Talk Story: The Role of Routines in Speech Events among Hawai'ian Children," in *Child Discourse*, ed. Claudia Mitchell-Kernan and Susan Ervin-Tripp (New York: Academic Press, 1977), 67–90; Kathryn Hu-Pei Au and Cathie Jordan, "Teaching Reading to Hawai'ian Children: Finding a Culturally Appropriate Solution," in *Culture in the Bilingual Classroom: Studies in Classroom Ethnography*, ed. Henry T. Trueba, Grace Pung Guthrie and Kathryn Hu-Pei Au (Rowley, MA: Newbury, 1981), 139–152.

19. Lynn A. Vogt, Cathie Jordan, and Roland G. Tharp, "Explaining School Failure, Producing School Success: Two Cases," *Anthropology and Education Quarterly* 18, no. 4 (Dec. 1987): 276.

20. R. Soleste Hilberg and Roland G. Tharp, "Theoretical Perspectives, Research Findings and Classroom Implications of the Learning Styles of Native American and Alaska Native Students," *ERIC Digest* EDO–RC–02–3, Charleston, WV, ERIC Clearinghouse on Rural Education and Small Schools, September 2002..

21. These examples are taken from Eliot A. Singer, "What Is Cultural Congruence, and Why Are They Saying Such Terrible Things About It?" (Occasional Paper no. 120, Institute for Research on Teaching, College of Education, East Lansing, Michigan State University, March 1988), https://files.eric.ed.gov/fulltext/ED292914.pdf.

22. John S. Zeuli and Robert E. Floden, "Cultural Incongruities and Inequities of Schooling: Implications for Practice from Ethnographic Research?," *Journal of Teacher Education* 38, no. 6 (1987): 9–15, https://doi.org/10.1177/002248718703800602.

23. Susan U. Philips, "Participant Structures and Communicative Competence: Warm Springs Children in Community and Classroom," in *Functions of Language in the Classroom*, ed. Courtney B. Cazden, Vera P. John, and Dell H. Hymes (New York: Teachers College Press, 1972), 392.

24. Robert E. Floden, Margret Buchmann, and John R. Schwille, "Breaking with Everyday Experience," *Teachers College Record* 88, no. 4 (1987): 491.

25. Shawn Malia Kana'iaupuni, Brandon Ledward, and Nolan Malone, "*Mohala i ka wai*: Cultural Advantage as a Framework for Indigenous Culture-Based Education and Student Outcomes," *American Educational Research Journal* 54, no. 1S (2017): 311S.

26. Savage et al. "Culturally Responsive Pedagogies in the Classroom," 192.

27. Angelina E. Castagno and Bryan M. J. Brayboy reviewed published syntheses of evidence, case studies, program descriptions, and anecdotal accounts regarding culturally responsive pedagogy, and they found weak to nonexistent causal links to academic performance. Angelina E. Castagno and Bryan M. J. Brayboy, "Culturally Responsive Schooling for Indigenous Youth: A Review of the Literature," *Review of Educational Research* 78, no. 4 (Dec. 2008): 941–993. https://doi.org/10.3102/0034654308323036. This verdict conforms to my reading of a more recent review by Brittany Aronson and Judson Laughter, "The Theory and Practice of Culturally Relevant Education: A Synthesis of Research Across Content Areas," *Review of Educational Research* 86, no. 1 (2016): 163–206. https://doi.org/10.3102/0034654315582066.

28. Bernard Lédéa Ouédraogo, *Entraide Villageoise et Développement: Groupements Paysans au Burkina Faso* (Paris: L'Harmattan, 1990).

29. Quoted in Pierre Pradervand, *Listening to Africa: Developing Africa from the Grassroots* (New York: Praeger, 1989), 19, 21.

30. For example, in the Right Livelihood Award Ouédraogo won in 1990: https://www.rightlivelihoodaward.org/laureates/bernard-ledea-oudraogo/.

31. Quoted in Pradervand, *Listening to Africa*, 101.

32. Pradervand, *Listening to Africa*, 22. Previous quotes are taken from 19–21.

33. Lecomte, *Project Aid*, 96.

34. Samba Guindo of Mali, quoted by Pradervand, *Listening to Africa*, 106.

35. Lecomte, *Project Aid*, 98.

36. Lecomte, *Project Aid*, 41.

37. Joseph Brunet-Jailly, *Où est, vu du Sud, l'obstacle au développement social?* (Paris: ORSTOM and Ministère des Affaires Etrangères, 1995), 15, 13.

38. Lecomte, *Project Aid*, 24. He cites sociologist Alfred Schwartz's characterization of the farmer in Côte d'Ivoire: "Readily on the defensive, he always looks very suspiciously at what is really behind the proposed innovation, and the real motives of its promoters. . . . Even when he appears to join in readily, he frequently does so only to gain time and defuse the initiative more effectively" (25).

39. Lecomte, *Project Aid*, 100.

40. Lecomte, *Project Aid*, 93.

41. A quick note on terminology. In the United States, words like Native Americans, American Indians, Indigenous Nations (capitalized or not), tribes, nations, reservations, Indian Country, and others have been variously accepted. "Perhaps the younger generation is comfortable with the words indigenous or Native, but we have never heard an elder say when asked who he or she is say, 'I am Native' or 'I am indigenous.' They always say I am Lakota or I am an Indian." Native Sun News Today Editorial Board, "Indian, Native or Indigenous. Which One Would You Choose?," *Native Sun News Today*, August 16, 2018. https://www.indianz.com/News/2018/08/16/indian-native-or-indigenous-which-one-wo.asp

42. Stephen Cornell, "Becoming Public Sociology: Indigenous Nations, Dialogue, and Change," in *Handbook of Public Sociology*, ed. Vincent Jeffries (Lantham, UK: Rowman & Littlefield, 2009), 263–264.

43. In the 2010 Census, about 1.2 million Native Americans resided on some 300 Indian reservations and 200 Alaska Native Villages. The Navajo (or Dine) Reservation is by far the largest, with about 175,000 residents.

44. Stephen Cornell and Joseph P. Kalt, *American Indian Self-Determination: The Political Economy of a Policy that Works* (Faculty Research Working Paper Series RWP10–043, Cambridge, MA, Harvard Kennedy School, 2010), 5. https://dash.harvard.edu/bitstream/handle/1/4553307/RWP10-043_Cornell_Kalt.pdf?sequence=1

45. Stephen Cornell and Joseph P. Kalt, "Reloading the Dice: Improving the Chances for Economic Development on American Indian Reservations," in *What Can Tribes Do? Strategies and Institutions in American Indian Economic Development*, ed. Stephen Cornell and Joseph P. Kalt. American Indian Manual and Handbook Series No. 4 (Los Angeles: American Indian Studies Center, UCLA, 1992), 21.

46. Cornell, "Public Sociology," 267.

47. Cornell and Kalt, "Reloading the Dice," 8–9.

48. Stephen Cornell and Joseph P. Kalt, "Where Does Economic Development Really Come From? Constitutional Rule among the Contemporary Sioux and Apache," *Economic Inquiry* 33, no. 3 (July 1995): 402–426, https://doi.org/10.1111/j.1465-7295.1995.tb01871.x.

49. Cornell and Kalt, "Where Does Economic Development Really Come From?"

50. Stephen Cornell and Joseph P. Kalt, "Where's the Glue? Institutional and Cultural Foundations of American Indian Economic Development," *Journal of Socio-Economics* 25, no. 5 (2000): 467.

51. Cornell and Kalt, "Reloading the Dice," 25.

52. "As for changes in tribal culture, even if tribes were willing to make significant changes—a highly questionable assumption—cultures cannot simply be fine-tuned to meet a set of predetermined criteria. Cultural changes that do occur often take a long time to accomplish, and changes that enhance well-being require leadership and vision that are themselves scarce in most societies." Cornell and Kalt, "Reloading the Dice," 10.

53. Cornell and Kalt, "Reloading the Dice," 26.

54. "'Success' in development activities does not mean solely jobs and income. The fact that American Indian tribes, like other societies, have goals of political and social sovereignty means that development success must also be assessed in political and cultural terms: Will this project bring large numbers of non-Indians onto the reservation who may challenge tribal sovereignty? Is this project going to introduce social or political strife among tribal members? Is factory work going to appeal to our young people? Would building that road up to the mine damage important religious sites? Will tribal members object to non-Indian hunters roaming the wilderness areas of the reservation?" Cornell and Kalt, "Reloading the Dice," 47.

55. "I also wish to resist the effort, so often apparent in central government policies toward Indigenous peoples in the CANZUS states, to idealize the Eurocentric 'good governance' mantra common in international development circles in recent decades. The principles often embedded in various versions of 'good governance' are generally laudable—for example, the rule of law, fairness, governmental

effectiveness, governmental accountability—and a number of them are amply apparent in Indigenous governance traditions. But we should make no assumption that capable Indigenous governance will conform to that mantra's boilerplate or to models of governance derived from contemporary liberal democracies." Stephen Cornell, "From Rights to Governance and Back: Indigenous Political Transformations in the CANZUS States," in *Reclaiming Indigenous Governance: Reflections and Insights from Australia, Canada, New Zealand, and the United States*, ed. William Nikolakis, Stephen Cornell, Harry W. Nelson, Sophie Pierre, and Gwen Phillips (Tucson: University of Arizona Press, 2019), 17.

56. Stephen E. Cornell and Joseph P. Kalt, "Successful Economic Development and Heterogeneity of Governmental Form on American Indian Reservations," in Merilee S. Grindle, ed., *Getting Good Government: Capacity Building in the Public Sector of Developing Countries* (Cambridge, MA: Harvard Institute for International Development, 1997), 257–296.

57. He went on to note: "Furthermore, my work on Indian political activism had persuaded me that few nations would talk to us unless they saw benefit in doing so. During my field research on Indian political movements, more than one tribal citizen had said something like, 'we've been studied to death and don't have much to show for it. If you don't help us, why should we help you?'" Cornell, "Public Sociology," 268.

58. Stephen Cornell, Miriam Jorgensen, Joseph P. Kalt, and Katherine A. Spilde, "Seizing the Future: Why Some Native Nations Do and Others Don't," in *Rebuilding Native Nations: Strategies for Governance and Development*, ed. Miriam Jorgensen (Tucson: University of Arizona Press, 2007), 296–323. The quote is from a 2005 preprint: https://hpaied.org/sites/default/files/publications/Seizing%20the%20 Future%20FOR%20PUB.pdf, 18.

59. For example, from the Native Nations Institute at University of Arizona: "Indigenous leaders and managers often identify two types of resources necessary for effective policy-making: (1) reliable, rigorous analyses that provide evidence about new approaches to governance and development, and (2) written accounts of Native nations' successes in various policy-making arenas." "Programs and Projects," n.d. https://nni.arizona.edu/programs-projects/policy-analysis-research

60. Dennis K. Norman and Joseph P. Kalt, eds. *Universities and Indian Country: Case Studies in Tribal-Driven Research* (Tucson: University of Arizona Press, 2015), vii, 6.

61. "The Toolboxes provide Nation Builders with learning activities and resources they can use to assist Indigenous communities in their drive for self-determination. The content is supplemented with case studies, lessons learned, and first-hand explanations by fellow decision makers who have tackled the challenges of strengthening their own communities." "What Are Nation Building Toolboxes," n.d.   https://sites.google.com/g.harvard.edu/nationbuildingtoolboxes/home#h.p_ DhcV8jCDpqqT/

62. The Harvard Project on American Indian Development, "About Honoring Nations," n.d. https://hpaied.org/honoring-nations

63. Cornell, "Public Sociology," 269.

64. Randall K. Q. Akee and Jonathan B. Taylor, *Social and Economic Change on American Indian Reservations. A Databook of the US Censuses and the American Community Survey 1990–2010* (Sarasota, FL: Taylor Policy Group, 2014), 11. http://taylorpolicy.com/us-databook.

65. Akee and Taylor, *Social and Economic* Change, 13. "Over that period, more than three-quarters of the reservations and nine-tenths of the reservation population saw their incomes grow at a pace exceeding that in the United States" (34).

66. Stephen Cornell and Joseph P. Kalt, "Two Approaches to Economic Development on American Indian Reservations: One Works, the Other Doesn't," in *Rebuilding Native Nations: Strategies for Governance and Development*, ed. Miriam Jorgensen (Tucson: University of Arizona Press, 2007), 16. https://www.honigman.com/media/site_files/111_imgimgjopna_2005-02_Approaches.pdf

67. Bayona-ba-Meya, *Facteurs Culturels.*

Chapter 9

1. Ishrat Husain, *Pakistan's Institutions of Accountability* (Islamabad: World Bank, 2012), 22.

2. Nonoptimal equilibriums manifest themselves beyond bribery to many sorts of behavior; and if pressed to define "underdevelopment," one might do worse than citing "a behavioral equilibrium where each of us underperforms according to our own standards because the rewards and punishments are set up that way."

3. Jonathan Watts, "Operation Car Wash: Is This the Biggest Corruption Scandal in History?," *The Guardian*, June 1, 2017. https://www.theguardian.com/world/2017/jun/01/brazil-operation-car-wash-is-this-the-biggest-corruption-scandal-in-history.

4. Juliana Bublitz, "Um Debate Sobre o Mal do País: A Corrupção," *Zero Hora*, April 2, 2016. https://gauchazh.clicrbs.com.br/geral/noticia/2016/04/um-debate-sobre-o-mal-do-pais-a-corrupcao-5712962.html.

5. Frank Jean Okot, "Fight Corruption at Presidency, Lira RDC Advises Museveni," *Saturday Monitor* (Kampala, Uganda), September 3, 2016, 2.

6. Pope Francis, "Address of Pope Francis to the Delegates of the International Association of Penal Law," October 23, 2014. https://w2.vatican.va/content/francesco/en/speeches/2014/october/documents/papa-francesco_20141023_associazione-internazionale-diritto-penale.html

7. Carlos Elizondo Mayer-Serra, "La Cultura de la Corrupción," *Excelsior*, August 28, 2014. https://www.excelsior.com.mx/opinion/carlos-elizondo-mayer-serra/2014/08/28/978645

8. Susan Rose-Ackerman, *Corruption: A Study in Political Economy* (New York: Academic Press, 1978), 1–2.

9. Bo Rothstein and Davide Torsello, "Bribery in Pre-Industrial Societies: Understanding the Universalism-Particularism Puzzle," *Journal of Anthropological Research* 70, no. 2 (2014): 279, 265.

10. "On average across the countries polled, nearly a quarter (24%) say they have discussed corruption over that period. Extreme poverty (20%), unemployment

(18%), and the rising cost of food and energy (17%) are the next most frequently discussed problems." In poor countries, the corresponding figure for corruption was 40%, with unemployment second at 28%. "Unemployment Rises as 'Most Talked-About' Problem: Global Poll," *Globescan*, December 11, 2011. https://globescan.com/unemployment-rises-as-qmost-talked-aboutq-problem-global-poll/

11. Daniel Jordan Smith, *A Culture of Corruption: Everyday Deception and Popular Discontent in Nigeria* (Princeton, NJ: Princeton University Press, 2007), 5–6.

12. Steven Pierce, *Moral Economies of Corruption* (Durham, NC, and London: Duke University Press, 2016).

13. Akhil Gupta, "Blurred Boundaries: The Discourse of Corruption, the Culture of Politics, and the Imagined State," *American Ethnologist* 22, no. 2 (1995): 375.

14. Leslie Holmes, *Corruption: A Very Short Introduction* (Oxford: Oxford University Press, 2015), xii.

15. John T. Noonan, Jr., *Bribes: The Intellectual History of a Moral Idea* (New York: Macmillan, 1984), xiv.

16. Annual reports and a description of the methodology can be found at Transparency International's CPI web page: https://www.transparency.org/research/cpi

17. OECD/EC JRC (Organisation for Economic Co-operation and Development/ European Commission Joint Research Centre), *Handbook on Constructing Composite Indicators: Methodology and User Guide* (Paris: OECD, 2008); Michaela Saisana, Andrea Saltelli, and Stefano Tarantola, "Uncertainty and Sensitivity Analysis Techniques as Tools for the Analysis and Validation of Composite Indicators," *Journal of the Royal Statistical Society A* 168 (Part 2) (2005): 307–323.

18. Saisana, Saltelli, and Tarantola, "Uncertainty and Sensitivity Analysis Techniques as Tools for the Analysis and Validation of Composite Indicators," 321.

19. Laarni Escresa and Lucio Picci, "A New Cross-National Measure of Corruption," *World Bank Economic Review* 31, no. 1 (Jan. 2017): 196–219.

20. Alberto Chong, Rafael La Porta, Florencio Lopez-de-Silanes, and Andrei Shleifer, "Letter Grading Government Efficiency," *Journal of the European Economic Association* 12, no. 2 (Apr. 2014): 277–299.

21. Bo Rothstein and Jan Teorell, "Defining and Measuring Quality of Government," in *Good Government: The Relevance of Political Science*, ed. Sören Holmberg and Bo Rothstein (Cheltenham, UK: Edward Elgar, 2012), 13–39.

22. World Justice Project, *Rule of Law Index 2019*, Washington, DC, World Justice Project, 2019. https://worldjusticeproject.org/our-work/research-and-data/wjp-rule-law-index-2019

23. Global Integrity, *Global Integrity Report 2013*, Washington, DC, Global Integrity.

24. PRS Group's website: https://www.prsgroup.com/explore-our-products/international-country-risk-guide/.

25. For example, Bo Rothstein and Sören Holmberg document significant correlations with such variables as GDP per capita, economic equality, country credit ratings, the Human Development Index, tax revenue as a percentage of GDP, average years of schooling, life expectancy, healthy life years, infant mortality rate, public health expenditures, CO_2 emissions per capita, access to drinking water, access to sanitation,

gender equality, measures of violence and crime, and various measures of happiness and satisfaction with life. Bo Rothstein and Sören Holmberg, "Correlates
of Corruption" (Working Paper Series 2014, Gothenburg, Sweden, Quality of
Government Institute, December 2014), 17.

26. Göran Hydén, *Beyond Ujamaa in Tanzania: Underdevelopment and an Uncaptured
    Peasantry* (Berkeley and Los Angeles: University of California Press, 1980); Göran
    Hydén, "The Economy of Affection Revisited: African Development Management in
    Perspective," 2014. http://ojs.ruc.dk/index.php/ocpa/article/view/3641.

27. For example, Ramón D. Rivas, "Instituciones Sociales y Cultura del Fraude en El
    Salvador," *Entorno* no. 44 (May 2010): 16–19. http://biblioteca.utec.edu.sv/entorno/
    index.php/entorno/article/viewFile/96/95.

28. Peter Hessler, "Letter from El-Bayana: Living-Room Democracy," *The New Yorker*,
    March 7, 2016; George Packer, "Afghanistan's Theorist-in-Chief," *The New Yorker*,
    July 4, 2016.

29. Edward Banfield, *The Moral Basis of a Backward Society* (New York: Free Press, 1958).

30. Alberto Alesina and Paola Giuliano, "Family Ties," in *Handbook of Economic Growth*,
    vol. 2A, ed. Philippe Aghion and Steven N. Durlauf, 177–215 (Oxford: North
    Holland, 2014).

31. Alesina and Giuliano, "Family Ties," 177 and Table 10.

32. Seymour Martin Lipset and Gabriel Salman Lenz, "Corruption, Culture, and
    Markets," in *Culture Matters: How Values Shape Human Progress*, ed. Lawrence E.
    Harrison and Samuel P. Huntington, 112–125 (New York: Basic Books, 2000).

33. Francis Fukuyama, *Political Order and Political Decay* (New York: Farrar, Strauss and
    Giroux, 2014), 88–89.

34. Sten Widmalm, "Explaining Corruption at the Village and Individual Level in
    India: Findings from a Study of the Panchayati Raj Reforms," *Asian Survey* 45, no. 5
    (Sept./Oct. 2005): 774.

35. Stephen D. Morris and Joseph L. Klesner, "Corruption and Trust: Theoretical
    Considerations and Evidence from Mexico," *Comparative Political Studies* 43, no. 10
    (Oct. 2010): 1267–8.

36. Human Rights Watch, *"Letting the Big Fish Swim": Failures to Prosecute High-Level
    Corruption in Uganda* (Washington, DC: Human Rights Watch, 2013), 1.

37. Olivier de Sardan, Bako, and Harouna, "Les Normes Pratiques en Vigueur dans les
    Secteurs de l'Éducation et la Santé au Niger."

38. Drucker never said exactly these widely cited words. Here's a valid quote from him,
    writing in 1991: "What these needs require are changes in behavior. But 'changing
    culture' is not going to produce them. Culture—no matter how defined—is singu-
    larly persistent. Nearly 50 years ago, Japan and Germany suffered the worst defeats
    in recorded history, with their values, their institutions and their culture discredited.
    But today's Japan and today's Germany are unmistakably Japanese and German in
    culture, no matter how different this or that behavior. In fact, changing behavior
    works only if it can be based on the existing 'culture.'" Peter Drucker, "Don't Change
    Corporate Culture: Use It," *Wall Street Journal*, March 28, 1991, A14.

39. On La Paz: Klitgaard, *Tropical Gangsters II*, Part II; on Mandaue: Melissa Mahoney and Robert Klitgaard, "Revitalizing Mandaue City: Obstacles in Implementing a Performance Governance System," *Policy Design and Practice* 2, no. 4 (online Aug. 2019); and Robert Klitgaard, "From Reform to Implementation: Overcoming Backsliding," Claremont Graduate University, CA, August 2019. http://scholar.cgu.edu/robert-klitgaard/wp-content/uploads/sites/22/2019/09/From-Reform-to-Implementation-C.pdf.

40. For references and evidence, see Robert Klitgaard, *Addressing Corruption Together* (Paris: OECD, 2015).

41. Smith, *A Culture of Corruption*, 5, 6.

42. Akhil Gupta, "Blurred Boundaries: The Discourse of Corruption, the Culture of Politics, and the Imagined State," *American Ethnologist* 22, no. 2 (1995): 397n46.

43. Donald W. Light, "Strengthening the Theory of Institutional Corruptions: Broadening, Clarifying, and Measuring" (Edmond J. Safra Research Lab Working Papers, no. 2, Cambridge, MA, Harvard University, March 2013, 3.

44. Cheyanne Scharbatke-Church and Diana Chigas, *Understanding Social Norms: A Reference Guide for Policy and Practice*, Henry J. Leir Institute of Human Security, Fletcher School of Law and Diplomacy, Tufts University, Medford, MA, 2019, 74–75.

45. Mancur Olson, *The Logic of Collective Action* (Cambridge, MA: Harvard University Press, 1971); Amy R. Poteete, Marco A. Janssen, and Elinor Ostrom, *Working Together: Collective Action, the Commons, and Multiple Methods in Practice* (Princeton, NJ: Princeton University Press, 2010).

46. Mark Pieth, ed., *Collective Action: Innovative Strategies to Prevent Corruption* (Zurich and St. Gallen: Dike Verlag AG, 2012); Klitgaard, *Addressing Corruption Together*.

47. For example, Chip Heath and Dan Heath, *Switch: How to Change Things When Change Is Hard* (New York: Broadway Books, 2010).

48. José Atilano, Pena López, and José Manuel Sánchez Santos found that Hofstede's individualism and power distance were significant predictors of the 2001 CPI in sixty countries. They concluded, fallaciously: "Since corruption depends on cultural variables, public intervention capabilities are greatly reduced, at least in the short term." José Atilano, Pena López, and José Manuel Sánchez Santos, "Does Corruption Have Social Roots? The Role of Culture and Social Capital," *Journal of Business Ethics* 122, no. 4 (July 2014): 705.

Chapter 10

1. Putnam, Leonardi, and Nanetti, *Making Democracy Work* and personal communication with Robert Putnam.

2. Pradervand, *Listening to Africa*, 19, 21, 22.

3. Bell, Fosse, Lamont, and Rosen, "Beyond the Culture of Poverty," 13.

4. Gruénais and Ouattara, "De L'Anthropologie dans un Projet de Santé Maternelle," 32

5. For his thoughts on applying such insights to developing countries, see Putnam, "Democracy, Development, and the Civic Community."

6. For example, United States Department of Agriculture, *Soil Quality Test Kit Guide* (Washington, DC: USDA, 2001). https://www.nrcs.usda.gov/Internet/FSE_DOCUMENTS/nrcs142p2_050956.pdf

7. And these categories had many variations—twenty-seven kinds of boundary rules and "112 different choice rules that were usually composed of two parts—an allocation formula specifying where, when, or how resource units could be harvested and a specific basis for the implementation of the formula (such as the amount of land held, historical use patterns, or assignment through lottery)." Elinor Ostrom, "Beyond Markets and States: Polycentric Governance of Complex Economic Systems," December 2009, 421. https://www.nobelprize.org/uploads/2018/06/ostrom_lecture.pdf.

8. Prachanda Pradhan, "Elinor Ostrom: From Nepal [*sic*] Perspective," *Hydro Nepal* no. 11 (July 2012): 69.

9. Elinor Ostrom, "'Nepal Has a Rich Tradition," interview with "A Correspondent." *Spotlight Nepal* 4, no. 13 (Dec. 20, 2010). https://www.spotlightnepal.com/2010/12/20/nepal-has-a-rich-tradition-nobel-laureate-elinor-ostrom/.

10. Ostrom, "Beyond Markets and States," 409.

11. Elinor Ostrom, "How Farmer Managed Irrigation Systems Build Social Capital to Outperform Agency Managed Irrigation Systems That Rely Primarily on Physical Capital," in *Trajectory of Farmer Managed Irrigation Systems*, ed. Prachanda Pradhan, Upendra Gautam, and Naveen Mangal Joshi (Kathmandu: Farmer Managed Irrigation Systems Promotion Trust, 2015), 25. https://fmistnepal.files.wordpress.com/2015/12/trajectory-of-fmis.pdf.

12. Angela R. McLean and Christopher Dye, "The Antimicrobial Commons," in "Tragedy Revisited," *Science* 362, Issue 6420 (Dec.2018): 1236–1241. https://doi.org/10.1126/science.aaw0911.

13. Elinor Ostrom, Larry Schroeder, and Susan Wynne, *Institutional Incentives and Sustainable Development: Infrastructure Policies in Perspective* (Boulder, CO: Westview Press, 1993).

14. Ostrom, "How Farmer Managed Irrigation Systems Build Social Capital," 23.

15. Michael Cox, Gwen Arnold, and Sergio Villamayor-Tomás, "A Review of Design Principles for Community-Based Natural Resource Management," *Ecology and Society* 15, no. 4 (2010): 38.

16. Tania Murray Li, "Anthropological Engagements with Development," *Anthropologie & Développement* 37–39 (2014): 227. http://journals.openedition.org/anthropodev/495.

17. James Ferguson and Tania Murray Li, *Beyond the "Proper Job": Political-Economic Analysis after the Century of Labouring Man* (PLAAS Working Paper 51, Cape Town, University of the Western Cape, April 2018).

18. Amy Chua and Jed Rubenfeld, *The Triple Package: How Three Unlikely Cultural Traits Explain the Rise and Fall of Cultural Groups in America* (New York: Penguin, 2014).

19. Li, *The Will to Improve*, 276–7, 240,

20. JoAnna Poblete, *Balancing the Tides: Marine Practices in American Sāmoa* (Honolulu: University of Hawai'i Press, 2020).

21. For an exemplary analysis, see California Environmental Associates, *Charting a Course to Sustainable Fisheries* (San Francisco: California Environmental Associates, 2012).

22. Lecomte, *Project Aid*, 93.

23. For some examples and more details, see Klitgaard, *Addressing Corruption Together*, and Robert Klitgaard, "Engaging Corruption: New Ideas for the International Monetary Fund." *Policy Design and Practice* 2, no. 3 (July 2019): 229–242.

24. Li, *The Will to Improve*, 55–56.

25. Olivier de Sardan, Diara, and Mora, "Travelling Models and the Challenge of Pragmatic Contexts and Practical Norms."

26. Gruénais, "L'anthropologie Sociale: Est-elle Inapplicable?"

27. Tonti, "The Model of Swiss Development Cooperation," 54.

28. Indeed, many exciting, diverse methods are in use, ranging from "problem-driven iterative adaptation" to participatory action research. "Convening" as I see it is distinguished by incorporating policy analysis, case studies, and data. And I'm hoping that cultural anthropology will enter in a variety of ways, including data, comparative analysis, case studies, and cultural science.

29. Ferguson, *Give a Man a Fish*, 213.

30. In the midst of her conclusion to *Balancing the Tides*, JoAnna Poblete inserts two rhetorical questions as if in an epiphany: "Despite occupying the lowest economic and social rungs of colonized societies, Pacific Islanders express high levels of personal comfort and fulfillment. What lessons can we all learn from *fa'a Sāmoa* and *vā* that can lead to more community-oriented fulfillment and move us beyond Western-based standards of achievement through individual materialism? How does one's outlook on life change when a balance in all relationships is the highest priority?" (138).

31. Marshall Sahlins, *Stone-Age Economics* (Chicago: Aldine, 1972), 3.

32. Clifford Geertz, "'From the Natives' Point of View': On the Nature of Anthropological Understanding," *Bulletin of the American Academy of Arts and Sciences* 28, no. 1 (Oct. 1974): 43.

33. Olivier de Sardan, Ali Bako, and Harouna, "Les Normes Pratiques en Vigueur dans les Secteurs de l'Éducation et la Santé," 131.

34. Robert Klitgaard, *Elitism and Meritocracy in Developing Countries* (Baltimore: Johns Hopkins University Press, 1986), chap. 1.

35. For example, Michel Leiris, *L'Afrique Fantôme* (Paris: Gallimard, 1950 [1934]); James Clifford and George E. Marcus, eds., *Writing Culture: The Poetics and Politics of Ethnography* (Berkeley and Los Angeles: University of California Press, 1986); Clifford Geertz, *Works and Lives: The Anthropologist as Author* (Stanford: Stanford University Press, 1988); and Marianna Torgovnic, *Gone Primitive: Savage Intellects, Modern Lives* (Chicago: University of Chicago Press, 1990), especially chaps. 5, 11, and 12.

36. James Clifford, *The Predicament of Culture: Twentieth Century Ethnography, Literature, and Art* (Cambridge, MA: Harvard University Press, 1988), 87–88.

37. Cuddihy, *The Ordeal of Civility*, 152.

38. Mary Ann Caws, "The Poetics of the Manifesto: Nowness and Newness," in *Manifesto: A Century of Isms*, ed. Mary Ann Caws (Lincoln: University of Nebraska Press, 2001), xxiii, xix.

39. Julian Hanna, *The Manifesto Handbook* (Alresford, UK: Zero Books, 2019). Provocation §37.

40. Lee Scrivner, "How to Write an AvantGarde Manifesto (A Manifesto," London, London Consortium, April 2006, 23. Maybe I should not share that the quote continues: "So perhaps the best bet would be to steer clear of publishing them or even writing them in the first place. Don't say anything at all." https://web.archive.org/web/20070615192751/http://www.londonconsortium.com/wp-content/uploads/2007/02/scrivneripmessay.pdf.

41. On his website, n.d., http://www.freemanpatterson.com/art_statement.htm.

42. Metamodernist Manifesto, n.d. http://www.metamodernism.org.

43. Luke Turner, "Metamodernism: A Brief Introduction," *Queen Mob's Teahouse*, January 5, 2015. https://queenmobs.com/2015/01/metamodernism-brief-introduction/.

44. Gérard Roland, "Culture, Institutions and Development," in *The Handbook of Economic Development and Institutions*, ed. Jean-Marie Baland, François Bourguignon, Jean-Philippe Platteau, and Thierry Verdier, 414–448 (Princeton, NJ: Princeton University Press, 2020), 23 of this preprint https://eml.berkeley.edu/~groland/pubs/Culturesurveyvf.pdf.

Bibliography

Ake, Claude. "Building on the Indigenous." In United Nations Economic Commission for Africa, International Conference on Popular Participation in the Recovery and Development Process in Africa, no pagination. Addis Ababa: United Nations Economic Commission for Africa, 1990. http://hdl.handle.net/10855/13951.

Akee, Randall K. Q., and Jonathan B. Taylor. *Social and Economic Change on American Indian Reservations. A Databook of the US Censuses and the American Community Survey 1990–2010.* Sarasota: Taylor Policy Group, 2014. http://taylorpolicy.com/us-databook.

Alesina, Alberto, and Nicola Fuchs-Schündeln. "Good Bye Lenin (Or Not?)—The Effect of Communism on People's Preferences." *American Economic Review* 97, no. 9 (Sept. 2007): 1507–1528.

Alesina, Alberto, and Paola Giuliano. "Culture and Institutions." *Journal of Economic Literature* 53, no. 4 (Dec. 2015): 898–944. https://doi.org/10.1257/jel.53.4.898.

Alesina, Alberto, and Paola Giuliano. "Family Ties." In *Handbook of Economic Growth*, vol. 2A, edited by Philippe Aghion and Steven N. Durlauf, 117–215. Oxford: North Holland, 2013.

Allik, Jüri, and Robert McCrae. "Toward a Geography of Personality Traits: Patterns of Profiles across 36 Cultures." *Journal of Cross-Cultural Psychology* 35, no. 1 (Jan. 2004): 13–28. https://doi.org/10.1177/0022022103260382.

Appadurai, Arjun. *The Future as Cultural Fact: Essays on the Global Condition.* London: Verso, 2013.

Aronson, Brittany, and Judson Laughter. "The Theory and Practice of Culturally Relevant Education: A Synthesis of Research Across Content Areas." *Review of Educational Research* 86, no. 1 (2016): 163–206. https://doi.org/10.3102/0034654315582066.

Aruga, Tadashi. "The Declaration of Independence in Japan: Translation and Transplantation, 1854–1997." *The Journal of American History* 85, no. 4 (Mar. 1999): 1409–1431.

Au, Kathryn Hu-Pei, and Cathie Jordan. "Teaching Reading to Hawai'ian Children: Finding a Culturally Appropriate Solution." In *Culture in the Bilingual Classroom: Studies in Classroom Ethnography*, edited by Henry T. Trueba, Grace Pung Guthrie, and Kathryn Hu-Pei Au, 139–152. Rowley, MA: Newbury, 1981.

Baez-Camargo, Claudia, and Lucy Koechlin. "Informal Governance: Comparative Perspectives on Co-optation, Control and Camouflage in Rwanda, Tanzania and Uganda." *International Development Policy/ Revue Internationale de Politique de Développement* 10 (2018): 78–100. https://journals.openedition.org/poldev/2646.

Bailey, F. G. "The Peasant View of a Bad Life." In *Peasants and Peasant Societies*, edited by Teodor Shann, 299–321. Middlesex: Penguin, 1971.

Balandier, Georges, ed. *Étude Comparée des Motivations et Stimulations Économiques en Milieu Coutumier et en Milieu "Moderniste" dans le Cadre des Pays Dits "Sous-développés."*

Bureau International de Recherche sur les Sociales du Progrès Technique (BIRISPT)/6-/ IS.1/54. Paris: Conseil International des Sciences Sociales, 1954.

Balandier, Georges. *L'Anthropologie Apliquée aux Problèmes des Pays Sous-Developpés*, Fasc. I and II. Prepared for a course at Institut d'Études Politiques, Université de Paris. Paris: Les Cours de Droit, 1954–1955.

Balandier, Georges. *Histoire d'Autres*. Paris: Stock, 1977.

Banfield, Edward, *The Moral Basis of a Backward Society*. New York: Free Press, 1958.

Barreca, Alan, Karen Clay, Olivier Deschenes, Michael Greenstone, and Joseph S. Shapiro. "Adapting to Climate Change: The Remarkable Decline in the U.S. Temperature-Mortality Relationship over the Twentieth Century." *Journal of Political Economy* 124, no. 1 (Feb. 2016): 105–159. https://doi.org/10.1086/684582.

Bass, Thomas A. *Camping with the Prince and Other Tales of Science in Africa*. Boston: Houghton Mifflin, 1990.

Bastide, Roger. *Anthropologie Appliquée*. Paris: Payot, 1971.

Bayona-ba-Meya, M., ed. *Facteurs Culturels et Projets de Développement Rural en Afrique Centrale: Points de Repère*. Paris: L'Harmattan, 1989.

Beaujean, A. Alexander. "Identifying Cultural Effects in Psychological Treatments Using Aptitude-Treatment Interactions." In *Cultural Competence in Applied Psychology*, edited by Craig L. Frisby and William T. O'Donahue, 473–497. New York: Springer, Cham, 2018.

Bebbington, Anthony. "Social Capital and Development Studies, II: Can Bourdieu Travel to Policy?" *Progress in Development Studies* 7, no. 2 (2007): 155–162. https://doi.org/ 10.1177/146499340600700205.

Becker, Anke, Benjamin Enke, and Armin Falk. "Ancient Origins of the Global Variation in Economic Preferences." *American Economic Review Papers and Proceedings* 110 (May 2020): 319–323. https://doi.org/10.1257/pandp.20201071.

Bell, Monica, Nathan Fosse, Michèle Lamont, and Eva Rosen. "Beyond the Culture of Poverty: Meaning-Making among Low-Income Population around Family, Neighborhood, and Work." In *The Blackwell Encyclopedia of Race, Ethnicity and Nationalism*, edited by John Stone, Rutledge Dennis, Polly Rizova, and Anthony Smith. New York: Wiley, 2014. https://doi.org/10.1002/9781118663202.wberen108.

Berche, Thierry. *Anthropologie et Santé Publique en Pays Dogon*. Paris: Karthala, 1998.

Besley, Timothy, and Maitreesh Ghatak. "Property Rights and Economic Development." In *Handbook of Development Economics*, vol. 5, edited by Dani Rodrik and Mark Rosenzweig, 4525–4595. Amsterdam: Elsevier, 2010.

Bien, Jacob, Jonathan Taylor, and Robert Tibshirani. "A Lasso for Hierarchical Interactions." *The Annals of Statistics* 41, no. 3 (2013): 1111–1141. https://doi.org/ 10.1214/13-AOS1096.

Bisin, Alberto, and Thierry Verdier. "On the Joint Evolution of Culture and Institutions." Working Paper 23375, National Bureau for Economic Research, April 2017; updated May 7, 2019, 16. https://s18798.pcdn.co/albertobisin/wp-content/uploads/sites/ 16384/2020/01/cirevision.pdf.

Bohren, Meghan A., Hedieh Mehrtash, Bukola Fawole, Thae Maung Maung, Mamadou Dioulde Balde, Ernest Maya, Soe Soe Thwin, Adeniyi K. Aderoba, Joshua P. Vogel, Theresa Azonima Irinyenikan, A. Olusoji Adeyanju, Nwe Oo Mon, Kwame Adu-Bonsaffoh, Sihem Landoulsi, Chris Guure, Richard Adanu, Boubacar Alpha Diallo, A. Metin Gülmezoglu, Anne-Marie Soumah, Alpha Oumar Sall, Özge Tunçalp. "How Women Are Treated During Facility-Based Childbirth in Four Countries: A

Cross-sectional Study with Labour Observations and Community-Based Surveys." *The Lancet*, October 8, 2019, 1–14. https://doi.org/10.1016/ S0140-6736(19)31992-0.

Borofsky, Robert. *An Anthropology of Anthropology*. Kailua, HI: Center for Public Anthropology, 2019. https://books.publicanthropology.org/an-anthropology-of-anthropology.pdf.

Bourdieu, Pierre. "Le Capital Social. Notes Provisoires." *Actes de la Recherche en Sciences Sociales*, no. 31 (Jan. 1980): 1 4. http://github.com/CCT416H5F SocialData Analytics-UToronto/2017-09-08/blob/master/Bourdieu%20-%20Le%20capital%20social.%20 Notes%20provisoires.pdf.

Bourdieu, Pierre. *The Social Structures of the Economy*. Translated by Chris Turner. Cambridge, MA: Polity Press, 2005.

Bowles, Samuel, and Herbert J. Gintis. *A Cooperative Species: Human Reciprocity and Its Evolution*. Princeton, NJ: Princeton University Press, 2011.

Braverman, Avishay, J. Luis Guasch, Monika Huppi, and Lorenz Pohlmeier. "Promoting Rural Cooperatives in Developing Countries: The Case of Sub-Saharan Africa." World Bank Discussion Papers WDP 121. Washington, DC, 1991.

Brown, Charles R. "Human Factors Problems in the Design and Evaluation of Key-Entry Devices for the Japanese Language." In *Ethnic Variables in Human Factors Engineering*, edited by Alphonse Chapanis, 207–224. Baltimore: Johns Hopkins University Press, 1975.

Brunet-Jailly, Joseph. *Où est, vu du Sud, l'obstacle au développement social?* Paris: ORSTOM and Ministère des Affaires Etrangères, 1995.

Bublitz, Juliana. "Um Debate Sobre o Mal do País: A Corrupção." *Zero Hora*, April 2, 2016. https://gauchazh.clicrbs.com.br/geral/noticia/2016/04/um-debate-sobre-o-mal-do-pais-a-corrupcao-5712962.html

Buijsrogge, Piet. *Initiatives Paysannes en Afrique de L'Ouest*. Paris: L'Harmattan, 1989.

Buskell, Andrew. "Looking for Middle Ground in Cultural Attraction Theory." *Evolutionary Anthropology* 28, no. 1 (2019): 14–17. https://doi.org/10.1002/evan.21762.

California Environmental Associates. *Charting a Course to Sustainable Fisheries*. San Francisco: California Environmental Associates, 2012.

Canavire-Bacarreza, Gustavo, Jorge Martínez-Vázquez, and Bauyrzhan Yedgenov. "Identifying and Disentangling the Impact of Fiscal Decentralization on Economic Growth." International Center for Public Policy Working Paper 19–03, Atlanta, Georgia State University, 2019.

Carroll, Raymonde. *Cultural Misunderstandings: The French-American Experience*. Translated by Carol Volk. Chicago: University of Chicago Press, 1988.

Castagno, Angelina E., and Bryan M.J. Brayboy. "Culturally Responsive Schooling for Indigenous Youth: A Review of the Literature." *Review of Educational Research* 78, no. 4 (Dec. 2008): 941–993. https://doi.org/10.3102/0034654308323036.

Cavell, Stanley. *Must We Mean What We Say?* Cambridge: Cambridge University Press, 1976.

Caws, Mary Ann. "The Poetics of the Manifesto: Nowness and Newness." In *Manifesto: A Century of Isms*, edited by Mary Ann Caws, xix–xxxii. Lincoln: University of Nebraska Press, 2001.

Chanda, Areendam, C. Justin Cook, and Louis Putterman. "Persistence of Fortune: Accounting for Population Movements, There Was No Post-Columbian Reversal." *American Economic Journal: Macroeconomics* 6, no. 3 (July 2014): 1–28. https://doi.org/10.1257/mac.6.3.1.

Chase, Stuart. *Mexico: A Tale of Two Civilizations*. New York: Macmillan, 1931.

Chong, Alberto, Rafael La Porta, Florencio Lopez-de-Silanes, and Andrei Shleifer. "Letter Grading Government Efficiency." *Journal of the European Economic Association* 12, no. 2 (Apr. 2014): 277–299. https://doi.org/10.1111/jeea.12076.

Christakis, Nicholas A. *Blueprint: The Evolutionary Origins of a Good Society.* New York: Little, Brown Spark, 2019.

Chua, Amy. *World on Fire: How Exporting Free Market Democracy Breeds Ethnic Hatred and Global Instability.* New York: Doubleday, 2002.

Chua, Amy, and Jed Rubenfeld. *The Triple Package: How Three Unlikely Cultural Traits Explain the Rise and Fall of Cultural Groups in America.* New York: Penguin, 2014.

Cleaver, Frances. "The Inequality of Social Capital and the Reproduction of Chronic Poverty." *World Development* 33, no. 6 (June 2005): 893–906. https://doi.org/10.1016/j.worlddev.2004.09.015.

Clifford, James. *The Predicament of Culture: Twentieth Century Ethnography, Literature, and Art.* Cambridge, MA: Harvard University Press, 1988.

Clifford, James, and George E. Marcus, eds. *Writing Culture: The Poetics and Politics of Ethnography.* Berkeley and Los Angeles: University of California Press, 1986.

Copans, Jean. *La Longue Marche de la Modernité Africaine: Savoirs, Intellectuels, Démocratie.* Paris: Karthala, 1991.

Cornell, Stephen. "Becoming Public Sociology: Indigenous Nations, Dialogue, and Change." In *Handbook of Public Sociology*, edited by Vincent Jeffries, 263–280. Lantham, UK: Rowman & Littlefield, 2009.

Cornell, Stephen. "From Rights to Governance and Back: Indigenous Political Transformations in the CANZUS States." In *Reclaiming Indigenous Governance: Reflections and Insights from Australia, Canada, New Zealand, and the United States*, edited by William Nikolakis, Stephen Cornell, Harry W. Nelson, Sophie Pierre, and Gwen Phillips, 15–37. Tucson: University of Arizona Press, 2019.

Cornell, Stephen, and Joseph P. Kalt. "American Indian Self-Determination: The Political Economy of a Policy that Works." Faculty Research Working Paper Series RWP10–043, Cambridge, MA, Harvard Kennedy School, 2010. https://dash.harvard.edu/bitstream/handle/1/4553307/RWP10-043_Cornell_Kalt.pdf?sequence=1.

Cornell, Stephen, and Joseph P. Kalt. "Reloading the Dice: Improving the Chances for Economic Development on American Indian Reservations." In *What Can Tribes Do? Strategies and Institutions in American Indian Economic Development*, edited by Stephen Cornell and Joseph P. Kalt, 2–59. American Indian Manual and Handbook Series No. 4. Los Angeles: American Indian Studies Center, UCLA, 1992.

Cornell, Stephen E., and Joseph P. Kalt. "Successful Economic Development and Heterogeneity of Governmental Form on American Indian Reservations." In *Getting Good Government: Capacity Building in the Public Sector of Developing Countries*, edited by Merilee S. Grindle, 257–296. Cambridge. MA: Harvard Institute for International Development, 1997.

Cornell, Stephen, and Joseph P. Kalt. "Two Approaches to Economic Development on American Indian Reservations: One Works, the Other Doesn't." In *Rebuilding Native Nations: Strategies for Governance and Development*, edited by Miriam Jorgensen. Tucson: University of Arizona Press, 2007. https://www.honigman.com/media/site_files/111_imgimgjopna_2005-02_Approaches.pdf.

Cornell, Stephen, and Joseph P. Kalt. "Where Does Economic Development Really Come From? Constitutional Rule among the Contemporary Sioux and Apache." *Economic Inquiry* 33, no. 3 (July 1995): 402–426. https://doi.org/10.1111/j.1465-7295.1995.tb01871.x.

Cornell, Stephen, and Joseph P. Kalt. "Where's the Glue? Institutional and Cultural Foundations of American Indian Economic Development." *Journal of Socio-Economics* 25, no. 5 (2000): 443–470.

Cornell, Stephen, Miriam Jorgensen, Joseph P. Kalt, and Katherine A. Spilde. "Seizing the Future: Why Some Native Nations Do and Others Don't." In *Rebuilding Native Nations: Strategies for Governance and Development*, edited by Miriam Jorgensen, 296–323. Tucson: University of Arizona Press, 2007.

Cornwall, Andrea, and Deborah Eade, eds. *Deconstructing Development Discourse: Buzzwords and Fuzzwords*. Rugby, UK: Practical Action, 2010.

Cox, Aimee Meredith. *Shapeshifters: Black Girls and the Choreography of Citizenship*. Durham, NC: Duke University Press, 2015.

Cox, Michael, Gwen Arnold, and Sergio Villamayor-Tomás. "A Review of Design Principles for Community-Based Natural Resource Management." *Ecology and Society* 15, no. 4 (Dec. 2010): Article 38. http://www.ecologyandsociety.org/vol15/iss4/art38/.

Cuddihy, John Murray. *The Ordeal of Civility: Freud, Marx, Lévy-Strauss, and the Jewish Struggle with Modernity*. Boston: Beacon, 1987 [1974].

Daftuar, Chittaranjan N. "The Role of Human Factors Engineering in Underdeveloped Countries, with Special Reference to India." In *Ethnic Variables in Human Factors Engineering*, edited by Alphonse Chapanis, 91–114. Baltimore: Johns Hopkins University Press, 1975.

De Munck, Victor C., and Giovanni Bennardo. "Disciplining Culture: A Sociocognitive Approach." *Current Anthropology* 60, no. 2 (Apr. 2019): 174–193. https://doi.org/10.1086/702470.

De Sousa Santos, Boaventura. *The End of the Cognitive Empire: The Coming of Age of Epistemologies of the South*. Durham, NC, and London: Duke University Press, 2018.

Santos, Boaventura de Sousa, and César A. Rodríguez-Garavito. "Introduction: Expanding the Economic Canon and Searching for Alternatives to Neoliberal Globalization." In *Another Production Is Possible: Beyond the Capitalist Canon*, edited by Boaventura de Sousa Santos, xvii–lxii. London and New York: Verso, 2006.

Deb, Joyee. "Cooperation and Community Responsibility." *Journal of Political Economy* 128, no. 5 (May 2020): 1976–2009. https://doi.org/10.1086/705671.

Dia, Mamadou. *Africa's Management in the 1990s and Beyond: Reconciling Indigenous and Transplanted Institutions*. Washington, DC: World Bank, 1996.

Doi, Takeo. *The Anatomy of Dependence*. Tokyo: Kodansha International, 1973.

Döring, Anna K. et al. "Cross-Cultural Evidence of Value Structures and Priorities in Childhood." *British Journal of Psychology* 106, no. 4 (Nov. 2015): 675–699. https://doi.org/10.1111/bjop.12116.

Douglas, Mary. "A History of Grid and Group Cultural Theory." Toronto, Canada: University of Toronto, 2007. https://semioticon.com/sio/files/douglas-et-al/douglas1.pdf.

Douglas, Mary, and Aaron Wildavsky. *Risk and Culture*. Berkeley and Los Angeles: University of California Press, 1982.

Downing, Theodore E., and Gilbert Kushner, eds. *Human Rights and Anthropology*. Cambridge, MA: Cultural Survival, 1989.

Drucker, Peter. "Don't Change Corporate Culture: Use It." *Wall Street Journal*, March 28, 1991, A14.

Ellis, Richard J., and Michael Thompson, eds. *Culture Matters*. Boulder, CO: Westview, 1997.

Eppig, Christopher, Corey L. Fincher, and Randy Thornhill. "Parasite Prevalence and the Worldwide Distribution of Cognitive Ability." *Proceedings of the Royal Society B:*

Biological Sciences 277 (Dec. 2010): 3801–3808. https://royalsocietypublishing.org/doi/full/10.1098/rspb.2010.0973.

Epstein, T. Scarlett. "How Can Ethnology Help to Promote Third World Development?" In *Ethnologische Beiträge zur Entwicklungspolitik 2*, edited by Frank Bliss and Michael Schönhuth, 205–213. Bonn: Politischer Arbeitskreis Schulen, 1990.

Escobar, Arturo. *Designs for the Pluriverse: Radical Interdependence, Autonomy, and the Making of Worlds*. Durham, NC, and London: Duke University Press, 2018.

Escobar, Arturo. *Encountering Development: The Making and Unmaking of the Third World*. With a new introduction by the author. Princeton, NJ: Princeton University Press, 2012.

Escresa, Laarni, and Lucio Picci. "A New Cross-National Measure of Corruption." *World Bank Economic Review* 31, no. 1 (Jan. 2017): 196–219. http://hdl.handle.net/10986/30134.

Esman, Milton J., and Norman Uphoff. *Local Organizations: Intermediaries in Rural Development*. Ithaca, NY: Cornell University Press, 1984.

Etounga-Manguelle, Daniel. *L'Afrique: A-t-elle Besoin d'un Programme d'Adjustement Culturel?* Ivry-sur-Seine: Éditions Nouvelles du Sud, 1990.

Etounga-Manguelle, Daniel. *Vers Une Société Responsable: Le Cas de l'Afrique*. Paris: L'Harmattan, 2009.

Evers, Hans-Dieter. "Optimizing the Use of Social Science Know-How in Development Cooperation." In *The Socio-Cultural Dimension in Development: The Contribution of Sociologists and Social Anthropologists to the Work of Development Agencies*, edited by Michael Schönhuth. Sonderpublikation der GTZ, no. 249, 22–27. Eschborn, Germany: Deutsche Gesellschaft für Technische, 1991.

Fedderke, Johannes W., and Robert Klitgaard. "Economic Growth and Social Indicators: An Exploratory Analysis." *Journal of Comparative Policy Analysis* 8, no. 3 (Sept. 2006): 283–303. https://doi.org/10.1080/13876980600858598. First published in *Economic Development and Cultural Change* 46, no. 3 (Apr. 1998): 455–489. https://doi.org/10.1086/452354.

Fedderke, Johannes W., Robert Klitgaard, and Valerio Napolioni. "Genetic Adaptation to Historical Pathogen Burdens." *Infections, Genetics and Evolution* 54 (July 2017): 299–307. https://doi.org/10.1016/j.meegid.2017.07.017.

Fehder, Daniel, Michael Porter, and Scott Stern. "The Empirics of Social Progress: The Interplay between Subjective Well-Being and Societal Performance." *American Economic Review Papers and Proceedings* 108 (May 2018): 477–482. http://dx.doi.org/10.1257/PANDP.20181036.

Ferguson, James. *The Anti-Politics Machine: "Development," Depoliticization, and Bureaucratic Power in Lesotho*. Minneapolis and London: University of Minnesota Press, 1994.

Ferguson, James. *Give a Man a Fish: Reflections on the New Politics of Distribution*. Durham, NC, and London: Duke University Press, 2015.

Ferguson, James, and Tania Murray Li. "Beyond the 'Proper Job': Political-Economic Analysis after the Century of Labouring Man." PLAAS Working Paper 51, Cape Town, University of the Western Cape, April 2018. http://repository.uwc.ac.za/xmlui/handle/10566/4538.

Fincher, Corey L., Randy Thornhill, Damian R. Murray, and Mark Schaller. "Pathogen Prevalence Predicts Human Cross-cultural Variability in Individualism/Collectivism."

Proceedings of the Royal Society B 275 (June 2018): 1279–1285. https://doi.org/10.1098/rspb.2008.0094.

Fischer, Edward F. *The Good Life: Aspiration, Dignity, and the Anthropology of Wellbeing.* Stanford: Stanford University Press, 2014.

Floden, Robert E., Margret Buchmann, and John R. Schwille. "Breaking with Everyday Experience." *Teachers College Record* 88, no. 4 (1987): 485–571.

Forbes, H. D. *Nationalism, Ethnocentrism, and Personality: Social Science and Critical Theory.* Chicago: University of Chicago Press, 1985.

Freedom House. *Freedom in the World 2020: A Leaderless Struggle for Democracy.* Washington, DC: Freedom House, 2020. https://freedomhouse.org/report/freedom-world/2020/leaderless-struggle-democracy.

Freilich, Morris. "Is Culture Still Relevant?" In *The Relevance of Culture*, edited by Morris Freilich, 1–26. New York: Bergin & Garvey, 1989.

Freilich, Morris, ed. *Marginal Natives: Anthropology at Work.* New York and London: Harper & Row, 1970.

Fuentes, Carlos. "La Socialización de la Política desde Abajo." *Ventana* (Nicaragua), no. 446 (Nov. 12, 1990): 8–9.

Fukuyama, Francis. *Political Order and Political Decay.* New York: Farrar, Strauss, and Giroux, 2014.

Fukuyama, Francis. "Social Capital and Development: The Coming Agenda." *SAIS Review* 22, no. 1 (Winter–Spring 2002): 23–37.

Galor, Oded. *Unified Growth Theory.* Princeton, NJ: Princeton University Press, 2011.

Gardner, Katy, and David Lewis. *Anthropology and Development: Challenges for the Twenty-First Century.* London: Pluto Press, 2015.

Gawande, Atul. *The Checklist Manifesto: How to Get Things Right.* New York: Macmillan, 2010.

Geertz, Clifford. "Distinguished Lecture: Anti Anti-Relativism." *American Anthropologist* 86, no. 2 (June 1984): 263–278.

Geertz, Clifford. "'From the Natives' Point of View': On the Nature of Anthropological Understanding." *Bulletin of the American Academy of Arts and Sciences* 28, no. 1 (Oct. 1974): 26–45. https://doi.org/10.2307/3822971.

Geertz, Clifford. *The Interpretation of Cultures.* New York: Basic Books, 1973.

Geertz, Clifford. *Works and Lives: The Anthropologist as Author.* Stanford: Stanford University Press, 1988.

Giuliagno, Felix. "Nobel Prize Winner Angus Deaton Shares 3 Big Ideas." *Financial Times*, October 12, 2015.

Givoni, Baruch. "Human Factors in Town Planning and Housing Design." In *Ethnic Variables in Human Factors Engineering*, edited by Alphonse Chapanis, 249–259. Baltimore: Johns Hopkins University Press, 1975.

Global Integrity. *Global Integrity Report 2013.* Washington, DC: Global Integrity.

Gorodnichenko, Yuriy, and Gérard Roland. "Culture, Institutions, and the Wealth of Nations." *Review of Economics and Statistics* 99, no. 3 (July 2017): 402–416.

Gorodnichenko, Yuriy, and Gérard Roland. "Understanding the Individualism-Collectivism Cleavage and Its Effects: Lessons from Cultural Psychology." In *Institutions and Comparative Economic Development*, edited by Masahiko Aoki, Timur Kuran, and Gérard Roland, 213–236. New York: Palgrave Macmillan, 2012.

Gorodnichenko, Yuriy, and Gérard Roland. "Which Dimensions of Culture Matter for Long-Run Growth?" *American Economic Review* 101, no. 3 (2011): 492–498.

Gow, David, Christine Haugen, Alan Hoben, Michael Painter, Jerry VanSant, and Barbara Wyckoff-Baird. *Social Analysis for the Nineties: Case Studies and Proposed Guidelines.* Bethesda, MD: Development Alternatives, 1989.

Grootaert, Christiaan, and Thierry van Bastelaer. "Conclusion: Measuring Impact and Drawing Policy Conclusions." In *The Role of Social Capital in Development*, edited by Christiaan Grootaert and Thierry van Bastelaer, 341–350. Cambridge: Cambridge University Press, 2002.

Gruénais, Marc-Éric. "L'anthropologie Sociale: Est-elle Inapplicable?" *Bulletin de l'APAD* 34–36 (2012). https://journals.openedition.org/apad/4109.

Gruénais, Marc-Éric, and Fatoumata Ouattara. "De L'Anthropologie dans un Projet de Santé Maternelle." In *Accompagner les Femmes à la Maternité au Burkina Faso: Anthropologie et Santé Publique dans un Projet D'Amélioration des Soins Obstétricaux*, edited by Fatoumata Ouattara, Marc-Éric Gruénais, Fabienne Richard, and Charlemagne Ouédraogo, 31–51. Paris: L'Harmattan, 2016.

Guiso, Luigi, Helios Herrera, and Massimo Morelli. "Cultural Differences and Institutional Integration." *Journal of International Economics* 99, Suppl. 1 (2016): 1013–1036.

Guiso, Luigi, Paola Sapienza, and Luigi Zingales. "Does Culture Affect Economic Outcomes?" *Journal of Economic Perspectives* 20, no. 2 (2006): 23–48.

Gupta, Akhil. "Blurred Boundaries: The Discourse of Corruption, the Culture of Politics, and the Imagined State." *American Ethnologist* 22, no. 2 (May 1995): 375–402. https://doi.org/10.1525/ae.1995.22.2.02a00090.

Hanna, Julian. *The Manifesto Handbook.* Alresford, UK: Zero Books, 2019.

Hannerz, Ulf. *Anthropology's World: Life in a Twenty-First Century Discipline.* London: Pluto Press, 2010.

Harrigan, Simon. "Relief and an Understanding of Local Knowledge: The Case of Southern Sudan." In *Culture and Public Action*, edited by Vijayendra Rao and Michael Walton, 307–327. Stanford: Stanford University Press, 2004.

Harris, Marvin. *Cultural Materialism: The Struggle for a Science of Culture.* New York: Vintage, 1980.

Hay, Simon I. et al. "Global, Regional, and National Disability-Adjusted Life-Years (DALYs) for 333 Diseases and Injuries and Healthy Life Expectancy (HALE) for 195 Countries and Territories, 1990–2016: A Systematic Analysis for the Global Burden of Disease Study 2016." *The Lancet* 390, no. 10100 (Sept. 2017): 1260–1344. https://doi.org/10.1016/S0140-6736(17)32130-X.

Heath, Chip, and Dan Heath. 2010. *Switch: How to Change Things When Change Is Hard.* New York: Broadway Books.

Helliwell, John F., Richard Layard, Jeffrey Sachs, and Jan-Emmanuel De Neve, eds. *World Happiness Report 2020.* New York: Sustainable Development Solutions Network, 2020.

Henrich, Joseph. *The Secret of Our Success: How Culture Is Driving Human Evolution, Domesticating Our Species, and Making Us Smarter.* Princeton, NJ and Oxford: Princeton University Press, 2016.

Hessler, Peter. "Letter from El-Bayana: Living-Room Democracy." *The New Yorker*, March 7, 2016.

Hilberg, R. Soleste, and Roland G. Tharp. "Theoretical Perspectives, Research Findings and Classroom Implications of the Learning Styles of Native American and Alaska Native Students." *ERIC Digest* EDO–RC–02–3. Charleston, WV, ERIC Clearinghouse on Rural Education and Small Schools, September 2002.

Hill, Polly. *Development Economics on Trial: The Anthropological Case for a Prosecution.* Cambridge: Cambridge University Press, 1986.

Hirschman, Albert O. *Development Projects Observed.* Washington, DC: Brookings Institution, 1967.

Hirschman, Albert O. "Obstacles to Development: A Classification and a Quasi-Vanishing Act." *Economic Development and Cultural Change* 13, no. 4, Part 1 (July 1965): 385–393.

Ilo, Karen, and Jill R. Cavanaugh. "What Happened to Social Facts? Introduction." *American Anthropologist* 121, no.1 (Feb. 2019): 160–167. https://doi.org/10.1111/aman.13184.

Hofstede, Geert. "Dimensionalizing Cultures: The Hofstede Model in Context." *Online Readings in Psychology and Culture* 2, no. 1 (2011): 1–26. https://doi.org/10.9707/2307-0919.1014.

Hofstede, Geert, Gert Jan Hofstede, and Michael Minkov. 2010. *Culture and Organizations.* 3rd ed. New York: McGraw-Hill, 2010.

Holmes, Leslie, *Corruption: A Very Short Introduction.* Oxford: Oxford University Press, 2015.

Horne, Robert, Lisa Graupner, Susie Frost, John Weinman, Siobhan Melanie Wright, and Matthew Hankins. "Medicine in a Multicultural Society: The Effects of Cultural Backgrounds on Beliefs about Medication." *Social Science & Medicine* 59, no. 6 (2004): 1307–1313. https://doi.org/10.1016/j.socscimed.2004.01.009.

Horowitz, Michael M. "Development Anthropology in the United States." In *Ethnologische Beiträge zur Entwicklungspolitik 2,* edited by Frank Bliss and Michael Schönhuth, 189–204. Bonn: Politischer Arbeitskreis Schulen, 1990.

Houtman, Gustaaf. "Interview with Maurice Bloch." *Anthropology Today* 4, no. 1 (Feb. 1988): 18–21. https://doi.org/10.2307/3032876.

Hubert, Henri, and Marcel Mauss. "Introduction à L'Analyse de Quelques Phénomènes Religieux." In Mauss, *Oeuvres,* edited by Victor Karady, vol. 1, 193–307. Paris: Éditions de Minuit, 1968 [1906].

Human Rights Watch. *"Letting the Big Fish Swim:" Failures to Prosecute High-Level Corruption in Uganda.* Washington, DC: Human Rights Watch, 2013.

Hydén, Göran. *Beyond Ujamaa in Tanzania: Underdevelopment and an Uncaptured Peasantry.* Berkeley and Los Angeles: University of California Press, 1980.

Hydén, Göran. "The Economy of Affection Revisited: African Development Management in Perspective." 2014. http://ojs.ruc.dk/index.php/ocpa/article/view/3641.

Hydén, Göran. "Reciprocity and Governance in Africa." In *The Failure of the Centralized State: Institutions and Self-Governance in Africa,* edited by James S. Wunsch and Dele Olowu, 249–269. Boulder, CO: Westview, 1990.

Inglehart, Ronald F. *Cultural Evolution: People's Motivations Are Changing, and Reshaping the World.* Cambridge and New York: Cambridge University Press, 2018.

Inglehart, Ronald, and Wayne E. Baker. "Modernization, Cultural Change, and the Persistence of Traditional Values." *American Sociological Review* 65, no. 1 (Feb. 2000): 19–51.

Ingold, Tim. *Anthropology: Why It Matters.* Cambridge: Polity Press, 2018.

Jones, Charles I., and Peter J. Klenow. "Beyond GDP? Welfare Across Countries and Time." *American Economic Review* 106, no. 9 (Sept. 2016): 2426–2457.

Jones, Garrett. *Hive Mind: How Your Nation's IQ Matters So Much More Than Your Own.* Stanford: Stanford University Press, 2015.

Kaaristo, Maarja, and Maurice Bloch. "The Reluctant Anthropologist. An Interview with Maurice Bloch." *Eurozine*, February 28, 2008. https://www.researchgate.net/publication/273451893_The_Reluctant_Anthropologist_An_Interview_with_Maurice_Bloch.

Kabou, Axelle. *Comment L'Afrique En Est Arrivée Là*. Paris: L'Harmattan, 2010.

Kabou, Axelle. *Et Si L'Afrique Refusait le Développement?* Paris: L'Harmattan, 1991.

Kana'iaupuni, Shawn Malia, Brandon Ledward, and Nolan Malone. "*Mohala i ka wai*: Cultural Advantage as a Framework for Indigenous Culture-Based Education and Student Outcomes." *American Educational Research Journal* 54, no. 1S (Apr. 2017): 311S–339S. https://doi.org/10.3102/0002831216664779.

Kennedy, Kenneth W. "International Anthropometric Variability and Its Effects on Aircraft Cockpit Design." In *Ethnic Variables in Human Factors Engineering*, edited by Alphonse Chapanis, 249–259. Baltimore: Johns Hopkins University Press, 1975.

Khan, Mohsin S. "Macroeconomic Adjustment in Developing Countries: A Policy Perspective." *World Bank Research Observer* 2, no. 1 (Jan. 1987): 23–42. https://doi.org/10.1093/wbro/2.1.23.

Kilani, Mondher. "Anthropologie du Développement ou Développement de L'anthropologie? Quelques Réflexions Critiques." In *La Culture, Otage du Développement?* edited by Gilbert Rist, 15–29. Paris: L'Harmattan, 1994.

Kleinfeld, Judith. "First Do No Harm: A Reply to Courtney Cazden." *Anthropology and Education Quarterly* 14, no. 4 (Winter 1983): 282–287.

Klitgaard, Robert. *Addressing Corruption Together*. Paris: OECD, 2015. https://www.oecd.org/dac/conflict-fragility-resilience/publications/FINAL%20Addressing%20corruption%20together.pdf.

Klitgaard, Robert. *Adjusting to Reality: Beyond "State versus Market" in Economic Development*. San Francisco: ICS Press and International Center for Economic Growth, 1991.

Klitgaard, Robert. *Elitism and Meritocracy in Developing Countries*. Baltimore: Johns Hopkins University Press, 1986.

Klitgaard, Robert. "Engaging Corruption: New Ideas for the International Monetary Fund." *Policy Design and Practice* 2, no. 3 (July 2019): 229–242. https://doi.org/10.1080/25741292.2019.1612542.

Klitgaard, Robert. "From Reform to Implementation: Overcoming Backsliding." Teaching Case. Claremont, CA, Claremont Graduate University, August 2019. http://scholar.cgu.edu/robert-klitgaard/wp-content/uploads/sites/22/2019/09/From-Reform-to-Implementation-C.pdf.

Klitgaard, Robert. *Tropical Gangsters*. New York: Basic Books, 1990.

Klitgaard, Robert. *Tropical Gangsters II: Adventures in Development in the World's Poorest Places*. Amazon KDP Books, 2013.

Kroeber, A. L., and Clyde Kluckhohn, with the assistance of Wayne Untereiner and Alfred G. Meyer. *Culture: A Critical Review of Concepts and Definitions. Papers of the Peabody Museum of American Archaeology and Ethnology*. Vol. XLVII, no. 1. Cambridge: Harvard University, 1952. http://www.pseudology.org/psyhology/culturecriticalreview1952a.pdf.

Kronenfeld, David B. *Culture as a System: How We Know the Meaning and Significance of What We Do and Say*. London and New York: Routledge, 2018.

Kuper, Adam. "Anthropology and Anthropologists Forty Years On." *Anthropology of This Century*, no. 11 (Oct. 2014). http://aotcpress.com/articles/anthropology-anthropologists-forty-years/.

Kyriacou, Andreas P. "Individualism-Collectivism, Governance and Economic Development." *European Journal of Political Economy* 42 (2016): 91–104. https://doi.org/10.1016/j.ejpoleco.2015.11.005.

Laland, Kevin, John Odling Smee, and Sean Myles. "How Culture Shaped the Human Genome: Bringing Genetics and the Human Sciences Together." *Nature Reviews Genetics* 11, no. 2 (Feb. 2010): 137–148. https://doi.org/10.1038/nrg2734.

Lanman, Jonathan, Hugh Turpin, and Samuel Ward. "Causes, Effects, and the 'Mush' of Culture." *Current Anthropology* 60, no. 2 (Apr. 2019): 187–188.

Lasch-Quinn, Elisabeth. *Race Experts: How Racial Etiquette, Sensitivity Training, and New Age Therapy Hijacked the Civil Rights Revolution*. New York: W. W. Norton, 2001.

Lawry, Steven, Cyrus Samii, Ruth Hall, Aaron Leopold, Donna Hornby, and Farai Mtero. "The Impact of Land Property Rights Interventions on Investment and Agricultural Productivity in Developing Countries: A Systematic Review." *Journal of Development Effectiveness* 9, no.1 (Jan. 2017): 61–68. https://doi.org/10.1080/19439342.2016.1160947.

Lecomte, Bernard J. *Project Aid: Limitations and Alternatives*. Paris: Development Centre, OECD, 1986.

Leiris, Michel. *L'Afrique Fantôme*. Paris: Gallimard, 1950 [1934].

Lenclud, Gérard. "La Question de L'application dans la Tradition Anthropologique Française." In *Les Applications de L'anthropologie: Un Essai de Réflexion Collective depuis la France*, edited by Jean-François Baré, 65–84. Paris: Éditions Karthala, 1995.

Light, Donald W. "Strengthening the Theory of Institutional Corruptions: Broadening, Clarifying, and Measuring." Edmond J. Safra Research Lab Working Papers, no. 2. Cambridge, Harvard University, March 2013.

Li, Tania Murray. "After Development: Surplus Labor and the Politics of Entitlement." *Development and Change* 48, no. 6 (Nov. 2017): 1247–1261. https://doi.org/10.1111./dech.12344.

Li, Tania Murray. "Anthropological Engagements with Development." *Anthropologie & Développement* 37–39 (2014): 227–240. http://journals.openedition.org/anthropodev/495.

Li, Tania Murray. *Land's End: Capitalist Relations on an Indigenous Frontier*. Durham, NC: Duke University Press, 2014.

Li, Tania Murray. *The Will to Improve: Governability, Development, and the Practice of Politics*. Durham, NC: Duke University Press, 2007.

Lipset, Seymour Martin, and Gabriel Salman Lenz. "Corruption, Culture, and Markets." In *Culture Matters: How Values Shape Human Progress*, edited by Lawrence E. Harrison and Samuel P. Huntington, 112–125. New York: Basic Books, 2000.

Lynn, Richard, and Susan Hampson. "The Rise of National Intelligence: Evidence from Britain, Japan and the U.S.A." *Personality and Individual Differences* 7, no. 1 (1986): 23–32. https://doi.org/10.1016/0191-8869(86)90104-2.

Mahoney, Melissa, and Robert Klitgaard. "Revitalizing Mandaue City: Obstacles in Implementing a Performance Governance System." *Policy Design and Practice* 2, no. 4 (online Aug. 12, 2019). https://doi.org/10.1080/25741292.2019.1642072.

Marcos, Silvia. "We Come to Ask for Justice, Not Crumbs." In *Indigenous Peoples and the Modern State*, edited by Duane Champagne, Karen Jo Torjesen, and Susan Steiner, 97–108. Walnut Creek, CA: AltaMira Press, 2005.

Marcus, George E., and Michael M. J. Fischer. *Anthropology as Cultural Critique: An Experimental Moment in the Human Sciences*. Chicago: University of Chicago Press, 1986.

Markus, Hazel R., and Alana Conner. *Clash!: 8 Cultural Conflicts That Make Us Who We Are*. New York: Penguin, 2013.

Markus, Hazel R., and Shinobu Kitayama. "Culture and the Self: Implications for Cognition, Emotion, and Motivation." *Psychological Review* 98, no. 2 (Apr. 1991): 224–253.

Mauss, Marcel. "Divisions et Proportions des Divisions de la Sociologie." *Année Sociologique*, Nouvelle Serie, vol. 2 (1927). In Mauss, *Oeuvres*, vol. 3, edited by Victor Karkady, 178–245. Paris: Éditions de Minuit, 1969.

Mauss, Marcel. *Manuel d'Ethnographie*. Paris: Payot, 1947.

Mayer-Serra, Carlos Elizondo. "La Cultura de la Corrupción." *Excelsior*, August 28, 2014. http://www.excelsior.com.mx/opinion/carlos-elizondo-mayer-serra/2014/08/28/978645.

Mazrui, Ali A. *Cultural Forces in World Politics*. London: James Currey, 1990.

McCalman, Janya, Crystal Jongen, Roxanne Bainbridge, and Antonio Clifford. *Cultural Competence in Health: A Review of the Evidence*. Singapore: Springer Singapore, 2017.

McLean, Angela R., and Christopher Dye. "The Antimicrobial Commons." In "Tragedy Revisited." *Science* 362, no. 6420 (Dec. 2018): 1236–1241. https://doi.org/10.1126/science.aaw0911.

Michalopoulos, Stelios, and Elias Papaioannou. "National Institutions and Subnational Development in Africa." *Quarterly Journal of Economics* 129, no. 1 (Feb. 2014): 151–213. https://doi.org/10.1093/qje/qjt029.

Mkandawire, Thandika. "Running While Others Walk: Knowledge and the Challenge of Africa's Development." *African Development* 36, no. 2 (2011): 1–36. https://www.jstor.org/stable/24484703.

Morawetz, David. *Why the Emperor's Clothes Are Not Made in Colombia: A Case Study in Latin American and East Asian Manufactured Exports*. New York: Oxford University Press, 1981.

Morris, Stephen D., and Joseph L. Klesner. "Corruption and Trust: Theoretical Considerations and Evidence from Mexico." *Comparative Political Studies* 43, no. 10 (Oct. 2010): 1258–1285. https://doi.org/10.1177/0010414010369072.

Murray, Gerald F. "A Haitian Peasant Tree Chronicle: Adaptive Evolution and Institutional Intrusion." In *Reasons for Hope: Instructive Experiences in Rural Development*, edited by Anirudh Krishna, Norman Uphoff, and Milton J. Esman, 241–253. West Hartford, CT: Kumarian Press, 1997.

Murray, Gerald F. "The Tree Gardens of Haiti: From Extraction to Domestication." In *Social Forestry: Communal and Private Management Strategies Compared*, edited by David Challinor and Margaret Hardt Frondorf, 35–44. Washington, DC: School of Advanced International Studies, Johns Hopkins University, 1991.

Murray, G. F., and M. E. Bannister. "Peasants, Agroforesters, and Anthropologists: A 20-Year Venture in Income-Generating Trees and Hedgerows in Haïti." *Agroforestry Systems* 61 (2004): 383–397.

Native Sun News Today Editorial Board. "Indian, Native or Indigenous. Which One Would You Choose?" *Native Sun News Today*, August 16, 2018. https://www.indianz.com/News/2018/08/16/indian-native-or-indigenous-which-one-wo.asp.

Noonan, John T., Jr., *Bribes: The Intellectual History of a Moral Idea*. New York: Macmillan, 1984.

Norman, Dennis K., and Joseph P. Kalt, eds. *Universities and Indian Country: Case Studies In Tribal-Driven Research*. Tucson. University of Arizona Press, 2015.

OECD/EC JRC (Organisation for Economic Co-operation and Development/European Commission Joint Research Centre). *Handbook on Constructing Composite Indicators: Methodology and User Guide*. Paris: OECD, 2008.

Ouédraogo, Bernard Lédéa. *Entraide Villageoise et Développement: Groupements Paysans au Burkina Faso*. Paris: L'Harmattan, 1990.

Okely, Judith. *Anthropological Practice: Fieldwork and the Ethnographic Method*. London: Bloomsbury Academic, 2013.

Okot, Frank Jean. "Fight Corruption at Presidency, Lira RDC Advises Museveni." *Saturday Monitor* (Kampala, Uganda): 2. September 3, 2016.

Olivier de Sardan, Jean-Pierre. *Anthropology and Development: Understanding Contemporary Social Change*. Translated by Antoinette Tidjani Alou. London and New York: Zed Books, 2005.

Olivier de Sardan, Jean-Pierre. "La Manne, les Normes et les Soupçons: Les Contradictions de L'aide Vue d'en Bas." *Revue Tiers Monde* 219, no. 3 (2014): 197–215. https://doi.org/10.3917/rtm.219.0197.

Olivier de Sardan, Jean-Pierre, Aïssa Diara, and Mahaman Mora. "Travelling Models and the Challenge of Pragmatic Contexts and Practical Norms: The Case of Maternal Health." *Health Research Policy and Systems* 15, Suppl. 1 (July 2017): 71–87. https://doi.org/10.1186/s12961-017-0213-9.

Olivier de Sardan, Jean-Pierre, Mahaman Tahirou Ali Bako, and Abdoutan Harouna. "Les Normes Pratiques en Vigueur dans les Secteurs de l'Éducation et la Santé au Niger: Une Base pour des Réformes Ancrées dans les Réalités?" *Etudes et Travaux du LASDEL*, no. 127. Niamey, Niger, Laboratoire d'Etudes et de Recherche sur les Dynamiques Sociales et le Développement Local, 2018. http://www.lasdel.net/index.php/nos-activites/etudes-travaux/271-n-127-les-normes-pratiques-en-vigueur-dans-les-secteurs-de-l-education-et-la-sante-au-niger-une-base-pour-des-reformes-ancrees-dans-la-realite-par-jean-pierre-olivier-de-sardan-mahaman-tahirou-ali-bako-et-abdoutan-harouna-2018.

Olowu, Dele. "African Economic Performance: Current Programs and Future Failures." In *The Failure of the Centralized State: Institutions and Self-Governance in Africa*, edited by James S. Wunsch and Dele Olowu, 100–129. New York and Abington, UK: Routledge, 2019.

Olson, Mancur. *The Logic of Collective Action*. Cambridge, MA: Harvard University Press, 1971.

Oltra, Joaquim. "Jefferson's Declaration of Independence in the Spanish Political Tradition." *The Journal of American History* 85, no. 4 (Mar. 1999): 1370–1379.

Ortner, Sherry B. "Dark Anthropology and Its Others: Theory Since the 80s." *HAU: Journal of Ethnographic Theory* 6, no. 1 (2016): 47–73.

Ortner, Sherry B. "Practicing Engaged Anthropology." *Anthropology of This Century*, no. 25 (May 2019). http://aotcpress.com/articles/practicing-engaged-anthropology/.

Ostrom, Elinor. "Beyond Markets and States: Polycentric Governance of Complex Economic Systems." Nobel Prize Lecture, 2009, 408–444. https://www.nobelprize.org/uploads/2018/06/ostrom_lecture.pdf.

Ostrom, Elinor. "How Farmer Managed Irrigation Systems Build Social Capital to Outperform Agency Managed Irrigation Systems that Rely Primarily on Physical Capital." In *Trajectory of Farmer Managed Irrigation Systems*, edited by Prachanda Pradhan, Upendra Gautam, and Naveen Mangal Joshi, 21–26. Kathmandu: Farmer Managed Irrigation Systems Promotion Trust, 2015. https://fmistnepal.files.wordpress.com/2015/12/trajectory-of-fmis.pdf.

Ostrom, Elinor. "Nepal Has a Rich Tradition," interview with "A Correspondent." *Spotlight Nepal* 4, no. 13 (Dec. 20, 2010). https://www.spotlightnepal.com/2010/12/20/nepal-has-a-rich-tradition-nobel-laureate-elinor-ostrom/.

Ostrom, Elinor, Larry Schroeder, and Susan Wynne. *Institutional Incentives and Sustainable Development: Infrastructure Policies in Perspective*. Boulder, CO: Westview Press, 1993.

Ouattara, Fatoumata, Marc-Éric Gruénais, Fabienne Richard, and Charlemagne Ouédraogo, eds. *Accompagner les Femmes à la Maternité au Burkina Faso: Anthropologie et Santé Publique dans un Projet D'Amélioration des Soins Obstétricaux*. Paris: L'Harmattan, 2016.

Ouattara, Fatoumata, Héléne Sam Tiendrébéogo, Caroline Yaméogo, and Domenique Pobel. "Des Rencontres entre des Usager et des Personnels de Santé: L'Anthropologie entre Médiation et Production de Donnees." In *Accompagner les Femmes à la Maternité au Burkina Faso*, edited by Fatoumata Ouattara, Marc-Éric Gruénais, Fabienne Richard, and Charlemagne Ouédraogo, 171–189. Paris: L'Harmattan, 2016.

Packer, George. "Afghanistan's Theorist-in-Chief." *The New Yorker*, July 4, 2016. http://www.newyorker.com/magazine/2016/07/04/ashraf-ghani-afghanistans-theorist-in-chief.

Page, Garitt L., Fernando A. Quintana, and Gary L. Rosner. "Discovering Interactions Using Covariate Informed Random Partition Models." arXiv preprint, October 2018. https://arxiv.org/pdf/1810.00121.pdf.

Pena López, José Atilano, and José Manuel Sánchez Santos. "Does Corruption Have Social Roots? The Role of Culture and Social Capital." *Journal of Business Ethics* 122, no. 4 (July 2014): 697–708. https://www.jstor.org/stable/42921466.

Percy, Sarah. "What Makes a Norm Robust: The Norm Against Female Combat." *Journal of Global Security Studies* 4, no. 1 (Jan. 2019): 123–138. https://doi.org/10.1093/jogss/ogy044.

Perrot, Marie-Dominique. "À Propos du Culturalisme: Du Super-flou au Superflu?" In *La Culture, Otage du Développement?* edited by Gilbert Rist. 31–49. Paris: L'Harmattan, 1994.

Philips, Susan U. "Participant Structures and Communicative Competence: Warm Springs Children in Community and Classroom." In *Functions of Language in the Classroom*, edited by Courtney B. Cazden, Vera P. John, and Dell H. Hymes, 370–394. New York: Teachers College Press, 1972.

Pierce, Steven. *Moral Economies of Corruption*. Durham, NC, and London: Duke University Press, 2016.

Pieth, Mark, ed., *Collective Action: Innovative Strategies to Prevent Corruption*. Zurich and St. Gallen: Dike Verlag AG, 2012.

Poblete, JoAnna. *Balancing the Tides: Marine Practices in American Sāmoa*. Honolulu: University of Hawai'i Press, 2020.

Pondi, Jean-Emmanuel. *Repenser le Développement à Partir de l'Afrique*. Yaoundé: Éditions Afrédit, 2011.

Pope Francis. "Address of Pope Francis to the Delegates of the International Association of Penal Law." October 23, 2014. https://w2.vatican.va/content/francesco/en/speeches/2014/october/documents/papa-francesco_20141023_associazione-internazionale-diritto-penale.html.

Posner, Richard A. "A Theory of Primitive Society, with Special Reference to Law." *The Journal of Law & Economics* 23, no. 1 (Apr. 1980): 1–53.

Postero, Nancy, and Eli Elinoff. "Introduction: A Return to Politics." *Anthropological Theory* 19, no. 1 (Mar. 2019): 3–28. https://doi.org/10.1177/1463499618814933.

Poteete, Amy R., Marco A. Janssen, and Elinor Ostrom. *Working Together: Collective Action, the Commons, and Multiple Methods in Practice*. Princeton, NJ: Princeton University Press, 2010.

Pradervand, Pierre. *Listening to Africa: Developing Africa from the Grassroots*. New York: Praeger, 1989.

Pradhan, Prachanda. "Elinor Ostrom: From Nepal [*sic*] Perspective." *Hydro Nepal*, no. 11 (July 9, 2012). https://doi.org/10.3126/hn.v11i0.7168.

Preacher, Kristopher J, and Sonya K. Sterba. "Aptitude-by-Treatment Interactions in Research on Educational Interventions." *Exceptional Children* 85, no. 2 (Jan. 2019): 248–264.

Psacharopoulos, George. *Higher Education in Developing Countries: A Cost-Benefit Analysis*. Washington, DC: World Bank, 1980.

Putnam, Robert D. "Democracy, Development, and the Civic Community: Evidence from an Italian Experiment." In *Culture and Development in Africa*, edited by Ismail Serageldin and June Tabaroff, 33–74. Washington, DC: World Bank, 1994. http://documents.worldbank.org/curated/en/303951468203676341/pdf/multi0page.pdf.

Putnam, Robert D., Robert Leonardi, and Raffaela Nanetti. *Making Democracy Work: Civic Traditions in Modern Italy*. Princeton, NJ: Princeton, University Press, 1994.

Putterman, Louis, and David N. Weil. "Post-1500 Population Flows and the Long-Run Determinants of Economic Growth and Inequality." *Quarterly Journal of Economics* 125, no. 4 (Nov. 2010): 1627–1682.

Rankin, Katherine N. "Social Capital, Microfinance, and the Politics of Development." *Feminist Economics* 8, no. 1 (Jan. 2002): 1–24. https://doi.org/10.1080/13545700210125167.

Rao, Vijayendra, and Michael Walton, eds. *Culture and Public Action*. Stanford: Stanford University Press, 2004.

Rew, Allen W. "The Link Between Advisory Work and Academic Research and Teaching: Perspectives from a Supplier Institution for Development Cooperation." In *The Socio-Cultural Dimension in Development: The Contribution of Sociologists and Social Anthropologists to the Work of Development Agencies*, edited by Michael Schönhuth. Sonderpublikation der GTZ, no. 249, 45–53. Eschborn, Germany: Deutsche Gesellschaft für Technische, 1991.

Richard, Fabienne, Charlemagne Ouédraogo, Georges Rouamba, Bruno Dujardin, and Vincente De Brouwere. "Conclusion: Que Reste-t-il Quatre Ans Après la Fin du Projet Aquasou?" In *Accompagner les Femmes à la Maternité au Burkina Faso*, edited by Fatoumata Ouattara, Marc-Éric Gruénais, Fabienne Richard, and Charlemagne Ouédraogo, 205–224. Paris: L'Harmattan, 2016.

Rigg, Jonathan. "Grass-Roots Development in Rural Thailand: A Lost Cause?" *World Development* 19, no. 2/3 (Feb./Mar. 1991): 199–211. https://doi.org/10.1016/0305-750X(91)90255-G.

Rivas, Ramón D. "Instituciones Sociales y Cultura del Fraude en El Salvador." *Entorno*, no. 44 (May 2010): 16–19. http://biblioteca.utec.edu.sv/entorno/index.php/entorno/article/viewFile/96/95.

Roland, Gérard. "Culture, Institutions and Development." In *The Handbook of Economic Development and Institutions*, edited by Jean-Marie Baland, François Bourguignon, Jean-Philippe Platteau, and Thierry Verdier, 414–548. Princeton, NJ: Princeton University Press, 2020.

Roland, Gérard. "The Deep Historical Roots of Modern Culture: A Comparative Perspective." Keynote Lecture at 2nd World Congress in Comparative Economics, revised December 2019.

Rosaldo, Renato. *Culture and Truth: The Remaking of Social Analysis*. Boston: Beacon, 1989.

Rose, David C. *Why Culture Matters Most*. New York: Oxford University Press, 2019.

Rose-Ackerman, Susan. *Corruption: A Study in Political Economy*. New York: Academic Press, 1978.

Ross, Cody T., and Peter J. Richerson. "New Frontiers in the Study of Human Cultural and Genetic Evolution." *Current Opinion in Genetics and Development* 29 (December 2014): 103–109. https://doi.org/10.1016/j.gde.2014.08.014.

Rothstein, Bo, and Sören Holmberg. "Correlates of Corruption." Working Paper Series 2014 no. 17. Gothenburg, The Quality of Government Institute, December 2014.

Rothstein, Bo, and Jan Teorell. "Defining and Measuring Quality of Government." In *Good Government: The Relevance of Political Science*, edited by Sören Holmberg and Bo Rothstein, 13–39. Cheltenham, UK: Edward Elgar, 2012.

Rothstein, Bo, and Davide Torsello. "Bribery in Pre-Industrial Societies: Understanding the Universalism-Particularism Puzzle." *Journal of Anthropological Research* 70, no. 2 (Spring 2014): 263–282.

Ruttan, Vernon W. "Cultural Endowments and Economic Development: What Can We Learn from Anthropology?" *Economic Development and Cultural Change* 36, no. S3 (Apr. 1988): S247–271. https://www.jstor.org/stable/1566545.

Ruttan, Vernon W. "What Happened to Political Development?" *Economic Development and Cultural Change* 39, no. 2 (Jan. 1991): 265–292. https://www.jstor.org/stable/1154082.

Sahlins, Marshall. *Stone-Age Economics*. Chicago: Aldine, 1972.

Saisana, Michaela, and Andrea Saltelli. "Corruption Perceptions Index 2012: Statistical Assessment." JRC Scientific and Policy Reports. Luxembourg, Publications Office of the European Union, 2012.

Saisana, Michaela, Andrea Saltelli, and Stefano Tarantola. "Uncertainty and Sensitivity Analysis Techniques as Tools for the Analysis and Validation of Composite Indicators." *Journal of the Royal Statistical Society A* 168 (Part 2) (2005): 307–23.

Salimans, Tim. "Variable Selection and Functional Form Uncertainty in Cross-Country Growth Regressions." *Journal of Econometrics* 171, no. 2 (2012): 267–280. https://doi.org/10.1016/j.jeconom.2012.06.007.

Santos, Henri C., Michael E. W. Varnum, and Igor Grossmann. "Global Increases in Individualism." *Psychological Science* 28, no. 9 (Sept. 2017): 1228–1239.

Savage, Catherine, Rawiri Hindle, Luanna Meyer, Anne Hynds, Wally Penetito, and Christine E. Sleeter. "Culturally Responsive Pedagogies in the Classroom: Indigenous Student Experiences across the Curriculum." *Asia-Pacific Journal of Teacher Education* 39, no. 3 (Aug. 2011): 183–198. https://doi.org/10.1080/1359866X.2011.588311.

Scharbatke-Church, Cheyanne, and Diana Chigas. *Understanding Social Norms: A Reference Guide for Policy and Practice.* Henry J. Leir Institute of Human Security, Fletcher School of Law and Diplomacy, Tufts University, Medford, MA, 2019. https://sites.tufts.edu/ihs/files/2019/10/SN_CorruptionRefGuide_AUG2019-linked.MR_.pdf.

Schwartz, Shalom H., and Anat Bardi. "Value Hierarchies across Cultures: Taking a Similarities Perspective." *Journal of Cross-Cultural Psychology* 32, no. 3 (2001): 268–290. https://doi.org/10.1177/0022022101032003002.

Scrivner, Lee. "How to Write an AvantGarde Manifesto (A Manifesto)." London, London Consortium, April 2006.

Seidman, Steven. "Substantive Debates: Moral Order and Social Crisis—Perspectives on Modern Culture." In *Culture and Society: Contemporary Debates*, edited by Jeffrey C. Alexander and Steven Seidman, 217–238. Cambridge: Cambridge University Press, 1990.

Shakow, Miriam. "The Rise and Fall of 'Civil Society' in Bolivia." *American Anthropologist.* Published online July 11, 2019. https://doi.org/10.1111/aman.13266.

Silverman, Lois H. *The Social Work of Museums.* Oxford and New York: Routledge, 2010.

Singer, Eliot A. "What Is Cultural Congruence, and Why Are They Saying Such Terrible Things About It?" Occasional Paper no. 120, Institute for Research on Teaching, College of Education, Michigan State University, East Lansing, March 1988. https://files.eric.ed.gov/fulltext/ED292914.pdf.

Small, Mario Luis, David J. Harding, and Michèle Lamont. "Reconsidering Culture and Poverty." *The Annals of the American Academy of Political and Social Science* 629 (May 2010): 6–29.

Smith, Daniel Jordan. *A Culture of Corruption: Everyday Deception and Popular Discontent in Nigeria.* Princeton, NJ: Princeton University Press, 2007.

Snow, C. P. *The Two Cultures.* With an Introduction by Stefan Collini. Cambridge and New York: Cambridge University Press, 1998.

Snow, Richard E. "Aptitude-Treatment Interaction as a Framework for Research on Individual Differences in Learning." In *Learning and Individual Differences: Advances in Theory and Research*, edited by Phillip L. Ackerman, Robert J. Sternberg, and Robert Glaser, 13–59. New York: W. H. Freeman/Times Books/Henry Holt, 1989.

Söderbom, Mats, and Francis Teal, with Markus Eberhardt, Simon Quinn, and Andrew Zeitlin. *Empirical Development Economics.* London and New York: Routledge, 2015.

Sowell, Thomas. *Migrations and Cultures: A World View.* New York: Basic Books, 1997.

Spolaore, Enrico, and Romain Wacziarg. "Ancestry, Language and Culture." In *The Palgrave Handbook of Economics and Language*, edited by Victor Ginsburgh and Schlmo Weber, 174–211. London: Palgrave Macmillan, 2016.

Spolaore, Enrico, and Romain Wacziarg. "How Deep Are the Roots of Economic Development?" *Journal of Economic Literature* 51, no. 2 (June 2013): 325–369.

Spolaore, Enrico, and Romain Wacziarg. "Long-term Barriers to Economic Development." In *Handbook of Economic Growth*, edited by Philippe Aghion and Steven N. Durlauf, 121–176. Amsterdam: Elsevier, 2014.

Stalder, Pia. "Management Interculturel: Entre Théorie et Anarchie." In *Le Défi Interculturel: Enjeux et Perspectives pour Entreprendre*, edited by Pierre-Robert Cloet, 141–149. Paris: Editions L'Harmattan, 2017.

Steel, Piers, Vasyl Taras, Krista Uggerslev, and Frank Bosco. "The Happy Culture: A Theoretical, Meta-Analytic, and Empirical Review of the Relationship Between Culture and Wealth and Subjective Well-Being." *Personality and Social Psychology Review* 22, no. 2 (2017): 128–169. https://journals.sagepub.com/doi/10.1177/1088868317721372.

Steele, Liza G., and Scott M. Lynch. "The Pursuit of Happiness in China: Individualism, Collectivism, and Subjective Well-Being During China's Economic and Social Transformation." *Social Indicators Research* 114, no. 2 (Nov. 2013): 441–451. https://doi.org/10.1007/s11205-012-0154-1.

Sumner, William Graham. *Folkways: A Study of the Sociological Importance of Usages, Manners, Customs, Mores, and Morals*. Boston: Ginn, 1899.

Szanton, David L. "Contingent Moralities: Social and Economic Investment in a Philippine Fishing Town." In *Market Cultures: Society and Morality in the New Asian Capitalisms*, edited by Robert W. Hefner, 257–267. Oxford and New York: Routledge, 2018.

Szanton, David L. *Estancia in Transition: Economic Growth in a Rural Philippine Community*. Manila: Ateneo de Manila University Press, 1971.

Tannen, Deborah. *You Just Don't Understand: Women and Men in Conversation*. New York: William Morrow, 2001.

Tax, Sol. *Penny Capitalism: A Guatemalan Indian Community*. Washington, DC: Smithsonian Institute of Social Anthropology, 1953.

Taylor, Charles. "The Politics of Recognition." In *Multiculturalism: Examining the Politics of Recognition*, edited by Amy Gutmann, 25–73. Princeton, NJ: Princeton University Press, 1994.

Tett, Gillian. *The Silo Effect: The Peril of Expertise and the Promise of Breaking Down Barriers*. New York: Simon & Schuster, 2015.

Thornhill, Randy, and Corey L. Fincher. "The Parasite-Stress Theory of Sociality and the Behavioral Immune System." In *Evolutionary Perspectives in Social Psychology*, edited by Virgil Zeigler-Hill, Lisa L. M. Welling, and Todd K. Shackelford, 419–437. Cham, Switzerland: Springer International, 2015.

Thornhill, Randy, and Corey L. Fincher. *The Parasite-Stress Theory of Value and Sociality: Infectious Disease, History, and Human Values Worldwide*. New York: Springer, 2014.

Tilley, Helen. *Africa as a Living Laboratory: Empire, Development, and the Problem of Scientific Knowledge, 1870–1950*. Chicago: University of Chicago Press, 2011.

Tinius, Jonas L., and Johannes Lenhard. "'Economy, Happiness, and the Good Life:' An Interview with Edward F. Fischer." *King's Review*, December 26, 2017.

Tobgay, Tshering. "The First Ten Years of Democracy: Reflections from Bhutan." Lecture at Oxford University, January 9, 2019. https://www.youtube.com/watch?v=HSrJGjkgaPg.

Tonti, Annick. "The Model of Swiss Development Cooperation." In *The Socio-Cultural Dimension in Development: The Contribution of Sociologists and Social Anthropologists to the Work of Development Agencies*, edited by Michael Schönhuth, 54–58. Sonderpublikation der GTZ, no. 249. Eschborn, Germany: Deutsche Gesellschaft für Technische, 1991.

Torgovnic, Marianna. *Gone Primitive: Savage Intellects, Modern Lives*. Chicago: University of Chicago Press, 1990.

Tsing, Anna Lowenhaupt. *The Mushroom at the End of the World: On the Possibility of Life in Capitalist Ruins*. Princeton, NJ: Princeton University Press, 2015.

Turner, Luke. "Metamodernism: A Brief Introduction." *Queen Mob's Teahouse*, January 5, 2015. https://queenmobs.com/2015/01/metamodernism-brief-introduction/.

UNESCO. "UNESCO Universal Declaration on Cultural Diversity." Adopted by the 31st Session of the General Conference of UNESCO. Paris, UNESCO, 2002.

United States Department of Agriculture. *Soil Quality Test Kit Guide*. Washington, DC: USDA, 2001. https://www.nrcs.usda.gov/Internet/FSE_DOCUMENTS/nrcs142p2_050956.pdf.

Uphoff, Norman. "Fitting Projects to People." In *Putting People First: Sociological Variables in Rural Development*, 2nd ed., edited by Michael M. Cernea, 467–512. New York: Oxford University Press, 1991.

Uphoff, Norman. "Why NGOs Are Not a Third Sector: A Sectoral Analysis with Some Thoughts on Accountability, Sustainability and Evaluation." In *Non-Governmental Organisations—Performance and Accountability: Beyond the Magic Bullet*, edited by Michael Edwards and David Hulme, 17–31. London: Earthscan, 1995.

Venot, Jean-Philippe, and Gert Jan Veldwisch. "Sociotechnical Myths in Development." *Anthropologie et Développment* 46–47 (2017): 7–26. https://doi.org/10.4000/anthropodev.582.

Veteto, James R., and Joshua Lockyear. "Applying Anthropology to What? Tactical/Ethical Decisions in an Age of Global Neoliberal Imperialism." *Journal of Political Ecology* 22, no.1 (2015): 357–367. https://doi.org/10.2458/v22i1.21113.

Vogt, Lynn A., Cathie Jordan, and Roland G. Tharp. "Explaining School Failure, Producing School Success: Two Cases." *Anthropology and Education Quarterly* 18, no. 4 (Dec. 1987): 276–286. http://dx.doi.org/10.1525/aeq.1987.18.4.04x0019s.

Watson-Gegeo, Karen Ann, and Steven T. Boggs. "From Verbal Play to Talk Story: The Role of Routines in Speech Events among Hawai'ian Children." In *Child Discourse*, edited by Claudia Mitchell-Kernan and Susan Ervin-Tripp, 67–90. New York: Academic Press, 1977.

Widmalm, Sten. "Explaining Corruption at the Village and Individual Level in India: Findings from a Study of the Panchayati Raj Reforms." *Asian Survey* 45, no. 5 (Sept./Oct. 2005): 756–776.

Wolfram, Sybil. "'Human Rights': Commentary." In *Human Rights and Anthropology*, edited by Theodore E. Downing and Gilbert Kushner, 107–114. Cambridge, MA: Cultural Survival, 1989.

Woolcock, Michael. "Culture, Politics, and Development." In *The Oxford Handbook of the Politics of Development*, edited by Carol Lancaster and Nicolas van de Walle, 107–122. New York: Oxford University Press, 2018. https://doi.org/10.1093/oxfordhb/9780199845156.013.11.

World Health Organization. *Global Health Estimates 2016: Disease Burden by Cause, Age, Sex, by Country and by Region, 2000–2016*. Geneva: WHO, 2018.

World Justice Project. *The World Justice Project Rule of Law Index® 2020*. Washington, DC, World Justice Project, 2020. https://worldjusticeproject.org/sites/default/files/documents/WJP-ROLI-2020-Online_0.pdf.

Wulff, Robert M., and Shirley J. Fiske, eds. *Anthropological Praxis: Translating Knowledge into Action*. Boulder, CO: Westview, 1987.

Wunsch, James S., and Dele Olowu. "The Failure of the Centralized African State." In *The Failure of the Centralized State: Institutions and Self-Governance in Africa*, edited by James S. Wunsch and Dele Olowu, 1–23 New York and Abington, UK: Routledge, 2019.

Zeuli, John S., and Robert E. Floden. "Cultural Incongruities and Inequities of Schooling: Implications for Practice from Ethnographic Research?" *Journal of Teacher Education* 38, no. 6 (Nov. 1987): 9–15.

Index

For the benefit of digital users, indexed terms that span two pages (e.g., 52–53) may, on occasion, appear on only one of those pages.

Tables and boxes are indicated by *t* and *b* following the page number.

Printed in the USA/Agawam, MA
March 19, 2021

771790.016